MIXED
METHODS IN
SOCIAL
INQUIRY

JB JOSSEY-BASS

MIXED METHODS IN SOCIAL INQUIRY

JENNIFER C. GREENE

BICENTENNIAL
1807
WILEY
2007
BICENTENNIAL

Published by Jossey-Bass
A Wiley Imprint
989 Market Street, San Francisco, CA 94103-1741—www.josseybass.com

Wiley Bicentennial Logo: Richard J. Pacifico.

Jossey-Bass books and products are available through most bookstores. To contact Jossey-Bass directly call our Customer Care Department within the U.S. at 800-956-7739, outside the U.S. at 317-572-3986, or fax 317-572-4002.

Jossey-Bass also publishes its books in a variety of electronic formats. Some content that appears in print may not be available in electronic books.

Library of Congress Cataloging-in-Publication Data

Greene, Jennifer C.
  Mixed methods in social inquiry/Jennifer Greene. — 1st ed.
     p. cm.
  Includes bibliographical references and index.
  ISBN-13: 978-0-7879-8382-6 (pbk.)
  1. Social sciences—Research—Methodology. I. Title.
  H62.G7514 2008
  300.72—dc22

                                                                    2007026831

10 9 8 7 6 5 4 3 2

CONTENTS

TABLES, FIGURES, & EXHIBITS

TABLES

FIGURES

EXHIBIT

To my mother and father, with profound gratitude for your gifts
of love and life

INTRODUCTION

This book offers a particular perspective on the dynamic field of mixed methods social inquiry, a perspective that emphasizes the rationales, purposes, and potentialities for mixing methods in social research and evaluation. It is centered on the generative value of mixed methods inquiry for the overall purpose of better, more insightful understanding of complex social phenomena. The perspective is further anchored in a distinctive stance regarding the role of science in society—a stance committed to meaningful engagement with difference and diversity. The book focuses on the contributions that mixed methods inquiry offers to this engagement.

The book aims to contribute to the mixed methods literature by grounding this recent methodological development in its historical context—specifically, the contentious and fractious debates in the latter part of the twentieth century between proponents of *qualitative* versus *quantitative* methodologies—and thereby advocating for thoughtful consideration of mixing not just methods or forms of data but also different ways of seeing, interpreting, and knowing. The "great qualitative-quantitative debate" was, at root, about these different ways of knowing. The book discusses in some depth the knotty issues and challenges of mixing at the levels of philosophy, conceptual theory, and ideology, in addition to mixing methods and forms of data. The discussion fully engages with the character of philosophical and conceptual assumptions that matter in social inquiry *and* with the nature of the relationship between such assumptions and inquiry practice, particularly practical decisions about methodology and method. The book also collects contemporary wisdom on the actual practice of mixed methods social inquiry. And the discussion in this book offers my views, alongside those of other contributors to the field, welcoming of shared and contrary standpoints alike.

The book has two primary sections. The first section, chapters One through Five, presents my own thinking about the domain of mixed methods social inquiry and situates this thinking historically (Chapter Three) and within the broader set of ideas that the mixed methods literature currently comprises. The second section, chapters Six through Ten, offers guidelines—both my own and those of others in the field—for practicing mixed methods inquiry. Examples of mixed methods practice are included in most chapters. In addition, three extended case examples are presented as interludes woven in between the conceptual and practical discussions. A final chapter offers my vision of the importance of a mixed methods approach to social inquiry.

The books' major conceptual themes from chapters One through Five include the following:

■ The book centrally engages the questions of just what is being mixed in mixed methods inquiry? And what are the options for mixing? I believe that the social inquirer's own lens, his or her particular way of seeing and making sense of the world, is inevitably, although often implicitly, invoked in the process and products of social inquiry. This lens includes assumptions about the character of the social world we are trying to understand and about the nature of the knowledge we can attain regarding that world, conceptual ideas from disciplines and scientific theories, self-understandings of one's role as a social scientist in society, life experience and wisdom, value commitments and beliefs. Denis Phillips (1996) and Mary Lee Smith (1997) call this lens a *mental model*—a concept that incorporates philosophical strands of scientific paradigms as well as disciplinary theories, life experiences, methodological traditions, values and beliefs (Chapter One). The discussion in this book actively engages the thorny questions associated with mixing not just methods or forms of data but also these multiple strands of inquirers' mental models. My stance in the book is that mixed methods inquiry is potentially most generative—of new insights and understandings—when the mixing happens at these multiple levels (chapters Two, Four, Five).

▪ The core meaning of mixed methods social inquiry is to invite multiple mental models into the same inquiry space for purposes of respectful conversation, dialogue, and learning one from the other, toward a collective generation of better understanding of the phenomena being studied. By definition, then, mixed methods social inquiry involves a plurality of philosophical paradigms, theoretical assumptions, methodological traditions, data gathering and analysis techniques, and personalized understandings and value commitments—because these are the stuff of mental models (chapters One, Two).

▪ The book promotes the adoption of a "mixed methods way of thinking" (Chapter Two). A mixed methods way of thinking involves an openness to multiple ways of seeing and hearing, multiple ways of making sense of the social world, and multiple standpoints on what is important and to be valued and cherished. A mixed methods way of thinking rests on assumptions that there are multiple legitimate approaches to social inquiry, that any given approach to social inquiry is inevitably partial, and that thereby multiple approaches can generate more complete and meaningful understanding of complex human phenomena. A mixed methods way of thinking means genuine acceptance of other ways of seeing and knowing as legitimate. A mixed methods way of thinking involves an active engagement with difference and diversity.

▪ Another conceptual theme in the book is that convergence, corroboration, confirmation—of the results from one method with the results from a different method—is overrated. Such convergence, reflecting the time-honored mixed methods purpose of triangulation, is an important component of the mixed methods repertoire. Yet it is only one component. Equally important is the generative potential of divergence, dissonance, difference—"the empirical puzzles" (Cook, 1985) that arise when the results of difference methods are not consonant.

- One aim of this book is to contribute to the developing theories of mixed methods social inquiry. My view is that the primary value or role of mixed methods theories is to give form, coherence, and additional possibilities to relatively longstanding practices of mixing methods, especially in applied social science fields like evaluation and educational research. Mixed methods theory aims to catch up with practice by providing organized and coherent guidance to mixed methods practitioners, so that mixed methods practice can be as well-planned and deliberate as other genres of social inquiry. In the discussions in this book, theory and practice are viewed as mutually informative, reciprocal, and ideally dialogic. Even so, I repeatedly make the point that the practice of social inquiry is substantially more complicated, contingent, and organic than any theory of methodology could ever hope to prescribe.

The practical part of the book, chapters Six through Ten, addresses the following topics in this order: purposes for mixing methods, mixed methods designs, mixed methods data analysis, criteria for judging the quality of mixed methods studies, and writing up and reporting mixed methods work. Each chapter aims to present my ideas and guidelines regarding these practical topics, as well as major ideas from others in the field. As will be clear to readers, guidelines for mixed methods practice are still in the development stage, and considerable opportunities remain for contributions from thoughtful and creative inquirers. Throughout chapters Six through Ten, I point out a number of key issues of practice warranting further development. These include the following, offered in the hope of whetting your appetite for further reading:

- One compelling rationale, both historically (Cook, 1985; Mark and Shotland, 1987b) and today (Onwuegbuzie and Johnson, 2006), for the mixing of methods in social inquiry is the opportunity to compensate for inherent method weaknesses, capitalize on inherent method strengths, and offset inevitable method biases. Yet little is known about methodological strengths and weaknesses, propensities and biases. And these are not only technical concerns, as in social desirability biases in survey responses or overestimates of pre-post gains due to regression to the mean. These are also contextual and political concerns, as in the varying credibility of some forms of data among different audiences for social inquiry and the differential capacity of different methods to meaningfully capture and represent the interests and perspectives of different members of a social context. Especially lacking is good empirical research on many of these issues (Chapter Six).

- It is quite common today for applied social inquirers to use a variety of methods in an empirical study, analyze the data from each independently, develop a set of conclusions or inferences that represent each method and data set, and then at the end of the study endeavor to make some linkages or connections among the various sets of results (a component mixed methods design). The kind of linkage made often reflects the purpose for mixing. Yet making such linkages effectively and defensibly remains a nontrivial task and constitutes an important area for further work in the mixed methods field (Chapter Seven).

- The mixed methods field remains ripe for further conceptual work on the challenges of analyzing, in well-planned and meaningful ways, multiple data sets of different form, content, and character. These challenges are especially important for integrated designs that intentionally incorporate a back-and-forth conversation among diverse methods and data sets (Chapter Eight).

- Contemporary computer software can facilitate the exporting of data files from qualitative to quantitative analyses and back again (Bazeley, 2003). Yet multiple challenges arise in this form of integrated analysis; for example, issues related to the fundamentally different meanings of codes in quantitative and qualitative data analysis tools. Quantitative codes are necessarily reductive, precise, and intended to have one constant meaning across respondents, whereas qualitative codes characteristically refer to multidimensional experiences that may take on different meanings in different contexts for different people. So "the critical issue from the point of view of mixed methods computing becomes the meaning of the code that is exported from one type of analysis program to another" (Bazeley, 2003, p. 415) (Chapter Eight).

- In mixed methods studies that intentionally mix different methodological traditions, each carrying its own distinctive criteria for judging inquiry quality (for example, internal validity or narrative coherence), are these different criteria and judgments of quality also mixed, and if so, how? Or are there alternative ways of approaching the challenges of judging quality in mixed methods social inquiry? There are few significant responses to these challenges of judging inquiry quality in the mixed methods literature (Chapter Nine).

- Challenges in writing up mixed methods inquiry remain considerable, as different methodological traditions involve quite different communication traditions that incorporate different technical criteria and norms, as well as different rhetorical and aesthetic criteria and norms for what makes a text compelling (Chapter Ten).

Overall, this book is intended as a guide to understanding and practicing mixed methods social inquiry. The book is written for applied social researchers and evaluators—practitioners, academicians, and graduate students. The particular challenges of evaluation will be featured in the book, as that is my own field of practice. Yet the discussion will include contextual issues and examples from multiple fields, and the discussion will generally be applicable to all fields. The use of the word *inquiry* is intended to signal this broad applicability. The book will be best understood by readers with some prior understanding of the conceptual logic and core constructs of methodologies from more than one tradition.

Jennifer C. Greene
October 2007

THE AUTHOR

Jennifer C. Greene has been an evaluation scholar-practitioner for more than thirty years. She received her doctorate in educational psychology in 1976 from Stanford University and has held academic appointments at the University of Rhode Island, Cornell University, and presently, the University of Illinois at Urbana-Champaign. Her evaluation scholarship has broadly focused on the intersections of social science method with policy discourse and program decision making, with the ambition of making evaluation useful and socially responsible. Greene has concentrated specifically on advancing responsive and democratic approaches to evaluation, both of which have been enriched by her two decades of work in the domain of mixing methods. Her evaluation practice has spanned multiple domains, concentrating on programs in the domains of education, youth development, and community-based family services. Greene has published widely in journals and books on program evaluation; she has held leadership positions in the American Evaluation Association and the American Educational Research Association, and she was coeditor-in-chief of *New Directions for Evaluation,* 1998 to 2003.

FRAMING MIXED METHODS SOCIAL INQUIRY: PARADIGMS AND PARADOXES

Just what is being mixed in mixed methods inquiry? And what are the options for mixing? In Part One, the reader is introduced to the philosophical and conceptual issues of particular importance in the mixed method arena and to one viable framework for mixed methods inquiry. This framework is anchored in the concept of the inquirer's mental model, which includes not just philosophical assumptions but also disciplinary perspectives, theoretical lenses, methodological traditions, contextual dimensions, as well as personalized understandings and value commitments. Mixing methods then ideally involves the respectful mixing of multiple mental models, as this is viewed as the most generative of understanding and insight.

Part One also locates this argument in its historical context and in the more contemporary landscape of stances on the sensibility and significance of mixing at these multiple levels when conducting mixed methods social inquiry.

CHAPTER

MENTAL MODELS AND MIXED METHODS INQUIRY

HERE THE journey begins, with a portrait of social inquiry planning in practice and an introduction to the concept of mental models. A mental model is the particular constellation of assumptions, theoretical commitments, experiences, and values through which a social inquirer conducts his or her work. In this first part of the journey, the traveler—you, the reader—will get a glimpse of the mental models of other social inquirers and be encouraged to be reflective about your own.

Imagine . . . It is a sunny and breezy day in early summer. You are seated around a scarred and stained oak wooden table in the meeting room of a downtown youth center. The wobbly seats are also made of oak and offer little comfort for the several middle-aged bodies at the table, although the younger youth counselors don't seem to be bothered. Pedro is in fact slouched way down in his chair as if it were a recliner. Robert is leaning far back in his chair, balancing it on the two back legs. And Latisha is sitting cross-legged on her chair, while you are struggling for space under the table just to cross your legs.

You have gathered here with these youth counselors, the director of the youth center, and several researchers from the local university to discuss plans for a study to be conducted in conjunction with an innovative mentoring program that will be implemented at the center beginning in the fall. (The mentoring program described in this constructed scenario is adapted from the actual TALKS Mentoring Program developed by the Reverend Harold Davis in Champaign-Urbana, Illinois [http://www.talksmentoring.org/champaign/index.htm]. In this program *urban* is a cultural term, rather than a term of population density, referring to the contemporary culture of urban African American youth, including hip-hop and rap music, particular fashion styles like oversized clothing for males, the contextual presence of drugs and associated crime, and at least some alienation from mainstream society. See also research on this program at http://www.talksmentoring.org/main_research.htm.)

This innovative mentoring program connects volunteer adult mentors with groups of three children or youth, all the same age (ranging from eight to sixteen) and gender, but differing in their developmental progress. One of the three children or youth is identified as generally "doing well" and one as generally "doing OK" across the developmentally important domains of academic achievement and school engagement, socioemotional relationships with peers and adults, athletic attainments and physical health, and behavioral adjustment and coping skills. The third child or young person is identified as "struggling" in one or more of these domains. The program is presented to the children and youth as an opportunity to develop their leadership potential. Mentors are expected to spend one hour a week with their group in the youth center during the after-school hours, following a well-developed curriculum. Mentors can spend additional time with their youth, but this is neither expected nor encouraged. This mentoring program is not about having fun but rather is focused on promoting positive youth development through high expectations, strong role modeling, and powerful peer relationships. Ideally, mentors continue with the same threesome for several years, or even until all the youth complete high school.

The program was originally developed for urban African American boys by a pastor in a nearby community. It was designed as an "in your face" program for boys lacking a strong male adult in their lives. After four years, the program was extended to African American girls, with a curriculum modified for their particular profile of assets and challenges. Now, another four years later, the curriculum has again been modified, this time for Latino boys and Latina girls, again in an urban culture. The city has recently experienced a sharp influx of working- and middle-class Latino families, both immigrants from Mexico and Central America and people choosing to resettle from a major city nearby into a smaller community. The new Hyundai automobile assembly factory built on the edge of the city is largely responsible for attracting these new workers to the community. And the population of children and youth served by the youth center has significantly diversified in recent years, although with little cross-group intermingling and even some racial tensions and incidents. The staff members hope that the mentoring program not only will support youth's overall development, but also could ease these tensions and promote healthy cross-group interactions, even though the mentoring takes place within same-race groups of children.

The mentoring program itself is not costly, as the mentors are all volunteers. Funds from the city, from the youth center's regular budget, and from a local community foundation are supporting the operational costs of the program. The three-year study to be conducted in conjunction with the mentoring program is funded by the W.T. Grant Foundation, under a grant to the university faculty present at the meeting, in cooperation with the center staff. The study is intended to learn more about the processes and outcomes of this highly promising positive youth development initiative. The data collected to date on the mentoring program—though of modest scope—do support its positive potential. Again, the purpose of today's meeting is to begin to plan the study.

GROUP DISCUSSION

As moderator of the group, you suggest that the eight people present (the center director, three youth counselors, and four university researchers—representing the fields of child and adolescent development, intergroup relationships, and program evaluation) pair up and begin to discuss (1) key foci and questions for the study and (2) initial ideas for the study's design and methods. Each pair should include one person from the center and one from the university. A discussion time of forty minutes is allotted, after which each pair will report out to the whole group. A summarized version of each pair's thinking is offered here, first for the priority study questions and then for the study design and methods.

What should this study focus on, what are some possible key inquiry questions, and why are these important to you?

The four pairs' ideas about priorities for empirical study follow.

Group 1—Youth Counselor Pedro and Developmental Psychologist Anne

"We think the study should concentrate on assessing important developmental markers across multiple domains," says Anne, "with special attention to school achievement and motivation, to behavior, and to the quality of the youth's relationships with their mentors and with their families. Contemporary developmental theory suggests that the presence of a strong, caring relationship with at least one adult is vitally important for positive youth development, so that is why we want to focus on mentor-mentee relationships."

Pedro adds, "And I know from my own life experience that *la familia* is really important for Latinos, and I think it is for African Americans, too. So this study should include taking a close look at how these kids get along with their families. It's also real important to Latino families that their kids do well in school, because we know that you can't have much of a life in this society without getting a good education."

Anne agrees and elaborates, "Also, the major 'work' of children and youth during middle childhood and early adolescence is indeed going to school and learning how to adapt one's behavior to the rules and norms of given contexts, so in addition to family relationships, we think achievement and behavior are high-priority parts of kids' lives to track over time."

Group 2—Youth Counselor Robert and Intergroup Relationship Specialist Frederick

"Our ideas are somewhat different," begins Frederick. "We both think that the most important aspects of the mentoring program to study are the relationships the mentees have with their peers—within the mentoring group and with other peers in school, in the youth center, and in the neighborhoods—including or even especially peers from different racial and ethnic groups. And we have various reasons for singling out peer relationships as a priority for the study."

Robert observes, "I've only been working with kids for a few years, but I have seen over and over again that the toughest part of their lives is resisting the pressure to be cool, even when being cool means doing bad things. If you don't act cool, then you're not cool, and you become a loser and a loner. Nobody wants to be friends with a loser. Finding good friends can be hard for so many kids."

Frederick comments, "While much of my work has been with older adolescents, like college students, I think the emphasis in the intergroup relationship community on peer-to-peer relationships extends to all ages. Our society and our world are getting more diverse, not less. One of our main societal agendas is to learn tolerance and acceptance, one of the other."

Group 3—Youth Counselor Latisha and Developmental Psychologist Gloria

"Our thinking is somewhat similar to what the first two groups have said," says Gloria. "We think it is really important to pay attention to the developmental progress of the children and youth in the mentoring program. And we would like to include all important domains of development—school achievement, behavior, peer and adult relationships, as well as physical health and well-being."

She continues, "You know, there is an epidemic of childhood obesity all over the country today, with especially high prevalence rates in poor and working-class minority communities. While there is no direct relationship between mentoring and obesity, I can't in good conscience study any group of children or youth today without attending to this issue."

Latisha adds, "Yeah, we have a lot of really heavy children who come to the center. Some of them can hardly walk across the gym. But for health and all the other parts of kids' lives we want to study, we think we have to use standards that make sense in each culture—what Gloria here said are called 'culturally adjusted developmental norms.' Though underneath kids are all the same, how kids from different groups show what they know or can do is really different. You see it every day here."

Group 4—Youth Center Director James and Program Evaluation Expert Linda

Linda states, "We would really like to emphasize all of the good things the other groups have already mentioned for this study. Many of those, however, are longer-term outcomes, and they may not show any measurable changes in the short time frame of this program. Our thinking concentrated on a shorter-term perspective and more on the program experience itself."

James continues, "We also believe that we must address questions of interest to the W. T. Grant Foundation because they are funding this study. So our priority questions address the quality of the mentoring experience for both the mentor and the mentees, the efficiency of the administration and operation of the program, and the short-term benefits of the program for participating children and youth in multiple relevant domains. Probably our own past experiences with program evaluation have influenced our thinking about these issues. It's not quite the same as research, and we understand this to be a program evaluation study."

Interlude

At this point in the conversation, please observe the various influences on these different ideas about priority concerns and questions for the mentoring program study. A sampling of these influences includes:

- Contemporary developmental theory ("Contemporary developmental theory suggests that the presence of a strong, caring relationship with at least one adult is vitally important for positive youth development"—Anne)

- Theory about intergroup relationships ("We both think that the most important aspects of the mentoring program to study are the relationships the mentees have with their peers"—Frederick)

- Personal life experiences ("And I know from my own life experience that *la familia* is really important for Latinos"—Pedro)

- Perceptions developed from repeated observations in context ("I have seen over and over again that the toughest part of their lives is resisting the pressure to be cool, even when being cool means doing bad things"—Robert; "You see it every day here"—Latisha)

- Values and beliefs ("One of our main societal agendas is to learn tolerance and acceptance, one of the other"—Frederick)

- Current trends and issues ("I can't in good conscience study any group of children or youth today without attending to this issue [of obesity]"—Gloria)

- Cultural sensitivity and respect ("We have to use standards that make sense in each culture—what Gloria here said are called 'culturally adjusted developmental norms'"—Latisha)

- Externalities ("We also believe that we must address questions of interest to the W. T. Grant Foundation because they are funding this study"—James)

- Contextual factors ("Many of those . . . longer-term outcomes . . . may not show any measurable changes in the short time frame of this program"—Linda)

- Professional experiences ("Our own past experiences with program evaluation have influenced our thinking about these issues"—James)

- Disciplinary perspectives (psychological development, Anne and Gloria; intergroup relationships, Frederick; program administration, James)

> *What are some of your thoughts about study design and methods, and what is your justification or rationale for these ideas?*

Next, the pairs' ideas about study design and methods are briefly summarized.

Group 1—Youth Counselor Pedro and Developmental Psychologist Anne

"The most important thing to study," begins Pedro, "is what difference the mentoring program makes for the kids involved. Anne has some fancy language to describe this kind of study."

Anne continues, "The ideal study, of course, is a randomized experiment. That would answer the priority question of what important outcomes are impacted by the mentoring program. But that won't be possible here, as the center wants to include as many youth as possible in the mentoring program, and do so without delay, thus ruling out a delayed control group that starts the program next year. The complex mix of three kids in each group also makes random selection and assignment problematic. So we think some kind of matched control group needs to be identified and tracked on key developmental markers along with the children and youth participating in the program.

"There is some interesting work coming out of Northwestern University on matched control groups that may be very relevant to this context. Ideally we could also get some process measures that help identify influential program mediators, but we may not have sufficient resources for this. More important than the process measures is establishing causal connections between the mentoring program and important outcomes, best studied with some kind of quasi-experimental design."

Group 2—Youth Counselor Robert and Intergroup Relationship Specialist Frederick

"As you all may recall, our inquiry priorities focused on the mentees' peer relationships. These are awfully difficult to study," notes Frederick. "I know because I have been trying to refine methods for studying peer relationships for years."

Robert continues, "We have two ideas for studying peer relationships. One is to use what Frederick said is a participatory methodology, involving the kids themselves as researchers in the study—collecting data and analyzing and interpreting it. Kids are more likely to be honest and authentic with other kids than they are with most adults. And it could be a really great experience for some of these kids to have this kind of responsibility for research. We also value the commitments of participation."

Frederick adds, "And there is some wonderful recent research on participatory inquiry with children and youth that could be very helpful to us. Our other idea is basically to use some kind of case study methodology, focusing intensively on just a few kids. I learned a lot about case studies from my own mentor and believe that they can offer rich insights not attainable with other methodologies."

Group 3—Youth Counselor Latisha and Developmental Psychologist Gloria

"Our design relies mostly on existing data plus a carefully designed survey, to be administered once or twice a year to all participating children and youth, and maybe another survey or perhaps some interviews with the mentors," says Gloria. "The existing data include school information like test scores, grades, absences and truancies, and suspensions and other behavioral infractions. For the older youth, there are also juvenile crime data available from the city. And if we do decide to include physical health and well-being, there are lots of health department data we can use. It just makes practical sense to use existing data whenever possible. The survey then would measure all other important developmental variables, plus culturally adjusted markers of development, as relevant."

Latisha observes, "Even though kids have to do a lot of surveys, I think we could make this one interesting and even fun to fill out. Maybe we could even get the kids to give it to each other, like Robert and Frederick were saying. That could make it quite special."

Gloria adds, "We think this survey methodology allows us to get consistent, standardized information with the minimum of error. Even though there are cultural variations, we believe that development is a universal process and thus best assessed via standardized and carefully administered measures."

Group 4—Youth Center Director James and Program Evaluation Expert Linda

"Our ideas combine some of the best thoughts of all of you," said Linda. "Please recall that we identified both program processes and short-term program outcomes as important foci for the study. We think that some kind of comparison—kids in the program to similar kids not in the program—will be important for the outcomes component of the study, both for us and for the W. T. Grant Foundation. And we believe that a realist, theory-driven framework for this outcomes component is appropriate."

James observes, "While development may not be universal, we believe that what counts as positive development in our community counts for all kids and can be assessed with high-quality, consistent measures (even as they are culturally responsive)."

Linda finishes, "At the same time, the experiences of the mentees and mentors in the program are likely to be quite variable and individual, best understood through a constructivist lens with accompanying open-ended, qualitative kinds of methods—interviews are likely to be most helpful here, although creative ideas like journaling and photography may also be quite useful."

Interlude

Again, please observe the various influences on these different ideas about study design and methods. A sampling of these influences includes:

- Methodological beliefs and traditions (causal understanding as most important and the experiment as the ideal design to obtain causal understanding, Pedro and Anne; the importance of standardized measurement, Latisha and Gloria)

- Methodological orientation (to research, the first three pairs; to program evaluation, the fourth pair)

- Contextual opportunities and constraints ("But that won't be possible here" —Pedro and Anne)

- The research literature ("Some interesting work coming out of Northwestern University"—Pedro and Anne; "Some wonderful recent research on participatory inquiry with children and youth"—Robert and Frederick)

- Professional experience ("I know because I have been trying to refine methods for studying peer relationships for years"—Frederick)

- Values ("We also value the commitments of participation"—Robert and Frederick)

- Education and training ("I learned a lot about case studies from my own mentor" —Frederick)

- Practicality ("It just makes practical sense to use existing data whenever possible" —Latisha and Gloria)

- Conceptual theories and beliefs ("We believe that development is a universal process"—Latisha and Gloria)

- Philosophy of science ("A realist, theory-driven framework . . . [and] best understood through a constructivist lens"—James and Linda)

- Creativity ("Creative ideas like journaling and photography may also be quite useful"—James and Linda)

MAKING SENSE OF THESE CONVERSATIONS: THE CONCEPT OF MENTAL MODELS

This group of youth development practitioners and researchers offered varied though not necessarily conflicting ideas for study foci and design—ideas that appear to be influenced by or rooted in an even greater variety of underlying predispositions, beliefs, and understandings. These underlying influences can be roughly grouped into the following (overlapping) clusters, with illustrations from the preceding scenario:

- *Substantive theory,* as in particular genres of developmental psychology or intergroup relationships, as well as *theoretical commitments* therein—for example, to universal or to culturally sensitive markers of development—along with *relevant research literature,* as in ongoing empirical work on youth development

- *Disciplinary perspectives,* mostly the psychology of positive youth development in the preceding scenario

- *Philosophy of science,* which includes beliefs about the nature of the social world, the nature of the knowledge we can have about that social world, and what is important to know—as in traditions of realism and constructivism

- *Methodological traditions,* as in experimentalism, case study inquiry, survey research, secondary data analysis, and participatory inquiry; as well as *methodological genres,* as in research and evaluation

- *Education and training,* as in the substantive and methodological orientations of one's formal education, as well as experiential influences from powerful mentors; along with *professional experience,* or ideas and commitments obtained from one's own practice over time

- *Contextual factors*—including issues of practicality and resources, opportunities, and constraints presented by the context at hand, important trends or issues in the larger community or society

- *Political factors,* as in sensitive issues of race and class, and issues of power and voice

- *Personal values,* as in a respect for diversity or a commitment to inclusive participation by all affected or a valuing of creativity; along with *personal experience,* or ideas and commitments obtained from one's own lived experience

These clusters, and probably others as well, represent important and intertwined strands of the individual *mental models* that guide the work of social inquirers. A mental model is the set of assumptions, understandings, predispositions, and values and beliefs with which all social inquirers approach their work. Mental models influence how we craft our work in terms of what we choose to study and how we frame, design, and implement a given inquiry. Mental models also influence how we observe and listen, what we see and hear, what we interpret as salient and important, and indeed what we learn from our empirical work. Speaking of evaluation, Mary Lee Smith (1997) observed, "A particular evaluation rests on the evaluator's mental picture of what the world is like, how evaluations ought to be, and what counts as knowledge. Because evaluation is a social action, an act of inquiry rests also on expectations of what standards the relevant community will likely apply to it" (p. 73); for example, the Joint Committee Standards for Educational Evaluation that are widely accepted by evaluators (http://www.wmich.edu/evalctr/jc/). Moreover, distinguishing relatively crude mental models from formalized statements of assumptions in the form of philosophical paradigms, Smith continued, "initial designs, as well as the day-to-day decisions, negotiations, and compromises that seem to characterize all inquiry projects, depend on the crude mental models of the people involved. . . . It is the crude mental model [rather than the formalized, logical paradigm] that gauges the potential meaning and usefulness of employing Method A or Method B or some combination of A and B.

Likewise, it is the crude model that embeds standards for considering the information yield of these methods" (M. L. Smith, 1997, p. 74).

Denis Phillips (1996) referred to the concept of mental models in a discussion of the connections between philosophical perspectives and the practice of social inquiry. He suggested that mental models comprise "assumptions, analogies, metaphors, or crude models that are held at the outset of the researcher's work . . . [that is, they] are present even before any [more formal or explicit] theories or models have been constructed" (pp. 1008–1009). For M. L. Smith, an inquirer's mental model is best revealed not by formally inquiring about her or his epistemological and ontological beliefs, but rather by "shaking an evaluator awake in the middle of the night and asking, Is it possible to have validity without reliability? Or, Can an evaluator know anything about a program without having seen it in action personally?" (1997, p. 74).

The stance taken in this book is wholly consonant with the ideas about mental models presented by M. L. Smith and Phillips. From these ideas, a mental model is understood as the complex, multifaceted lens through which a social inquirer perceives and makes sense of the social world. Each inquirer's mental model is unique, just as each human being in the world is unique. At the same time, facets of mental models are commonly shared across inquirers—as when the inquirers have similar educational backgrounds, professional experiences, and personal values and beliefs, or when the meanings of these mental model facets are socially constructed. Mental models thus subsume philosophical paradigms, as well as substantive theories, disciplinary perspectives, and a whole host of more personalized experiences, values, and ways of knowing.

Furthermore, it is inquirers' mental models that importantly frame and guide social inquiry. Decisions about what to study, how to study it, and why are all rooted in the complex tangle of substantive frameworks, methodological training, philosophical stances, practical experience, personal commitments, and so forth that an inquirer brings to a social scientific study. Just as important, the interpretive sense that inquirers make of their data is also guided by their understandings of meaning and of the rules of interpretation they have embraced, and by their self-understandings of themselves as social inquirers—in short, by their mental models.

MIXED METHODS SOCIAL INQUIRY AS MIXING MENTAL MODELS

Moreover, in the emerging tradition of mixed methods approaches to social inquiry that is the subject of this book, the concept of mental models has a central role. The core meaning of mixing methods in social inquiry is to invite multiple mental models into the same inquiry space for purposes of respectful conversation, dialogue, and learning one from the other, toward a collective generation of better understanding of the phenomena being studied. By definition, then, mixed methods social inquiry involves a plurality of philosophical paradigms, theoretical assumptions, methodological traditions, data gathering and analysis techniques, and personalized understandings and value commitments—because these are the stuff of mental models.

But by extension, the mixed methods conversation is not fundamentally about paradigm commensurability or the compatibility of rival theoretical explanations or even the consonance of various methodological traditions. Of course, these considerations feature in the conversation, because they are part of the mix. Considered and thoughtful attention to various ways of knowing and various ways of conducting social inquiry is, in fact, a central and defining characteristic of mixed methods inquiry as presented in this book. Most fundamentally, to mix methods in social inquiry is to set a large table, to invite diverse ways of thinking and valuing to have a seat at the table, and to dialogue across such differences respectfully and generatively toward deeper and enhanced understanding. This view positions mixed methods inquiry as a practice of active engagement with difference. "In good mixed methods evaluation, difference is constitutive and generative" (Greene, Benjamin, & Goodyear, 2001, p. 32).

AN INVITATION TO READ THIS BOOK

Anchored in the concept of mental models and in the importance of engaging with difference in social inquiry, this book presents a particular conceptualization of the rationale, location, and practice of mixed methods social inquiry. In the book, I retain the label of *mixed methods* social inquiry, because of the historical legacies of this label (as further discussed in Chapter Three). But in my view, mixed methods social inquiry is *not* chiefly about mixing different ways to gather, analyze, and interpret empirical data about social life. Rather, the various ways in which different methods can be mixed represent the practice of this genre of social inquiry, but not its purpose or role in society. Practice is, of course, critically important, and the field of mixed methods inquiry currently embraces a rich array of creative ideas about how to mix diverse methods in social research and evaluation. The authors of these creative ideas have contributed thoughtfully to the mixed methods conversation about design (Creswell, 2002; Maxwell & Loomis, 2003; Tashakkori & Teddlie, 1998), language and terminology (Teddlie & Tashakkori, 2003), and analysis (Bazeley, 2003; Onwuegbuzie & Teddlie, 2003). Many of their ideas are included in the practice sections of this book (chapters Six through Ten).

But distinctively, this book emphasizes the rationales and purposes for mixing methods in social inquiry. It is centered on the value of mixed methods inquiry for the overall purpose of *better understanding* social phenomena, which are inherently complex and contextual (as elaborated in Chapter Six). In this book, mixed methods practice becomes defined and directed by mixed methods purpose. The discussion in the book is also resolutely grounded in a distinctive stance regarding the role of science in society—a stance committed to *meaningful engagement with difference*—and the book focuses on the particular, even unique contributions that mixed methods inquiry offers to this engagement (as elaborated in Chapter Two). Moreover, what is importantly mixed in mixed methods inquiry—or the differences that are engaged—goes well beyond method to include the myriad other strands entangled in inquirers' mental models. As illustrated previously, some of these strands are the inquirer's philosophical assumptions, theoretical commitments, political beliefs, personal wisdom, and professional experience; other strands are represented in specific data gathering and analysis tools. (See chapters Four and Five for further discussion of all that can be mixed in mixed methods inquiry, and why social inquirers should seriously and thoughtfully consider these multiple mixes in their work.)

In these ways, the discussion in this book offers a counterpoint to two trends in the broader contemporary mixed methods conversation. In one trend, mixed methods inquiry is importantly defined by its *design* alternatives, which comprise various methods (usually labeled *qualitative* and *quantitative*) arranged in various sequences and priorities. Discussions of these design alternatives—again while contributing creatively to ideas about mixed methods practice—too often give only passing attention to the many other dimensions of difference that are inherently part of social inquiry. Muted by the emphasis on design typologies are the possible contributions to better understanding that could come from mixes of differences in philosophy, substantive theory, and disciplinary thinking, alongside mixes of differences in personal experience, education, values, and beliefs. This book is a clear and unequivocal argument in favor of the richness of mixing multiple dimensions of social inquirers' mental models, as this best serves the generative potential of mixed methods inquiry. Moreover, a priority focus on design and method in the mixed methods conversation is misplaced, as methods are always the servants of substance, not vice versa.

The second trend popular in current mixed methods discourse features the advancement of an "alternative" philosophical paradigm for mixed methods social inquiry; that is, alternative to extant "quantitative" and "qualitative" paradigms. *Paradigm* in this discussion refers to an integrated set of assumptions about the nature of the social world, about the character of the knowledge we can have about the social world, and about what is important to know. Social science in most Western societies was dominated by a post-positivist paradigm (Phillips & Burbules, 2000) through much of the twentieth century. The assumptions of this paradigm characteristically invoke standardized, a priori, quantitative designs and methods. During the last three decades of the twentieth century, persistent challenges to post-positivist thought generated an explosion of interest in other philosophical paradigms more consonant with qualitative methodologies, including interpretivism, various forms of constructivism, and phenomenology (Schwandt, 2000, 2001). A smaller explosion of interest occurred in ideologically oriented philosophical paradigms—notably, critical social science and multiple forms of feminist thought. And more recently, postmodern and poststructural challenges to all previous "meta-narratives" (Lyotard, 1984)—such as philosophical paradigms—have crowded the spaces where philosophical assumptions are engaged and contested. These are heady and difficult debates, as the issues are complex and abstract. Is the social world really there, or is it constructed by people in interaction with one another? Are there only contextual truths, or are there some understandings about human behavior that are true across different settings? How are the predispositions and standpoints of the inquirer present in the knowledge that is generated in a given study, and is this really a problem? And so forth. It is understandably tempting to locate the mixed methods discussion in a space uncluttered by such complexities and unfettered by such abstractions. It is understandably tempting to identify an "alternative" philosophical paradigm that somehow dissolves or resolves these long-standing debates, a paradigm like American pragmatism (Biesta & Burbules, 2003) or critical realism (Maxwell, 2004a).

In this book, I enthusiastically support the consideration of possible alternative paradigms for mixed methods social inquiry. I consider this a viable stance on the challenging issue of mixing what can be different, even incompatible philosophical assumptions in a mixed methods study. But I reject this as the only viable response to this challenge, embracing instead several other stances on mixing paradigms while mixing methods. Again, because I believe that the generative and creative potential of mixed methods social inquiry requires full engagement with differences of all kinds, I resist trends or ideas that seek to paper over potentially important differences or to homogenize mixed methods thought along just one channel. (Again, these ideas about how philosophy of science is engaged in mixed methods inquiry are elaborated in chapters Four and Five.)

WHO IS INVITED

Applied social inquirers from multiple fields are the intended audiences for this book—academicians, graduate students, and practitioners alike. Although the examples presented favor the fields I know, particularly educational program evaluation, the ideas are applicable to all fields of applied social inquiry.

The next four chapters of the book address conceptual issues in mixed methods social inquiry, followed by five chapters devoted to mixed methods practice and then a concluding final chapter. Small examples are sprinkled throughout the book. Three extended examples are also included as concrete illustrations of the conceptual ideas presented. The examples both illustrate and reinforce two final premises of this book—that mixed methods practice is one of artful craftspersonship and that practice is ever so much harder than theory (Schwandt, 2003). Mixed methods "theory" today consists of several organized sets of concepts and ideas that offer important guidance but not prescriptive instructions for mixed methods practice. The mixed methods practitioner must indeed be a craftsperson, making sense of these conceptual ideas in the context at hand, and patiently weaving and reweaving them into a meaningful pattern and a practically viable blueprint for generating better understanding of the social phenomena being investigated.

CHAPTER

ADOPTING A MIXED METHODS WAY OF THINKING

A CRITICAL part of the journey is encountered in this chapter, which presents the major stances and strands of a mixed methods way of thinking, which in turn forms the core rationale for the journey itself. A mixed methods way of thinking aspires to better understand complex social phenomena by intentionally including multiple ways of knowing and valuing and by respectfully engaging with differences, both those presented by other inquirers' mental models and those located in the social world. The traveler on this leg of the journey will engage with a mixed methods way of thinking and begin to craft his or her own portrait of it.

Social inquiry begins with purpose. From purpose come specific inquiry questions, and from questions, particular inquiry designs and methods (I. Newman, Ridenour, C. Newman, & DeMarco, 2003). At this juncture in time, there are a variety of legitimate purposes for social inquiry, both research and evaluation. Research and evaluation purposes overlap but also have distinctive characters and justifications. Research purposes tend to be rooted in the philosophical paradigm that is framing the research study, explicitly or, perhaps more commonly, implicitly. Historically, the dominant purpose for social research has been to develop sound explanations for social phenomena in order to better predict and control them, following the model of the natural sciences. The idea of societal improvement through social engineering well captures this purpose, which is firmly anchored in post-positivist principles and assumptions. With the proliferation and general acceptance of multiple other paradigms for research came other purposes. For example, research in an interpretivist or a constructivist framework characteristically seeks in-depth contextual understanding with an eye to legitimization of local and practitioner knowledge. Critical social scientific research aims for social critique in the interests of greater justice or equity in society. And action-oriented research typically seeks actionable knowledge in service of concrete changes in the context being studied, toward greater participation and empowerment, particularly of those with less power and privilege.

In evaluation, purposes can be grouped into four primary clusters (Greene, 2000). (Although evaluations can be conducted on programs, policies, proposals, products, performances, and personnel, among other entities [Scriven, 1999], throughout this book evaluations of programs will be the primary type of evaluation discussed.) The four clusters of evaluation purpose can be roughly aligned with different philosophical paradigms, but more importantly are aligned with different audiences for evaluation studies, as follows:

- Evaluations that are conducted to inform decision making or to provide accountability information characteristically serve the information needs and interests of policy and other decision makers.

- Evaluations that are conducted to improve the program being evaluated or to enhance the development of the organization in which the program is located typically provide information of value to managers and others responsible for day-to-day program operations.

- Evaluations that are conducted to develop a more in-depth and contextualized understanding of the program and its practices—perhaps from the different perspectives of administrators, board members, direct service staff members, and program participants—usually serve the information needs and interests of program staff members, and sometimes of participants as well.

- Evaluations that are designed to promote greater justice and equity in the program and context being evaluated—for example, to make the decision making about the program more inclusive of diverse perspectives or to democratize program decision making (House & Howe, 1999)—characteristically serve the interests of program participants, their families, and communities.

Collectively, these multiple and diverse purposes for social research and evaluation are all considered legitimate and are all broadly accepted by the research and evaluation communities, though not by all individual inquirers. Disputes about these purposes accompanied their emergence and proliferation and still continue today. To illustrate, the historically and still dominant primary inquiry purpose of explanation, for subsequent uses of prediction and control, has been challenged in a number of ways. Questions about the nature of "scientific explanation" have been raised, as have related questions about the nature of causality in the social world (Maxwell, 2004b; Salmon, 1998). Is the only or the most important form of explanation in social inquiry one that causally and linearly links A to B—for example, linking participation in a problem-based learning program to the development of critical thinking skills in young children, the presence of a strong adult role model to youth's abstinence from substance abuse, or the provision of adequate sensory stimulation to an infant's speech development? What kind of inquiry is invoked by a model of causality that is more recursive, iterative, and reciprocal? Or more spatial and temporal? Or more contextual and storied? And what *is* the role of context in causal ascription? Can causal claims from a given study be unproblematically generalized to other locales and settings? Or are particular features of a context constitutive of the causal relationships found in an inquiry study, so that the same causal pattern is not likely to show up in a different context? Further, what is the role and nature of values in social inquiry? Are values separately identifiable entities that can be studied empirically, somehow interwoven into the very fabric of inquiry findings and thus our claims to know, or are these issues better left to the clerics and the politicians?

These disputes and contestations about the purposes of social inquiry are important. Yet they are not likely to be resolved any time soon, as they are rooted in quite different, even incommensurable assumptions and stances about reality, knowledge, and especially the purpose and role of social science in society. So all social inquirers today need to figure out how to engage this disputed territory of inquiry purpose *and* to justify their stance. This is a distinct responsibility of contemporary social inquiry, and it is twofold. First, inquirers today need to identify the inquiry purpose and accompanying approach that best fit their own mental models and substantive work. In past eras, one became a bona fide social researcher or evaluator by learning about the "proper methods, properly applied" (J. K. Smith, 1983, 1985). Today, however, given the multiplicity of perspectives and stances regarding social inquiry, responsible inquirers need to become educated about the various options and make a carefully considered and justified choice about what approach to inquiry they will take in their work and for what purpose, or in service of whose interests. Second, inquirers today need to decide whether or not and in what ways they will participate in the continuing debates about inquiry purpose and role in society, and again, why or with what justification. Some contemporary inquirers choose to join a community of like-minded scholars or practitioners and "do their own thing," without undue concern for or preoccupation with those with different views and perspectives. Other inquirers choose to fully engage the disputes themselves by mounting eloquent arguments for their own point of view. These ongoing debates are, for the most part, a sign of healthy vitality within the social science community. And still other contemporary social inquirers seek to acknowledge contested spaces and ideas without trying to assert the supremacy of any given one, but rather with intentions of actively engaging in dialogue with "others," of dialoguing across difference (Burbules & Rice, 1991), toward enhanced and more generative understanding. This latter response to continuing debates about the purpose and character of social inquiry represents a mixed methods way of thinking. With this book, I extend an invitation to all readers to learn more about this way of thinking about applied social research and evaluation and to reflectively contemplate its relevance for your own work.

A MIXED METHODS WAY OF THINKING

A mixed methods way of thinking is a stance or an orientation toward social research and evaluation that is rooted in a multiplistic mental model and that actively invites to participate in dialogue—at the large table of empirical inquiry—multiple ways of seeing and hearing, multiple ways of making sense of the social world, and multiple standpoints on what is important and to be valued and cherished. A mixed methods way of thinking rests on assumptions that there are multiple legitimate approaches to social inquiry and that any given approach to social inquiry is inevitably partial. Moreover, social phenomena are extraordinarily complex. The esteemed educational researcher David Berliner recently observed that educational phenomena are ever so much more complex than most natural phenomena in domains like physics and astronomy. In fact, he encouraged a variation on the common phrase, "It's not rocket science!"—a new phrase acknowledging and honoring the complexities of teaching and learning: "Well, at least it's not educational research" (Berliner, 2002).

Given this complexity, better understanding of the multifaceted character of educational and other social phenomena can be obtained from the use of multiple approaches and ways of knowing. A mixed methods way of thinking is thus generative and open, seeking richer, deeper, better understanding of important facets of our infinitely complex social world. A mixed methods way of thinking generates questions, alongside possible answers; it generates results that are both smooth and jagged, full of relative certainties alongside possibilities and even surprises, offering some stories not yet told (Greene, 2005a).

Three critical features of a mixed methods way of thinking—its orientation around the broad purpose of generating better understanding of social phenomena, its roots in a multiplistic mental model, and its dialogic value commitment to engaging with difference—are previewed in the discussion that follows.

Toward Better Understanding

The primary purpose of a study conducted with a mixed methods way of thinking is to better understand the complexity of the social phenomena being studied. In a mixed methods way of thinking, *better understanding* can take various forms, more than one of which may be invoked in a given study. Better understanding in a mixed methods study can mean:

- Getting it right, enhancing the validity or credibility of our findings

- Doing our work better, generating understandings that are broader, deeper, more inclusive, and that more centrally honor the complexity and contingency of human phenomena

- Unsettling the settled; probing the contested; challenging the given; engaging multiple, often discordant perspectives and lenses

- Foregrounding the political and value dimensions of our work, to not just illuminate them but also to engage with each other about our differences, to advance our dialogues

Different mixed methods purposes—that is, different forms of "better understanding"—are connected to different inquiry questions, different combinations of methods, and different approaches to mixed methods analysis. These variations on mixed methods purpose are further discussed and illustrated in Chapter Six.

Example. Patricia Phelan (1987) presents an early mixed methods study that demonstrates in practice how the use of both qualitative and quantitative methods generated better understanding. Her work, in particular, illustrates the "dialectical tacking" between different perspectives advanced by Geertz (1983).

Phelan's study investigated the "systems of meaning" surrounding incidents of incest. She initiated the study as an intensive ethnography in an educational treatment program serving about five hundred families with histories of incest. Phelan had to spend many months as an intern counselor in the program, establishing rapport and credibility and learning the culture and language of the program context, prior to beginning her life history interviews with program participants. Her initial interviews were conducted with participants with whom she had the most rapport. Even so, she began to develop several hunches about differences in the incestuous relationships of birth fathers and stepfathers. For example, some stepfathers talked about this relationship in romantic terms, compared to birth fathers' statements that indicated objectification of their daughters.

Phelan then wanted to confirm or disconfirm these hunches in a more systematic and representative manner, so she interviewed counselors and intensively studied the case descriptions of 102 program participants, representing all the families the program had worked with in the preceding year. She developed a quantitative database of the characteristics of the incestuous relationships for these 102 families; for example, number of children involved, how old the children were when the molestation began, and if the abuse reached full sexual intercourse. For each of these variables, there were statistically significant differences between birth fathers and stepfathers.

Phelan concludes,

> The quantitative differences found in this investigation would not have emerged had they not been preceded by the gathering of qualitative data. Further, the quantitative differences alone have little meaning. It was necessary to return to ideas . . . [in] the qualitative analysis to begin to build a coherent picture of the process of incest in these two family types." (p. 40)

On Multiplism

In a highly regarded and highly influential book chapter published in 1985, Thomas Cook shared his vision of "post-positivist critical multiplism" (Cook, 1985). Said Cook,

> In a world where one way of conducting research was universally considered to be "correct," scientific practice would be easy. Researchers would simply do what is correct. It is the current absence of total certainty about what constitutes correct practice that leads to the advocacy of multiplism in perspectives and methods. (p. 22)

> This chapter is concerned with what I think is the most pressing methodological problem of our day: How can scientific practice be justified in light of the cogent criticisms of its most basic premises by philosophers, historians, and sociologists of science? . . . [a problem felt] most acutely by those who have worked at the [evaluation] interface between social science and social policy. (p. 21)

Cook's chapter first historically traces the philosophical attacks on "positivism" and the serious challenges faced by social scientists when they tried to use the experimentalist methodologies of positivism to evaluate the U.S. social reforms of the 1960s Great Society—antipoverty programs. Both of these histories are well documented in the general social science and evaluation literatures (see, for example, Cronbach & Associates, 1980; Gage, 1989; Pressman & Wildavsky, 1979; Weiss, 1972). In Cook's analysis, these philosophical and evaluative histories both witnessed a decrease in the authority of social scientific theory and conventional method, notably the randomized experiment and the survey, among other consequences. But, argued Cook, "declines are not disappearances;" that is, these histories led to "old certainties unthroned, but not abolished" (pp. 37–38).

In the remainder of the chapter, Cook presents his theory of multiplism.

> The fundamental postulate of multiplism is that when it is not clear which of several options for question generation or method choice is "correct," all of them should be selected so as to "triangulate" on the most useful or the most likely to be true. If practical constraints prevent the use of multiple alternatives, then at least more than one should be chosen, preferably as many as span the full range of plausible alternative interpretations of what constitutes a useful question or a true answer. (p. 38)

This theory extended the established practice of multiple operationalism (Campbell & Fiske, 1959; Webb, Campbell, Schwartz, & Sechrest, 1966) to nine other dimensions of social inquiry practice, making a total of ten:

1. Measure important constructs in multiple ways (multiple operationalism), and measure multiple types of constructs (for example, behavioral and mentalist).

2. Use multiple methods in research (including both quantitative and qualitative methods).

3. Plan multiple interconnected studies in research programs, rather than rely on the illusive single definitive study.

4. Synthesize multiple studies conducted outside planned research programs (using literature reviews or meta-analyses).

5. Construct complex multivariate causal models, instead of simple univariate ones.

6. Competitively test multiple models and multiple rival hypotheses, rather than just one.

7. Use multiple stakeholders, rather than policymakers alone, to formulate research questions.

8. Use multiple theoretical and value frameworks to interpret research questions and findings.

9. Use multiple analyses and multiple analysts to examine important datasets.

10. Implement multitargeted research that probes many different issues in a single study.

Cook's multiplistic conceptualization of social research and the knowledge it can generate is both bold and conservative—bold in acknowledging that contextual contingency, complexity, and value plurality are inherent in human affairs, yet conservative in retaining commitments to "multiple verification and the falsification of identified alternative interpretations" (1985, p. 40). "Multiplism is mean to raise consciousness about what should be learned to help increase the likelihood that knowledge claims are true" (p. 46). Cook's multiplism thus privileges convergent truths through triangulation even as it provides spaces for divergence and difference, regarding such occurrences as troublesome "empirical puzzles." Cook's multiplism represents a significant step toward the multiplistic mental model that underlies a mixed methods way of thinking and has indeed helped to shape my own thinking.

Yet Cook remains quite firmly grounded in the realist and truth-seeking commitments of post-positivist thought and—while open to multiple inquiry questions, methods, analyses, theories, and values—does not embrace alternative philosophical ways of knowing or kinds of knowledge. There does not seem to be a place in Cook's multiplism for socially constructed meaning or hermeneutic dialogic understanding or critical race theory critique—at least, not as forms of knowledge.

A mixed methods way of thinking, as presented in this book, respects and actively embraces multiple philosophical and theoretical stances on knowledge and legitimizes diverse claims to know. Mixed methods multiplism, at root, accepts the legitimacy of multiple and diverse ways of knowing, the partiality of any one way of knowing, and thus the desirability of multiple stances on knowledge in service of more comprehensive insights and understandings. Sharing considerable justificatory space with Cook's multiplism and owing an important intellectual debt to his ideas, my multiplistic mental model is more expansive and more inclusive.

Moreover, multiplism as a grounding for a mixed methods way of thinking does not privilege convergence, consonance, or consensus and thereby triangulation, but views with equal regard divergence, dissonance, and Cook's "empirical puzzles." There are two reasons for this. First, the idea of divergence or dissonance captures the full generative potential of mixed methods social inquiry. Done thoughtfully, mixed methods inquiry can generate puzzles and paradoxes, clashes and conflicts that, when pursued, can engender new perspectives and understandings, insights not previously imagined, knowledge with originality and artistry. Surely the continuing crises that plague our world need all of our creativity and insight. Classic case studies in the literature also illustrate this mixed methods promise (Jick, 1983; Louis, 1981; Maxwell, Bashook, & Sandlow, 1986; Phelan, 1987; Trend, 1979). A second reason that multiplism in mixed methods thinking embraces dissonance alongside consonance is the importance of positioning social inquiry as meaningful engagement with difference. And it is this latter reason that rescues multiplism from extreme relativism.

Following a presentation of a mixed methods classic, the importance of engaging with difference is elaborated.

Example. An early mixed methods policy evaluation well illustrates the contributions of multiplism to a mixed methods way of thinking. For this reason, among others, this study is considered a mixed methods classic (Trend, 1979).

In 1972, the U.S. Department of Housing and Urban Development (HUD) sponsored a social experiment in which low-income families were given a direct cash housing allowance instead of housing subsidies. The underlying idea was to use existing housing stock more efficiently and to provide low-income families with freedom of housing choice, rather than continuing to rely on highly concentrated blocks of public housing. Three studies were conducted on this social experiment. One studied effects on housing markets, a second investigated how recipients used their housing allowances, and a third—the focus of the mixed methods example—examined management practices associated with the direct cash allowance approach. For the third study, eight local public agencies, located in different parts of the country, designed and implemented their own versions of this housing allowance program. Abt Associates was awarded the contract for this administrative study, which used twelve analytic and management functions—for example, "audit and control"—to guide data collection and analysis aimed at identifying the most effective administrative practices.

The study design included a substantial investment in both quantitative and qualitative methods. Standardized forms were used to track families in the program. Families were also surveyed at regular intervals, and their housing was assessed both before and after program entry. In addition, an observer was assigned to each site for the first year of the experiment. The observer's job was to generate a holistic picture of each site, emphasizing administrative practices and daily rhythms in the office. Most of the observers were anthropologists. Separate reports were planned for quantitative program outcomes and qualitative program processes. In addition, a report that synthesized all relevant information and offered policy recommendations was planned.

The mixed methods story relates to substantial discrepancies in the quantitative and qualitative data reports for one site, called Site B. Site B included three subsites—two rural counties and one medium-sized city—each with its own branch office and with the urban office designated as the headquarters. The challenges arose in the urban branch of Site B. Quantitative data from year one indicated that the urban branch of Site B had served a large number of families efficiently, whereas the observation report signaled serious problems with actual program implementation and with internal office relationships and morale. These problems included (1) tensions with the overall contracting agency overseeing this site, which focused almost exclusively on getting the maximum number of families processed (nine hundred); (2) worries among the service staff about substandard housing being approved and about not being allowed to provide any counseling or support services to enrolled families; and (3) accusations, over time, of racial discrimination as the urban office was instructed by the contracting agency to curtail enrollments of African Americans in order to attain greater population balance in the families served. It is noteworthy that a number of housing counselors in this office resigned after this first year of the program.

Meanwhile, back in Cambridge (home of Abt Associates), the Site B observer's first written account of the dynamics of the site focused on overall site discord, particularly the conflicts between the contracting agency and the urban office, as well as managerial incompetence and insensitivity. Internal reviewers of this first report were concerned that it emphasized idiosyncratic tensions that were of little policy relevance and did not adequately describe the operation of the twelve management functions in this office. At this point, quantitative data beyond number of families served were not yet available. The Site B observer was instructed to begin the full case study report and to try to cover management functions more completely.

Five months later, the Site B draft case study report was again rejected. This report de-emphasized site discord and instead concentrated on staff overwork and "the heavy-handed interference of the contracting agency that wanted to succeed at any price" (Trend, 1979, p. 76). However, quantitative analyses now in hand indicated that not only did Site B serve a large number of families, but it did so with cost efficiency and with an appropriate representation of minorities. So even if "heavy-handed," this contracting agency did achieve results! Still out were data on actual improvements in housing quality for Site B families. And the credibility of the Site B observer was beginning to be questioned.

Several more drafts of the case study report for Site B were generated, each rejected by the core project analysts. A final version portrayed the issue as one of differing opinions on what the program should accomplish. The contracting agency prioritized outcomes, whereas the local office prioritized services and quality of living conditions. Just at that moment, however, the data analyses on housing quality showed that "Site B recipients enjoyed an improvement in housing quality that ranked second in the [overall project]" (p. 77).

Sides began to be chosen. The Site B observer insisted that his interpretation was basically correct. He knew what he had seen. . . . Another [observer] asserted that outcome measures did not tell the whole truth, that quantitative techniques were "garbage" and that human behavior could not be reduced to "mere numbers." [But the Site B] observer was by now thoroughly discredited in the eyes of the Cambridge staff. (p. 77)

The empirical puzzle presented to the author of this account, who both believed in the observer and felt responsible for his work, was this: how could a program "produce such admirable results . . . when all of the observation data indicated the program would be a failure?" (p. 78). This puzzle was pursued with further analyses of critical points of divergence in the qualitative and quantitative data sets, including staff workload, monitoring of family data such as income and family size, and the office's efficiency. Comparisons of the urban office with the two rural offices were conducted. Other data were analyzed; for example, trends in housing markets. New hypotheses were generated—notably, that the efficiency of the urban office was illusory and that the housing counselors were alienated from the service-oriented work many wanted to do. The final case study report included many of these additional analyses and interpretations and hedged on the program outcome of housing quality, noting that families found whatever housing they did with no assistance from the program. Then it was discovered that the quantitative data on housing quality were actually faulty and not trustworthy.

In reflecting on this experience, Trend says

The difficulty lay in conflicting explanations or accounts, each based largely on a different kind *of data. The problems we faced involved not only the nature of observational* versus *statistical inferences, but two sets of preferences and biases within the entire research team. The solution was to overturn the existing explanations by offering a third. This required no brilliance, some ingenuity, and a good amount of tenacity. (p. 83, emphasis in original)*

The reader is encouraged to read the full account of this mixed methods classic.

Engaging with Difference

Just as social inquirers today must thoughtfully select and justify their own inquiry purposes and approaches from among the multiple contenders, so must contemporary inquirers wrestle with the politics and values of social inquiry. It is widely recognized that different inquiry traditions embrace different value commitments. For example, post-positivism remains committed to neutrality, objectivity, and open critique of empirical truth claims (Phillips, 1990; Phillips & Burbules, 2000), whereas many feminist traditions centrally advance commitments to the well-being of women and girls through the dismantling of patriarchy (Harding & Hintikka, 1983). In fact, for many post-positivists, values of objectivity, neutrality, and open critique are *the* values of science, whereas all other values are to remain separated out from science, as they are not subject to empirical examination or rational debate and adjudication (Phillips, 1990). Moreover, for the domain of evaluation, is it also widely recognized that evaluation practice is situated in inherently contested and politicized contexts and is thus imbued with strands of political and policy debate (Cronbach & Associates, 1980; Weiss, 1998). Some evaluators even contend that evaluation importantly helps not just to inform but to actually constitute the character and content of political discourse about contested issues (House, 1993).

In this section I offer the value commitments that inspire and motivate my own work as a social scientist, most particularly as an evaluator of social and educational public programs in the United States. These commitments color my own vision of a mixed methods way of thinking. In fact, these commitments pivotally influenced the evolution of my thinking about mixed methods social inquiry. I offer them to inform readers about my stances—not to try to persuade readers to my point of view, but rather so the other words and ideas in this book can, I hope, be interpreted more in line with their intentions. This is the section of narrative scholarship that I require all of my students to include and that I call "locating one's self in one's work."

My commitment to engaging with difference as fundamental to a mixed methods way of thinking has three intertwined dimensions: philosophy, methodology, and ideology. It is motivated overall by a commitment to positioning social inquiry in service of the public good (Greene, 2005b), as elaborated in the discussion that follows.

First, with respect to philosophy, a mixed methods way of thinking actively engages with epistemological differences in order to (1) respect multiple ways of knowing, from the post-positivist proposition to the Marxist-feminist social critique; and (2) understand and respect some of the deep contradictions posed by different epistemological traditions; yet (3) not get stuck in these contradictions *nor* feel forced to choose sides—that is, to choose just one way of knowing—but instead, (4) invite multiple ways of knowing into the same study so that it may be deeply and generatively enriched (Greene & Caracelli, 1997a). Yes, multiple and diverse ways of knowing are likely to invoke some tensions. Yet it is precisely in these tensions that the generative potential of mixed methods inquiry might best be realized (Greene, 2001; Greene & Caracelli, 1997a). Moreover, some of these tensions can be reframed from highly abstract philosophical stances, such as objectivism and subjectivism, to less irreconcilable and more tangible features of social inquiry, such as particularity and generality, closeness and distance, the unusual and the representative (Bryman, 1988; Greene & Caracelli, 1997a). This idea is elaborated further in chapters Four and Five. Thus, my mixed methods epistemological stance is one of actively engaging with epistemological tensions and of actively resisting the false need to pick just one side. This engagement is not intended to be a contest or competition, but more of a conversation. The point is to see not who wins, but what can be learned, one from the other.

Joe Kincheloe (2001) recently made a similar argument for qualitative social research, using the concept of *bricolage* (from Denzin & Lincoln, 2000) and the importance of conducting inquiry that crosses traditional disciplinary boundaries:

The process at work in the bricolage involves learning from difference. Researchers employing multiple research methods are often not chained to the same assumptions as individuals operating within a particular discipline. As they study the methods of diverse disciplines, they are forced to compare not only methods also differing episte-mologies and social theoretical assumptions. . . . Bricolage does not simply tolerate *difference but* cultivates *it as a spark to researcher creativity. (pp. 686–687, emphasis in original)*

Second, with respect to methodology, mixed methods social inquiry, by definition, includes a diversity of methodological traditions, inquiry designs, methods for data gathering and analysis, and forms of interpretation and reporting. This methodological diversity is the signature character of a mixed methods approach to social research and evaluation. In the field of evaluation and in some domains of applied social research, inquirers have been mixing methods for some decades now, often as a practical response to multiple demands in the inquiry context. If it is important to gauge both the frequency and intensity of a phenomenon *and* its experiential meaningfulness, it simply makes good methodological sense to use both a survey and a case study design, perhaps analyzing existing administrative data and conducting a small set of intensive interviews. In fact, the emerging literature on mixing methods in social inquiry is precisely intended to offer some guidance and structure to what some inquirers have been doing for some time now in practice, so that methods are mixed with intention and thoughtfulness. What methodologically distinguishes a mixed methods way of thinking as presented in this book—specifically in terms of engaging with difference—is the privileging of mixing methods that are quite different from one another. As elaborated in Chapter Seven, one important dimension of mixed methods design is the kind and extent of difference among the methods selected for a given study. Closed-ended questions on a standardized, paper-and-pencil survey share many features with open-ended questions on the same instrument. Similarly, open-ended personal interviews share many features with semistructured focus group interviews. Yet ethnographic participant observation of the rhythms, events, and interactions in a school classroom is quite different from administering a standardized instrument assessing "classroom climate" along predetermined dimensions to the students in that classroom. Engaging methodologically with difference in mixed methods inquiry implies that, as possible and appropriate, methodologies and methods that are different in important ways are included in a mixed methods study, as this enhances not only the generative potential of mixed methods inquiry but also its potential to respect, appreciate, and accept variation and diversity in the substance of what is being studied.

Third, and perhaps most important, my commitment to a mixed methods way of thinking as a dialogic engagement with difference reflects my own ideological stances, substantiated by the recognition that epistemology, methodology, and ideology are intertwined, that ways of knowing and understanding are also ways of valuing. In my view, contemporary American society, and other societies as well in this post–September 11 world, are seriously fractured and even ruptured by differences in race, class, religion, culture, disability status and other demographic markers of diversity. Radical inequities and injustices of access and opportunity persist, based on nothing more substantial than historical legacies of discrimination and continuing prejudices. There is no more urgent national or global priority than to engage with this diversity, to learn how to live with, appreciate, and accept our differences. To conduct social inquiry with an intention to locate, attend to, and engage with the differences manifest in a given context is to conduct social inquiry in service of the public good.

A serious engagement with difference requires the rejection of old myths, stereo-typed images, and racialized code words like *urban* and *inner city* (Lee, 2003). It also requires rejection of race, ethnicity, culture, social class, religion, able-bodiedness, sexual orientation, and other markers of historical disadvantage as fixed or essential-ized categories rather than as multifaceted, situated, dynamic, and socially constructed dimensions of experience and identity (Orellana & Bowman, 2003).

> [We need to] resist simplistic assumptions about the meaning of group membership and develop more nuanced and complex research agendas [and evaluation questions] that work from a basic assumption that human beings always have agency, always have resources, and make meaning of their experience in varied ways. . . . (Lee, 2003, p. 4)

> [We need to disrupt and challenge persistent] folk theories about groups in the human family that are inextricably tied to relationships of power and dominance. . . . [We need to use] a dynamic view of culture as located in history, in belief systems, and as carried forward through institutional practices [to better understand, respect, and accept the Other]. (Lee, 2003, pp. 3)

That is to say, the idea of difference or diversity embraced in this book extends beyond historical markers of disadvantage in our contemporary society to include the infinite, astonishing other ways in which human beings are different from one another. In this conceptualization of difference, traditional social categories are both respected—because to do otherwise is to ignore past injustices and risk perpetuating them—and also troubled as but social constructions. Troubling traditional markers of diversity opens spaces for getting beyond them to other more personalized and meaningful dimensions of the human character and spirit.

Engaging with diversity and difference in social inquiry is thus both a substantive and a moral commitment. It is enacted in what issues we as inquirers address, what methods we use, what kinds of reports we craft—that is, where we locate our work in society—*and* in who we are as inquirers, where we position ourselves in our work, what kinds of relationships we forge with others, and what we attend to and what matters in those relationships (Greene, 2005b). A mixed methods way of thinking, as enacted in a mixed methods approach to inquiry, offers considerable promise for conducting social inquiry that meaningfully engages with difference and that is thus positioned in service to the public good, toward a noble vision of a pluralistic society characterized not by radical disparities in power and privilege, but by tolerance, understanding, and acceptance.

LOOKING AHEAD

Given this view of a mixed methods way of thinking, mixed methods inquiry is defined in this book as the planned and intentional incorporation of multiple mental models—with their diverse constituent methodological stances, epistemological understandings, disciplinary perspectives, and habits of mind and experience—into the same inquiry space for purposes of generatively engaging with difference toward better understanding of the phenomena being studied. Mixed methods inquiry thus defined has valuable potential to contribute to better understanding that is distinctively marked by greater tolerance, acceptance, and respect for difference.

Chapter Three presents some of the history of the contemporary interest in mixed methods social inquiry, including the "great quantitative-qualitative debate" of the 1960s, 1970s, and 1980s. Yet in this historical discussion, and throughout the remainder of this volume, the terms "qualitative" and "quantitative" will be reserved to refer to methodological traditions, methods, and forms of data, *not* to philosophical paradigms. Paradigms will be labeled with their appropriate monikers; for example, post-positivism and constructivism. This usage is intended to reinforce the importance of attending to philosophical assumptions, disciplinary perspectives, and other substantive components of mental models when conversing about mixing methods. The quantitative and qualitative labels make it too easy to focus on designs, methods, and data alone. They make it too easy to position the conversation at a technical level only, rather than at a level that encompasses issues related to the nature of knowledge, different ways of seeing and knowing, and varied purposes for social inquiry.

THE HISTORICAL ROOTS OF THE CONTEMPORARY MIXED METHODS CONVERSATION

A BIT of time travel into the recent past awaits the traveler in this chapter. The primary purpose of this time travel is to engender a thoughtful understanding of the origins of the contemporary interest in mixed methods social inquiry, under the premise that history is always instructive. Travelers thus will revisit the character of and issues constituting the qualitative-quantitative debate that occupied several decades of ferment in multiple social science communities during the latter half of the twentieth century.

For as long as I can remember, quantitative, qualitative, and mixed-model evaluations have co-existed. In the early days of the U.S. Office of Economic Opportunity, for example,

there were quasi-experimental designs (for instance, both the Westinghouse-Ohio study and the Head Start Longitudinal Study . . . used quasi-experimental designs). There were mixed-model designs, such as the classic Head Start Community Impact Study. [And] there were qualitative studies, such as Greenberg's The Devil Wears Slippery Shoes, a report on the Mississippi Community Action Program. . . . (Datta, 1994, p. 54)

The practice of mixing methods in empirical studies is not a new phenomenon, especially in the highly applied domains of social science that are dedicated to understanding and improving human practices in the real world, including education, social psychology, sociology, organizational studies, and evaluation. I have long surmised that methodological openness to new ideas—qualitative inquiry in the 1970s and mixed methods inquiry more recently—is more characteristic of highly applied domains than domains centered on laboratory research, precisely because the complex and messy demands of inquiry in the real world compel acceptance of multiple strategies and tools for understanding. Lois-ellin Datta's (1994) storied reflections on her decades of evaluative inquiry in service to public programs attest to this observation. But the current buzz about mixing methods in social inquiry *is* a more recent phenomenon—one that gradually took root in the 1980s, sprouted a few buds during the 1990s, and then started to blossom at the turn of the century. The current conceptual work in mixed methods inquiry is dedicated to giving some theoretical form to these burgeoning ideas about mixed methods inquiry. Indeed, many contemporary mixed methods concepts arose from reflective scrutiny of early pioneering empirical work (Greene, Caracelli, & Graham, 1989). And indeed, mixed methods "theory" proceeds well only in respectful conversation with practice.

The contemporary interest in mixed methods approaches to social inquiry is a natural and logical development, given the recent history of social scientific thought and practice—a history that spans the latter half of the twentieth century, with roots in prior eras. Understanding the main outlines of this history is essential to a full appreciation of the continuing issues and controversies in mixed methods inquiry. Historical grounding can significantly enrich meaningfulness and understanding. This chapter presents these historical outlines of the contemporary mixed methods conversation. The discussion starts with the seeds of discontent—sown mid-century both in the rarified realms of the philosophy of science as well as in the nitty-gritty trenches of applied social science practice, particularly program evaluation. This discontent shortly (in the 1960s and 1970s) took the form of a full-fledged battle of words and ideas, known then and now as the "great qualitative-quantitative debate" ("great," of course, only to those in the social scientific community who cared about it). The substance of this debate will be only briefly recounted, as there are already numerous excellent reconstructions of the arguments at hand. Some of the character and contours of the debate will also be shared, as those were intellectually challenging and very exciting times. The rapprochement that signaled the end of this great debate will then be discussed, with a particular focus on the logical emergence of rapprochement in the form of mixing methods; that is, as the inclusion of qualitative and quantitative methods in the same study. This idea had appeal in part because of the fairly long-standing acceptance of methodological triangulation in *both* qualitative and quantitative methodological traditions. The concept of triangulation and its origins in both traditions will be described as part of this history.

So a truce, if not a peace, was declared, although not all at once, not among all combatants, and not forever. And troubled waters remained. If one mixes methods, does that mean one also mixes paradigms? Is such an idea possible, sensible, practical? What are the politics of mixing methods? Is this just a ruse to silence those qualitative upstarts once and for all (Smith and Heshusius, 1986)? Witness the recent reengagement of these issues in the scholarly community in reaction to a reprivileging of quantification, standardization, outcomes, and even experimentation in some arenas by many western governments' wholesale adoption of new managerial practices and accountability-oriented policies during the past two decades (Power, 1999). Further, if methods are mixed, does this threaten the integrity and the quality of each method? And what about all the other paradigms and methodologies that have emerged in recent decades? Can one mix methods with a feminist paradigm? A participatory approach to social inquiry? A post-modern reading of social life as radically contingent and uncertain, best conceptualized as text and cinema? These and other questions that accompanied the emergence of the idea of mixing methods helped to catalyze further interest in and development of this approach to social inquiry.

Now to the brief recounting of the recent history in social scientific methodology that gave birth to the current mixed methods conversation.

THE PHILOSOPHICAL SEEDS OF DISCONTENT

At their beginnings, social sciences in many western societies, including the United States, were modeled after the natural sciences. Like their natural science colleagues, social scientists sought to induce theory from pristine observations and then test this theory under carefully controlled experimental conditions, toward empirically sound and generalizable propositions about how the social world worked. The purpose of this experimentalist social science, that is, was to explain and thereby predict and control the social world, just as physicists explain and endeavor to predict and control the worlds of quarks and quasars.

This way of thinking about social science was implicitly framed by a positivist and later a post-positivist paradigm. Post-positivism retained the ideals of positivism—the assumption that the social world exists independent of our knowledge of it (realism), a commitment to objective methods and to methodological sophistication, and the setting of questions of value outside the perimeter of scientific questions of fact, all in service of causal explanation as universal truth—but post-positivists retained these ideals with more humility, less faith in the power of method, and better acceptance of the inevitable fallibility of human beings as observers than their forbearers had. For example, acknowledging this fallibility, Donald Campbell, an exceptionally eloquent spokesperson for post-positivist thought during the twentieth century, advocated the submission of all social scientific knowledge claims to a "disputatious community of scholars" (Campbell, 1984, p. 44) to see which survive the tests of intellectual challenge, empirical replication, and time. (For further discussion of the philosophical evolution from positivism to post-positivism, see Cook, 1985; Phillips, 1990; and Phillips & Burbules, 2000.) This framing of social science by the tenets of post-positivism was implicit because this framework was neither acknowledged nor articulated, so it could not be challenged. One became a social science investigator mainly by acquiring strong skills in the accepted methods of inquiry of the day. And methods in post-positivism continue to be designed to serve, in large part, to protect the data from the particular predispositions and stances of the inquirer. Given this vitally important role, post-positivist methods grow ever more sophisticated with each advance in knowledge and technology.

Meanwhile, on the heights of erudite thinking about the nature of science, philosophers were fully engaged in conversations and debates about other frameworks for social science and had been since the latter part of the nineteenth century. At that earlier time, the philosopher Wilhelm Dilthey contended that there was a fundamental difference in subject matter between the natural sciences and the social sciences.

> *Whereas physical sciences dealt with a series of inanimate objects that could be seen as existing outside of us (a world of external, objectively knowable facts), [social] sciences focused on the products of the human mind with all its subjectivity, emotions, and values. From this [Dilthey] concluded that since social reality was the result of conscious human intention, it was impossible to separate the interrelationships of what was being investigated and the investigator. There was no objective social reality as such divorced from the people, including investigators, who participated in and interpreted that reality. . . . [So] the investigator of the social world could only attain an understanding of that world through a process of interpretation—one that inevitably involved a hermeneutical method. [Further] the meaning of human expression was context-bound and could not be divorced from context. (Smith & Heshusius, 1986, p. 5)*

Dilthey's interpretive stances for the social sciences stimulated multiple projects in the philosophy of science, as these stances raised considerable challenges to post-positivist assumptions. Instead of objective, realist, and generalizable claims of truth, interpretive knowledge was viewed as inherently and inevitably subjective, contextual, contingent, and value-laden.

By the middle of the twentieth century, these philosophical disputes had made their way to the communities of social science theorists and methodologists, quite a number of whom jumped into the fray. Social scientists' willingness to engage these complicated issues was encouraged by practical difficulties with the methods of post-positivist science (as discussed in the next section) and also, for some, by the general revolutionary temperament of the 1960s and 1970s, at least in the United States. Social movements abounded in that era—movements that sought to end the Vietnam War, shatter the shackles of discrimination and prejudice, and experiment with new social mores and norms. Disrupting the canons of high science, initiating conversations about the politics of method, and envisioning new horizons and possibilities for social science—these were easily embraced by those already wearing multicolored armbands of protest.

As will be elaborated in the discussion that follows on the great debate, these weighty issues about the very nature of social science were engaged both at the level of philosophy or worldview and at the level of methodology and technique. This is partly because many methodologists were quite comfortable engaging with the merits and limitations of standardized surveys compared to contextualized participant observation, but less comfortable engaging with the perennial philosophical debates about objectivism versus relativism or realism versus idealism. In fact, one indelible feature of that era was the heady immersion of many methodologists and practitioners in the abstractions of philosophy and the steep learning curve such immersion entailed. Again, one learned how to be a social scientific inquirer at that time by mastering method, not by pondering paradigms—because the exclusively dominant paradigm remained unspoken.

THE SEEDS OF DISCONTENT IN PRACTICE

The midpoint of the twentieth century in the United States was also the era of the War on Poverty, a massive social welfare campaign mounted by the federal government. Programs supported by considerable federal funding were initiated in nearly all sectors of social well-being—including education, employment, health, welfare, community development—with the collective intention of eradicating poverty in the country once and for all. A number of highly esteemed applied social scientists of that era—sociologists, psychologists, educators, and economists, including esteemed scholars Donald Campbell, Lee Cronbach, Carol Weiss, Peter Rossi, among others—were sufficiently beguiled and challenged by this enormously ambitious attempt at societal change to offer their expertise in studying its effects. Also, some of the federal initiatives were actually developed in tandem with evaluative mandates—perhaps most notably, the Elementary and Secondary Education Act of 1965.

So accompanying the War on Poverty were policy-oriented investigations of the quality and effectiveness of its many innovations and interventions—investigations that used the best and most sophisticated methodologies of that time, which were still the experimentalist methods of the post-positivist paradigm. But as has been well documented (with a near-legendary reputation), experimental methodologies did not, and in fact could not do the job. The need for randomization of potential program participants into control and experimental groups raised substantial ethical issues; even when possible, randomization was vulnerable to contamination. The important requirements of experiments for careful control over and standardization of the conditions under which participants experienced the intervention simply did not work in the real world of social interaction. In particular, defensible experimental research required standardized strategies in tightly controlled contexts, but good practice required constantly adjusting strategies to changing circumstances (Marris and Rein, 1982, p. 206). In programs such as Community Action Agencies this mismatch was clear. Peter Marris and Martin Rein explain,

As soon as the staff, through experimentation or trial and error, discovered a better way of serving trainees they adapted their procedures, methods and techniques accordingly. It was impossible to be inventive, flexible and expedient on the one hand and at the same time do careful, scientific, controlled research on the other (1982, p. 198).

Critics further argued that confining social inquiry to observable phenomena constrained, indeed even biased research on social programs and problems to the finite ability of research methods to capture such phenomena. Such a requirement also privileged the assessment of program inputs and outcomes, with but scant attention to program processes or experiences—a criticism later dubbed the "black box" approach to evaluation. Cook's post-positivist critical multiplism (1985), presented in Chapter One, is in significant part a response to this failure of the methods of experimental science in real world contexts. He summarizes,

We can see in the attack on [post-]positivist methods a rejection of the primacy of observation over introspection, quantification over understanding, micro-level over macro-level analysis, control over naturalism, theory testing over discovery, and crucial experiments conducted on select parts of nature over more tentative probing of all of nature. (p. 29)

In short, the experimental methods of post-positivist social science were not able to provide sound empirical data on the quality and effectiveness of the War on Poverty programs. In the field of evaluation, the time period following these failed experimental studies of the innovations of the War on Poverty (1970s and 1980s) saw an explosion of new ideas and theories about evaluation, some of which embraced the qualitative methodologies of the newly understood interpretive and constructivist paradigms and, some a bit later, more ideologically oriented paradigms of participation, social action, and social justice.

These seeds of discontent, in the form of serious challenges to standard social science practice, were experienced perhaps most acutely in the policy and program evaluation communities, but were certainly repeated elsewhere. The field of educational research, for instance, was fully engaged in these issues and controversies. The social science methodology pendulum was swinging hard and fast toward qualitative approaches to social inquiry, toward studies of people's contextualized experiences, toward inquiry rendered as narratives. But it wasn't swinging without opposition. Rather, what ensued was fifteen to twenty years of intense and sometime rancorous debate about the relative merits of comfortingly familiar quantitative methodologies compared with the discomforting strangeness of qualitative methodologies—along with their philosophical roots and rationales.

THE GREAT QUALITATIVE-QUANTITATIVE DEBATE

So conventional wisdom was being challenged in both theory and practice. When the assumptions and stances of post-positivism were articulated and held up for scrutiny, they were found wanting by some social scientists of the era. They were found wanting also because of the practical challenges they encountered on the ground, in the real world outside the laboratory. Experimental methods did not work as well with human beings as they did with crops or chemicals or magnetic forces. Human beings behaved with unpredictable intentionality, whereas crops and chemicals and magnetism appeared to behave in accordance with manipulated conditions. And the contexts inhabited by humans were not nearly as controllable as soil in fields or equipment in laboratories. Yet the assumptions and stances of interpretivism, constructivism, phenomenology, and other paradigms favoring qualitative methodologies appeared radical, even ludicrous to other social scientists—clearly an instance of throwing the baby out with the bathwater. What kinds of explanations and theories could be developed from single intensive case studies? How could empirical results be trusted if derived so subjectively? And what was really accomplished anyway by one interview with one person in one place at one time?

> What distinguishes the debate that gained ground in the 1970s was the systematic and self-conscious intrusion of broader philosophical issues into discussions of methods of research. . . . [And] there seem, then, to be two fairly distinct versions of the nature of the difference between quantitative and qualitative research which might usefully be referred to as the "epistemological" and the "technical" accounts. However, there is a tendency for many writers to oscillate between these two versions. (Bryman, 1988, p. 2, 107)

As astutely observed by Bryman, the qualitative-quantitative debate occurred on two main levels—the philosophical and the methodological—even as participants intermingled these two levels while contesting the issues and even as the debate also involved politics and values. A sampling of the key issues—philosophical, methodological, and political—that constituted the debate includes the following. (See also Greene & Henry, 2005.)

Issues at the Philosophical Level

As previewed earlier by Dilthey's ideas, central to the debate were different assumptions about the nature of the social world and the nature of social knowledge. In post-positivism, the social world is assumed to be real; that is, it exists independent of our knowledge of it. And it is assumed to operate much like the physical or natural world; that is, just as plants predictably react to varying environmental conditions of moisture, light, and temperature, so do humans predictably react to varying forces and factors in the external environment. Figuring out just what these forces and factors are, which is most influential, and how they interact is precisely the job of social scientists. In contrast, in most interpretive paradigms, the social world is assumed to be importantly constructed, at least in part. Human beings, unlike plants, act with intentionality. This intentionality is rooted in the meanings that people construct of various phenomena they encounter in their daily lives as they interact with others in varied settings. And it is these constructed meanings that significantly guide and shape human behavior, more so than external forces and factors. Moreover, because different contexts present different constellations of people, interactions, and events, what is meaningful to a given individual or group is, in important measure, context-specific rather than universal.

Post-positivist knowledge claims ideally constitute generalizable causal explanations of observed human phenomena. Post-positivists aim to generate, test, and substantiate theories about human behavior, which comprise empirically warranted propositions about what causes people to do particular things, such as learn well, become a star athlete, or engage in active citizenship or in criminal behavior. Interpretivists aim for contextualized understanding of the meaningfulness of humans' lived experiences. This form of social knowledge is not generalizable nor propositional in form, but rather multiplistic, dynamic, and contingent. Peer tutoring may help one child learn well but not help another, because these two children experience and make meaning of peer relationships in very different ways. Interpretivist knowledge claims are also characteristically textual, narrative, and holistic.

And post-positivists' knowledge claims are warranted by their correspondence with social reality. Truth is attained when theoretical predictions are supported by empirical data. Central to strong knowledge claims, or claims to truth, is excellence in method, so warrants are also constituted by evidence of methodological excellence. Interpretivists' knowledge claims are warranted by the persuasive power of the account. Interpretivists do not claim truth-status for what they come to know, because there are multiple truths or multiple meanings of human experience in any given context. Good method supports persuasive interpretive accounts. But such accounts are at core interpretations—by the person of his or her experience, by the inquirer of the person's interpretation of his or her experience, and then by the reader of the inquirer's interpretation of the person's interpretation of his or her experience (Van Maanen, 1995). These three moments of interpretation encapsulate the nonfoundationalist epistemology that significantly distinguishes interpretive paradigms from the foundational premises of post-positivism. (See J. K. Smith, 1989, for further discussion of this critical difference.)

Issues at the Methodological Level

As Bryman noted about this grand debate, intermingled with claims and counterclaims about the nature of the social world, the knowledge we can have about that social world, and thus what is important to know, were charges and countercharges about which set of methods for social inquiry was superior and why. Some of this intermingling was not by design, but some was. In fact, one contested issue in the debate was the necessary coupling of philosophical assumptions with particular methodologies. Do post-positivist beliefs require quantitative methods, and do constructivist commitments mandate the use of qualitative methods? This particular issue is discussed further in chapters Four and Five, as it bears on the role of philosophical assumptions in mixed methods inquiry. Although not yet settled—as few philosophical issues ever are—there emerged some common understandings about the relationship between philosophy and methodology, understandings central to the mixed methods movement and continuing conversation.

The contours of the overall debate at the methodological level are certainly now well known and familiar to the applied social science community. Quantitative methodologies were touted for their perceived superiority as carefully controlled and standardized assessments of human phenomena, as studies of samples carefully and randomly drawn from identified populations, and thus as capable of yielding generalizable claims about the human phenomena under study. Quantitative methods rely on a priori definitions (conceptual and operational) of what is being studied; on a priori designs, methods, and representative samples; and on limits to the number of statistical tests that can be conducted without violating error parameters established for purposes of confidence. Setting up the study in advance fulfills the deductive conditions and expectations of hypothesis testing. Social inquiry, after all, serves the primary purpose of theory testing and refinement. So quantitative methods, properly done, generate propositional findings with confidence, if not total certainty.

In contrast, qualitative methodologies were advanced for their perceived superiority as thoughtful studies of lived human experience, as intense and in-depth studies of a few cases or a few people—purposefully, not randomly selected, and thus as capable of yielding holistic understanding of human behavior in all of its contextuality and complexity. Qualitative methods are emergent and flexible, as they endeavor to be responsive to what is learned as the study proceeds. Qualitative methods center around the perceptive acuity and relational capabilities of the inquirer, as the inquirer is the primary instrument of data generation, analysis, and interpretation. Not setting up the study completely in advance fulfills the inductive, emergent, and contextual challenges of understanding lived experience, which is, after all, the primary purpose of social inquiry. Qualitative methods endeavor to generate this understanding from the perspective of those living the experience, but as necessarily interpreted through the lens of the observer-inquirer.

While these and other contrasting lists of key characteristics of quantitative and qualitative methodologies occupied many pages and hours of the debate, some of the most hotly contested and critical issues concerned this last point: the ways in which and the extent to which the predispositions and stances of the inquirer matter to the quality of inquiry findings. This point encompasses issues related to objectivity and subjectivity, bias and interpretation, independence and engagement, distance and closeness. In quantitative methodological traditions, controlling for bias of all kinds is of vital importance to the quality of the study and is in fact a driving force underlying methodological advancements. In quantitative traditions it is method that protects the data and thus the inquiry findings from the idiosyncrasies of the inquirer. Quantitative inquiry findings are credible only if and when they can be defended as unbiased, objective, independent of the particular stances of the inquirer and of particular theoretical or policy ideas. Quantitative findings tainted by the favored theories or stances of the inquirer are rejected as biased and as unsubstantiated by independent and objective methods and critique.

In qualitative traditions, recalling Dilthey, "it [is] impossible to separate the interrelationships of what was being investigated and the investigator. There [is] no objective social reality as such divorced from the people, including investigators, who participated in and interpreted that reality" (Smith & Heshusius, 1986, p. 5). Distinctive to social inquiry, say the qualitative methodologists, is the inevitable participation of the inquirer in the "social reality" being studied and thus the inevitable presence of the inquirer's own perspectives and understandings in the findings and understandings generated. Human inquiry is inherently subjective and interpretive, they argue. No particular kind or number of sophisticated methods can insulate social knowledge from the particular predispositions of the knower. It is not possible for human inquirers to stand outside their own sociocultural history and location in the world and observe human phenomena with complete impartiality. It is only possible to observe from within one's own historical location; thus human inquiry is inevitably interpretive and inherently subjective. Subjectivity is not bias; rather, it intrinsically defines the very character of human understanding.

As does the intertwinement of "values" with "facts," maintain qualitative methodologists. The fact-value dichotomy long embraced by quantitative methodologists—and its rejection by qualitative methodologists—remains an issue of continuing contestation and debate (House & Howe, 1999; Phillips, 2005). Issues of values are important, argue quantitative methodologists, but not really subject to empirical investigation and so not appropriate for the work of social scientists. Rather, values are best allocated to the domains of policy and politics, religion and rhetoric, leaving science to concentrate on matters of fact. Nonsense, say the qualitative methodologists. Human experience and its meaningfulness are intrinsically imbued with values; it is thus not possible to separate values out from understandings of human phenomena. To strip human experience of its beliefs, commitments, principles, and passions is to render it other than uniquely social, uniquely human.

Enter Politics

Beyond the arguments about the presence and role of values in social inquiry, the great qualitative-quantitative debate also included strands of political arguments related to the role of social inquiry in society, or, more bluntly, whose interests should be served by social research and evaluation. This is perhaps best illustrated by the character of these political disputes in the evaluation field, as audiences are explicitly named in evaluation studies.

Post-positivist, quantitative evaluation characteristically provides information on the degree to which a given social or educational intervention attained intended outcomes, or the outcomes established by decision makers and program developers. For example, an evaluation of teen pregnancy support and prevention program might be quantitatively evaluated using a quasi-experimental design to assess program impact on the identified outcomes of staying in school, not having a repeat pregnancy, participating in prenatal care, and taking steps toward economic independence. Post-positivist evaluation thus has traditionally served the interests of policy makers and other decision makers charged with the responsibility of setting directions for resource allocation in the service of social problem solving. In the public arena, these are our elected and appointed officials and staff.

Interpretivist, qualitative evaluation characteristically provides information on the quality and meaningfulness of a program experience, from the multiple perspectives of program staff, participants, and associated family and community members. For example, a qualitative evaluation of the same teen pregnancy support and prevention program might use a mini case study design to illuminate and understand the significance and meaningfulness of these program experiences in the lives of its participants, along possibly emergent dimensions of caring, safety, nurturing, and hope, as well as concrete and material benefits in daily life. This information is most likely to be of value to members of the setting being studied—the staff responsible for program implementation, the local officials responsible for program oversight, and those the program is intended to benefit. These different audiences for evaluation, and social inquiry more broadly, invoked in the great debate a political strand about the role of inquiry in society and about whose questions and interests should be addressed by our work.

Reprise

Those were heady times—exceptionally intellectually demanding, as many of us were challenged to learn a whole host of new concepts and ideas, many of them highly abstract and deep. We read widely, eager for any books or articles that could help us learn as we strove to be among the enlightened. We jammed into conference sessions that featured people in the know. We met in revolt and in protest against revolt, establishing new interest groups and convening small conferences to advance our disparate interests (Eisner and Peshkin, 1990). Heroes and heroines emerged, as did antiheroes and antiheroines. Which was which obviously depended on your point of view. And we argued, sometimes with civility and manners, and sometimes not. One excerpt from an exchange between two presidents of the American Evaluation Society, both evaluation scholars, illustrates the sometimes contentious tenor and contours of this great debate.

> *Whatever it is we have now, it is clearly not working. . . . We need to move beyond cost benefit analysis and objective achievement measure to interpretive realms . . . to begin talking about what our programs mean, what our evaluations tell us, and what they contribute to our understandings as a culture and as a society. We need literally begin to shape . . . the dreams of all of us into realities. (Lincoln, 1991, p. 6)*

> *Groundwater contamination may be simply a construction of some scientist's fertile mind and not real at all, as the Fourth Generation appears to insist, but I would not drink that constructed water myself. If we want to have the maximum likelihood of our results being accepted and used, we will do well to ground them, not in theory and hermeneutics, but in the dependable rigor afforded by our best science and accompanying quantitative analyses. (Sechrest, 1992, p. 3)*

For more in-depth discussions of the substantive issues being debated, see these references, among others: Bernstein (1983); Bryman (1988); Cook and Reichardt (1979); Cronbach (1975); Denzin, Van Maanen, and Manning (1989); Filstead (1970, 1979); Guba (1985, 1990); Hammersley (1992); Hargreaves (1985); Kuhn (1970); Lincoln and Guba (1985); McCarthy (1981); Phillips (1990); Rist (1980); and Smith (1989).

RAPPROCHEMENT AND THE EMERGENCE OF THE IDEA OF MIXING METHODS

Gradually, and grudgingly in some quarters, a truce in the great debate emerged, a truce that legitimized multiple rationales for and multiple ways of practicing social inquiry. Although most social inquirers maintained an allegiance to one particular methodological tradition, most also accepted a plurality of legitimate traditions. And many had substantially deeper understandings of and rationales for their own methodological allegiance or home base as part of their acceptance of other traditions. For example, Nathaniel Gage, an esteemed senior educational researcher, observed that

> It was finally understood that nothing about objective-quantitative research precluded the description and analysis of classroom processes with interpretive-qualitative methods. Classroom processes need not be described solely in terms of behaviors or actions; they could also be described in terms of meaning-perspectives. (Gage, 1989, p. 7)

And Lee Cronbach, one of the twentieth century's social science geniuses, observed, regarding evaluation, that "merit lies not in form of inquiry but in relevance of information . . . [and] the evaluator will be wise not to declare allegiance to either a quantitative-scientific-summative methodology or a qualitative-naturalistic-descriptive methodology" (Cronbach & Associates, 1980, p. 7). Typical of this truce was the idea that qualitative methods were good for gathering data on some aspects of human behavior, and quantitative methods were good for gathering data on other aspects of human behavior. That is, the two methodological traditions could function in a complementary fashion, each contributing uniquely to the results (see, for example, Kidder & Fine, 1987; Rossman & Wilson, 1985; Salomon, 1991; A. G. Smith & Louis, 1982; M. L. Smith, 1986). This kind of thinking presaged the turn to the idea of mixed methods social inquiry. In many ways, this turn was one logical outcome of the great debate.

Traditions of Triangulation

The social science community was also receptive to mixed methods ideas because of strong commitments to ideas related to the concept of triangulation in both quantitative and qualitative traditions. From its classic sources, triangulation refers to the intentional use of multiple methods, with offsetting or counteracting biases, in investigations of the same phenomenon to strengthen the validity of inquiry results. The core premise of triangulation is that all methods have inherent biases and limitations—for example, the social desirability known to plague social science surveys and many personal interviews—so that use of only one method to assess a given phenomenon will inevitably yield biased and limited results. However, when two or more methods that have offsetting biases are used to assess a given phenomenon, and the results of these methods converge or corroborate one another, then the validity or credibility of inquiry findings is enhanced. This idea of triangulation is derived from other fields, like surveying and astronomy, where more precise results are achieved by taking measurements from two or more positions.

In quantitative methodological traditions, the concept of triangulation is usually traced first to the multitrait, multimethod (MTMM) matrix conceptualization offered by Campbell and Fiske (1959) for the development and validation of new psychological measures. With this matrix conceptualization, the validity of inferences from a new measure could be convincingly established through a combination of divergent validity (with inferences from measures of different constructs) and convergent validity (with inferences from measures of the same construct), controlling for or separating out shared variance due to similar methods. The actual triangulation label was first used in quantitative traditions by the authors of the highly creative idea of using unobtrusive measurement to support, substantiate, and especially to "cross-validate" more intentional measurement (Webb, Campbell, Schwartz, & Sechrest, 1966).

In qualitative traditions, the triangulation concept is nearly always traced to sociologist Norman Denzin's 1978 text on sociological methods. In this text, Denzin proposed four forms of triangulation—of data sources, methods (specifically interview and observation), investigators, and theories—as ways to overcome limitations of any single data generation perspective or event. Of special focus in this conceptualization of triangulation was the importance of both asking inquiry participants for their interpretations of their experiences and observing the same individuals in action. What people say and what people do are not always the same, and understanding each can inform an understanding of the whole. That is, in qualitative methodological traditions, triangulation was a vehicle to develop a more coherent and comprehensive account or story of the phenomena being studied, as this constituted the interpretive version of validity or credibility.

As noted by Greene and McClintock (1985), the classic triangulation argument requires that the two or more methods be (1) intentionally used to assess the same phenomenon, conceptualized the same way; (2) therefore implemented simultaneously; and (3) also implemented independently, to preserve their counteracting biases. Challenges of triangulation have persisted in the mixed methods literature, as have misunderstandings of what this concept means (Mark & Shotland, 1987b; Mathison, 1988).

And although familiarity with the idea of triangulation may have helped, in some important ways, to support early ideas about mixing methods, the lingering effects of the triangulation concept in the mixed methods conversation have not always been as productive. In particular, triangulation seeks enhanced validity or credibility through convergence and corroboration. There is sometimes a conflation of the very notion of mixed methods social inquiry with the ideas of convergence and corroboration. For example, in my review of early mixed methods evaluation studies, conducted with colleagues Valerie Caracelli and Wendy Graham (Greene, Caracelli, & Graham, 1989), the value of mixing methods for purposes of triangulation was widely promoted, across very different kinds of studies. Triangulation was the dominant stated rationale for using a mix of methods in these studies, even when convergence for purposes of increased validity was not the actual intent of mixing methods in the study's implementation. And a chapter on making inferences in mixed methods inquiry in the *Handbook of Mixed Methods in Social and Behavioral Research* focuses the discussion primarily on triangulated inferences (Erzberger & Kelle, 2003). Muted by this emphasis on convergence and corroboration is the potential value of divergence and dissonance. As noted previously, one important stance in this book is that mixed methods social inquiry can substantially enhance our understanding of social phenomena by generating empirical puzzles—results that do not converge and thereby warrant further study and contemplation (see also Mathison, 1988).

Moreover, the great qualitative-quantitative debate had left simple methodologists with newfound knowledge, if not complete understanding, about the philosophical foundations of their craft. Early on in the mixed methods conversation, questions about the possibility and the sensibility of cross-paradigm triangulation were raised. Greene and McClintock (1985), for example, conducted a self-consciously mixed methods, mixed-paradigm study of the ways in which evaluative data are used in learning and decision making in the educational institution of the Cooperative Extension System. Although each component of the study was conducted relatively independently (meeting one important condition of triangulation), the various sets of qualitative and quantitative results were carefully, even painstakingly integrated at the point of making conclusions and inferences. My colleague Charles McClintock and I then reflectively wondered, what exactly did we do during the process of integration? We knew that different sets of philosophical assumptions had guided the data-gathering processes for each component—because that was an intentional strand of this study— but we did not know what philosophical assumptions had framed and guided the integration process. Our reflections suggested that the integration had occurred in a mostly post-positivist framework, possibly denying the sensibility of cross-paradigm triangulation. Questions about these issues persist today.

Early Mixed Methods Ideas

In addition to renewed scholarly and practical interest in the concept of triangulation, the early mixed methods conversation was imbued with abundant seeds of creative ideas, marking the generative potential of this way of thinking about and conducting social inquiry. Some of these are introduced here as snapshots of the times and as harbingers of the material in the chapters to follow.

First, a handful of instant empirical classics were cited in nearly every early mixed methods article and discussion. These included the Phelan (1987) and Trend (1979) studies featured in Chapter Two. What made a mixed methods empirical study an instant classic was its clear, unequivocal demonstration of insights and inferences that were attained from the mix of methods and that would not have been attained with only one type of method. This notion of an empirical classic is still true today and is well illustrated by Tom Weisner's (2005) edited collection of exciting mixed methods empirical studies from the field of child development. Weisner's collection was assembled for the express purpose of illustrating the innovations of thought possible with intentional and methodologically rigorous mixes of methods in practice. Several of the early classics—perhaps most notably the housing policy study reported by Trend—were additionally augmented by the drama of overt conflict and contestations about data and even investigator credibility. These early mixed methods studies, though not labeled as such, were thus tantalizing enticements of an exciting new approach to social inquiry, with possibly high demands in terms of emotional angst but also potentially important rewards in terms of creative and insightful understandings.

Second, also frequently cited in these early mixed methods conversations were the ideas of sociologist Samuel Sieber (1973), who sought early on to create spaces for the joint use of the two dominant methodological traditions in sociology: surveys and field work. Doren Madey (1982) extended these ideas to the field of program evaluation, with many useful examples. The primary idea promoted by Sieber and later Madey was the value of using one kind of method to help develop the other method, where development included not just actual instrumentation but also sample identification and selection, as well as direction for data analyses. One analysis example offered by Madey was the use of data from qualitative observations and interviews to help construct various indices from the quantitative data sets. The qualitative data served to signal important components of the constructs for which indices were constructed. Just as important, Sieber and Madey also presented these ideas as not only how qualitative methods can strengthen and enhance quantitative methods, but also—in a rare balanced and evenhanded manner—how quantitative methods can strengthen and enhance qualitative methods. An analytic example of this from Madey (drawn from Sieber) was the use of quantitative data to help correct the "holistic fallacy" of many qualitative analysts. The holistic fallacy is the tendency on the part of field observers to perceive all aspects of a situation as congruent. In Madey's evaluation, for example, a site director's positive report about the efficiency of the program's administrative operations at the director's site could have been holistically (mis)understood by the qualitative interviewer, a misunderstanding revealed when the quantitative administrative data indicated site problems with low client participation and high staff turnover. In sum, the work of Sieber and Madey highlighted the contributions possible with a sequential and balanced use of both qualitative and quantitative methods in social inquiry.

Third, other strands of the early discussions of mixing methods in social inquiry featured other possible roles or purposes for mixing methods and other facets of mixed methods design of possible importance. Gretchen Rossman and Bruce Wilson (1985) identified three functions or purposes for a mixed methodology: *corroboration* or convergence, *elaboration* or providing richness and detail (later relabeled *complementarity* by Greene et al., 1989), and *initiation*, which "prompts new interpretations, suggests areas for further exploration, or recasts the entire research question. Initiation brings with it fresh insight and a feeling of the creative leap. . . . Rather than seeking confirmatory evidence, this [initiation] design searches for the provocative" (p. 637 and 633). Extending Rossman and Wilson's ideas from an analysis of evaluation studies that used a mix of methods, Greene et al. (1989) suggested two additional purposes: the use of one method to help develop the other (called *development*, from Sieber & Madey) and the use of different methods for different components of an evaluation study; for example, assessments of program implementation and program outcomes (labeled *expansion*). Bryman (1988) presaged important continuing conversations about the value of multiple perspectives potentially captured by a mix of methods—notably, those of structure and process, outside-researcher and inside-participant, macro and micro levels, and cause and meaning. And John Brewer and Albert Hunter (1989) drew attention to the importance of a mixed methods design that features integration of the different methods throughout the study. (The more recent book by these authors revisits these ideas; Brewer & Hunter, 2005.)

Fourth, Charles Ragin helped to initiate discussions on analysis of mixed data sets. Ragin, an international comparative researcher who studies, for example, the emergence of democracy around the globe, posited two primary approaches to such research: variable-oriented and case-oriented, each with its strengths and limitations. In *The Comparative Method: Moving Beyond Qualitative and Quantitative Strategies* (1987), Ragin invented a methodological procedure involving Boolean algebra that enables data from both variable- and case-oriented studies to be combined. Ragin later developed software to support this procedure, foreshadowing contemporary work by Patricia Bazeley on computer software that facilitates iterative exchanges of analyses of quantitative data with SPSS and qualitative data with NVivo (Bazeley, 2003, 2006).

The final snapshot of these early mixed methods discussions returns to the "paradigm issue" in mixed methods inquiry. Rossman and Wilson (1985) offered three stances on the questions of whether and how philosophical paradigms can be mixed in mixed methods research: (1) the purists who say "Absolutely not," (2) the pragmatists who say "Of course, what's the problem here?" and (3) the middle-ground situationalists who say "Maybe, especially if we reframe the notion of philosophical paradigm." These ideas are engaged in some detail in Chapter Five. Related to these issues, Reichardt and Cook (1979) presented a catalytic set of ideas regarding the nature of philosophical paradigms and their relationships to practice. They challenged both the inviolability of philosophical paradigms and their directive role in social research. This set of issues is taken up in the next chapter as a prelude to Chapter Five's direct engagement with the paradigm issue.

Additional influential contributors to these early conversations about mixed methods social inquiry include Mark and Shotland (1987a), Fielding and Fielding (1986), Smith and Louis (1982), and M.L. Smith (1986), some of which were anchored in more general seminal work such as Mary Kennedy's (1979) paper on generalizing from the case study and Donald Campbell's classics on qualitative knowing in action research (1978) and on degrees of freedom in the case study (1979).

FOR EXAMPLE

An illustration of an exciting mixed methods study being conducted at this time of early rapprochement is the dissertation on understanding hunger conducted by Kathy Radimer (1990). Radimer positioned her study in the midst of a highly politicized debate about the existence of hunger in America during the 1980s. She argued that the debate was rooted in "lack of agreement as to what constitutes hunger and what indicators are considered to signify it" (p. 50). She then argued that the meanings of hunger should be grounded in the contextualized experiences of those who "go hungry," and it is these meanings that should be translated into measurable indicators for national survey purposes.

Radimer's dissertation then proceeded to enact this argument through a two-part study. In part one, she conducted in-depth interviews with thirty-two women identified through community-based organizations serving low-income families. Extensive and iterative analysis of these qualitative data yielded a complex portrait of the meanings of hunger for this sample. This portrait included three major dimensions of the experience of being hungry, each with multiple facets and characteristics: problems with the quantity of food intake, problems with the quality of food intake, and problems with food supply for the household overall. A fourth dimension or closely related construct described by the interviewees was food anxiety. The interview data also yielded rich information on how these women manage food insecurity and the threat of going hungry, which Radimer included, along with still other significant dimensions and events, in her overall conceptual framework for hunger.

In part two of her dissertation, Radimer developed survey items based on the conceptual framework for hunger that emerged from the qualitative data and pilot tested these items on a sample of women with a broader range of hunger experiences, from none to substantial. Extensive psychometric analyses were used to assess the congruence of the pilot test results with the conceptual framework and to assess the reliability and validity of intended inferences about hunger from the survey. Survey results were also used to make modest revisions in the conceptual framework, which was then used to recommend a small set of hunger indicators for use on national surveys assessing the state of hunger in the nation.

Radimer's study is exemplary in its in-depth engagement with the complexities of a major public health issue like hunger. Her study well illustrates the conceptual and practical value of a mixed methods approach and especially one with open respect for the legitimacy of multiple ways of knowing and understanding.

BUT TROUBLED WATERS REMAINED

These snapshots from the early conversations about mixing methods in social inquiry are intended to convey some of the exciting sense of potential that followed the proclaimed rapprochement of the great qualitative-quantitative debate. But murmurs of challenge remained, some of which continue as critical strands of the mixed methods conversation today. These include the following:

- Some inquirers with allegiance to qualitative traditions were concerned that their particular way of knowing was actually being silenced by the interest in mixing methods, which they perceived as a thinly disguised advocacy for continued post-positivist and quantitative dominance.

- Some participants wondered what all the fuss was about, as some social inquirers, like program evaluators, had been fruitfully mixing methods for quite some time (Datta, 1994).

- Other participants in the early conversations were concerned that the rush to rapprochement and partnership (Reichardt and Rallis, 1994) left many important issues and concerns by the wayside. Philosophically, for example, the long-standing challenges of incommensurability (Howe, 1988, 2003; J. K. Smith, 1989) were not sufficiently well engaged at that time.

These and other issues will be pursued as this conversation moves on from history. The next two chapters specifically engage the paradigm issue in mixed method social inquiry.

CHAPTER

CONTESTED SPACES: PARADIGMS AND PRACTICE IN MIXED METHODS SOCIAL INQUIRY

THE LEGACIES of the qualitative-quantitative debate in applied social science persist today, as do some of the tensions, especially regarding the nature and role of philosophical assumptions and stances in social inquiry practice. Back from the quick trip to the past, in this chapter the traveler will venture out into the abstract and roughly textured landscape of philosophical paradigms and mental models. The traveler will explore a number of different routes through this landscape *to* the domain of social inquiry practice and will begin to map the route most congruent with his or her own travel modes, speeds, and destinations. The traveler will further be encouraged to share his or her own story of how he or she developed an interest in mixed methods social inquiry.

Epistemological purity doesn't get research done.

—Miles and Huberman, 1984, p. 21

■ ■ ■

In the introductory chapter (2003) to the well-received *Handbook of Mixed Methods in Social and Behavioral Research* (2003a), Charles Teddlie and Abbas Tashakkori (who are also the editors of the *Handbook*) identify "six major unresolved major issues and controversies" in the mixed methods field. These include the following:

1. The nomenclature and basic *definitions* used in mixed methods research
2. The *utility* of mixed methods *research* (why we do it) [or mixed methods *purposes;* see Chapter Six]
3. The *paradigmatic foundations* for mixed methods research
4. *Design* issues in mixed methods research
5. Issues in *drawing inferences* in mixed methods research
6. The logistics of conducting mixed methods research [or mixed methods *practice*] (p. 4, emphases added)

Teddlie and Tashakkori then offer a thoughtful elaboration of each of these issues, to which the present discussion will return in subsequent chapters. In particular, Chapter Five of this book takes up the third issue in the preceding list, that of the "paradigmatic foundations" for mixed methods research, or what to do with paradigms when mixing methods.

The present chapter sets the stage for the Chapter Five discussion of the paradigm issue in mixed methods social inquiry. Following on from the contentious qualitative-quantitative debate, disagreements remain regarding the nature of philosophical paradigms and especially regarding their role in applied social inquiry. Engaging with these disagreements is important for a meaningful understanding of just what is at stake in the different stances taken on the paradigm issue in mixed methods social inquiry. So this chapter takes up these issues by framing them as contested spaces in which philosophy meets practice. The discussion specifically pursues two issues: (1) What is the nature of a philosophical paradigm or a set of assumptions that is relevant to social inquiry? (2) What is the role of paradigms or assumptions in making practice decisions? The discussion thus probes whether or not indeed, and in what ways—if at all—"philosophical purity" serves to "get the research done."

ON THE NATURE OF PHILOSOPHICAL PARADIGMS FOR SOCIAL INQUIRY, AND MENTAL MODELS, TOO

The philosopher Denis Phillips (2005), in a treatise on the contested definition of "scientific" educational research in the United States, presents several key characteristics of paradigms for social inquiry. A paradigm, says Phillips, comprises a model for inquiry that specifies particular inquiry purposes or uses. A paradigm also includes a stance or position regarding what constitute warranted conclusions "and about whether any conclusions—rather than opinions or political stances—can be formulated at all" (p. 2). And a paradigm privileges particular methodologies, takes a stance on the desirability and possibility of achieving objectivity in social inquiry, and offers a position on the nature of truth and on the character of reason and its efficaciousness. A paradigm further incorporates particular presuppositions about social reality, about how the social world works, about the causative agents in the social world, and about whether regularities in the social world are uncovered by inquirers or constructed by them. As is customary in philosophy, Phillips includes in his conception of a paradigm assumptions related to ontology or the nature of the social world, epistemology or the nature of the knowledge we can have about that world, methodology, as well as inquiry purpose or role in society. (In this paper, as well as other writings, Phillips also offers excellent descriptions and critiques of different paradigms for social inquiry; see Phillips, 2000; Phillips & Burbules, 2000.)

Reichardt and Cook (1979) also discussed attributes of paradigms in a provocative statement about the sensibility of using both qualitative and quantitative methods in the same evaluation study. They acknowledged that the great qualitative-quantitative debate that was being waged at that time engaged underlying paradigmatic issues, and they offered their own tabulation of prominent attributes of each paradigm:

> In brief, the quantitative paradigm is said to have a positivistic, hypothetico-deductive, particularistic, objective, outcome-oriented, and natural science world view. In contrast, the qualitative paradigm is said to subscribe to a phenomenological, inductive, holistic, subjective, process-oriented, and social anthropological world view. (pp. 9–10)

These attributes overlap the presentation by Phillips and are not controversial.

Are Paradigms Fixed and Immovable?

But Reichardt and Cook also advanced one idea that was controversial and that was to reject the assumption that paradigms are "rigid and fixed . . . cast in stone so that modifications . . . are not possible"*and so* the only choice is to choose between them (p. 11). Instead, they proposed that

> All of the attributes which . . . make up the paradigms are logically independent. . . . The attributes themselves are not logically linked to one another. . . . [So] there is nothing to stop the researcher, except perhaps tradition, from mixing and matching

the attributes from the two paradigms to achieve that combination which is most appropriate for the research problem and setting at hand. (p. 18)

This challenge to mix and match paradigm attributes to meet the particular demands of the context is, on the one hand, attractive, especially for social inquirers like evaluators whose work is intrinsically responsive to context. Yet on the other hand, this idea trivializes beliefs and assumptions that are fundamentally important to the character *and* to the practice of social inquiry. Reichardt and Cook's mix-and-match proposal undervalues the ways in which philosophical assumptions, beliefs, and stances frame and guide what counts in a given social inquiry. This proposal also underplays the power of these underlying assumptions, beliefs, and stances in generating and warranting inquiry findings as claims to know.

Reichardt and Cook reminded us that social inquiry paradigms are themselves intellectual constructions and so are not inviolate, immovable, static, or unshakeable. At the same time, paradigms cannot be whimsical or arbitrary; they cannot change character or composition from context to context. Rather, inquiry paradigms or logics of justification must each offer a strong, plausible, coherent, internally consistent framework for arguing and substantiating the warrants of given inquiry findings (Phillips, 2005).

[That is] scientific research [and social inquiry] can be regarded as parallel to the work of a trial lawyer—what is crucial is the way the case is built up, how evidence or arguments are marshaled to fill in the "holes," how the final argument hangs together including whether it can stand up to the scrutiny of peers (trial lawyers working for the other side) and the independent jurors who need to be convinced "beyond all reasonable doubt." (p. 21)

Argumentation is "generalized jurisprudence" [such that] our extra-legal claims have to be judged . . . before the Court of Reason. (Toulmin, 2003, p. 8, as cited in Phillips, 2005, p. 21)

Are Different Inquiry Paradigms Completely or Mostly Incompatible (Incommensurable), One with the Other?

Lincoln and Guba (2000), in one of their several discussions of social inquiry paradigms, present three sets of attributes of five different paradigms (positivism, post-positivism, critical theory, constructivism, and participation). The first set of attributes includes the basic philosophical beliefs related to the nature of the social world (ontology), the nature of the social knowledge (epistemology), and the ways in which such knowledge can be developed or constructed (methodology). The second set of paradigmatic attributes includes "paradigm positions on selected practical issues": nature of knowledge, knowledge accumulation, quality criteria, values, ethics, inquirer posture, and training. For example, in post-positivism, values are excluded and their influence denied, whereas in constructivism values are included and their influence viewed as formative. Lincoln and Guba's third set of paradigm attributes is labeled "critical issues of the time": axiology; accommodation and commensurability; action; control; relationship to foundations of truth and knowledge; extended considerations of validity and goodness criteria; and voice, reflexivity, postmodern textual representation. To give an example of paradigmatic positions on a critical issue that is directly relevant to the present discussion, Lincoln and Guba asserted that critical theory, constructivist, and participatory paradigms are not commensurable with positivist or post-positivist paradigms because they rest on radically different assumptions, beliefs, and stances. Issues of paradigm commensurability are part of a longstanding and classic philosophical debate and are directly relevant to the paradigm issue in mixed methods social inquiry. The stance of incommensurability taken by Lincoln and Guba renders the mixing of paradigms while mixing methods not possible. In Chapter Five, this is labeled a *purist* position on the mixed methods paradigm issue.

But a stance of incommensurability is inconsistent with a mixed methods way of thinking (presented in Chapter Two) and with much of the potential of mixed methods practice as presented in this book. If the assumptions and logics of justification underlying different paradigms present irreconcilable views of the social world and our knowledge of it, then there is no possibility of mixing paradigms while mixing methods. One could only mix methods *within* a given paradigm or across paradigms with considerable shared assumptive space. And what a missed opportunity that would be—a missed opportunity for fresh perspectives, new insights, ideas previously unimagined!

Respecting Multiple Paradigms (and Mental Models), Dialogically

So how can paradigms be simultaneously respected, honored, and understood, on the one hand, as vitally important anchors for inquiry findings and their warrants, and on the other, as open, dynamic, and inviting of dialogue with other perspectives and stances? The answer—which *is* the argument of this book—is twofold. First, broaden the rarefied, abstract notion of philosophical paradigm to reflect the more grounded, intuitive, dialogic notion of a mental model as the underlying framework or logic of justification for social research. As presented in Chapter One, a mental model is the set of assumptions, understandings, predispositions, and values and beliefs with which a social inquirer approaches his or her work. A mental model includes the basic philosophical assumptions (ontology, epistemology, methodology) but also includes inquirer stances, values, beliefs, disciplinary understandings, past experiences, and practical wisdom (much like Phillips' portrayal of paradigms). Although one philosophical paradigm may be incommensurable with another, most mental models are inherently dialogic, as most social inquirers seek connection, conversation, understanding—one with the other. Second, redirect attention away from fundamentally incommensurable attributes of paradigms—including objectivism-subjectivism and realism-idealism—and toward different and distinctive but not inherently incompatible attributes, such as distance-closeness, outside-insider view, figure-ground, generality-particularity, the representative and the unusual, and so forth (Greene & Caracelli, 1997a). That is, leave to the philosophers the challenges of incommensurability. And meanwhile, get on to the work of applied social inquiry by intentionally and thoughtfully employing the full extent of our methodological repertoire. This is not to argue, as do Miles and Huberman (1984), that attention to philosophy and its assumptions should be set aside in order to get our work done. Rather, the argument is for setting aside philosophical purity and its incommensurability in abstract form in favor of active engagement with the diversity of philosophical assumptions and stances in their dialogic form. The urgency of today's social problems demands no less.

INTERLUDE

In the discussion so far, I have endeavored to develop a portrait of social inquiry mental models as anchored in the classic assumptions of philosophical paradigms (ontology, epistemology, and methodology) but also embracing inquirer experiences, values and beliefs, theoretical commitments, understandings about the purpose of social inquiry, and more. Moreover, as vitally important frameworks for social inquiry, mental models must be strongly coherent, internally consistent, and defensible. In the second part of this two-part discussion, I will take up the issue of whether, and if so how paradigms and mental models influence social inquiry practice decisions. I introduce that discussion with a set of vignettes from the field, presented next.

Susan Jones, a public health researcher, is excited about her forthcoming intervention study. She is planning to assess the effectiveness of new program designed to combat the current epidemic of childhood obesity (Institute of Medicine, 2004, 2006) by changing social norms that influence healthy eating among middle and high school youth. The program is modeled after a highly successful program that trains diverse school leaders (in academics, athletics, the arts, government, and social influence) to model anti–sexual harassment behaviors and thereby influence their peers to do the same. Susan is especially pleased to have developed a defensible quasi-experimental design for this intervention study. Eating behaviors among children and youth are influenced by the complex interaction of multiple environmental and structural factors and personal characteristics, including but not limited to powerful social norms. This complexity makes a true randomized experimental all but impossible, so Susan is quite pleased with the creative and plausible quasi-experiment she has designed.

➤   What accounts for Susan's allegiance to experimentation? Is it an underlying commitment to conducting social inquiry for the purpose of establishing causal relationships and an acceptance of experiments as the most defensible method for this purpose? What else might be influencing her design decisions?

Brenda Morales is planning a study on recidivism patterns among poor rural residents of the county she works for as a planner. Although urban populations have been studied repeatedly, less is known about the post-prison experiences of the rural poor. Brenda decides to first conduct a discriminant analysis of the Department of Corrections database for county residents who have been in prison at least once in the last fifteen years. She thinks this analysis may generate distinct groups or clusters of residents who have served time, based on demographic and other descriptive factors. She then plans to purposefully sample one or two individuals within each cluster for mini-case studies of their prison and post-prison experiences.

➢ What accounts for Brenda's choice of a case study methodology? Is it an understanding of prison and post-prison experiences as highly contextual and dynamic and an acceptance of case study methods as the most appropriate way to gather data on such experiences? What else might be influencing her design decisions?

Sam Johnson is dreading the evaluation he has been assigned by his supervisor in the international development agency in which he works. This assignment involves the comprehensive evaluation of an HIV/AIDS education and health care program that has been implemented recently in Tanzania by a European aid organization. Sam has worked in the HIV/AIDS field for over twenty years, and he has developed clear ideas about what is needed for an effective program. Centrally important, he thinks, is the fostering of community responsibility for the care of the sick *and* their children. Sam believes that it is irresponsible if not immoral to use resources without attending seriously to the needs of the growing population of AIDS orphans. Yet the program he has been asked to evaluate has no provisions for orphan care or placement. Sam decides that he can position the evaluation to critically engage these issues while also addressing questions of policy.

➢ What accounts for Sam's apparent lack of concern about the possible biasing influences of his own views on the program and issues being evaluated? Is it an inquiry stance that values the subjective lens and experience of the inquirer and a view of evaluation as an opportunity for social critique? What else might be influencing Sam's inquiry decisions?

ON THE RELATIONSHIPS OF MENTAL MODELS (AND PARADIGMS) TO PRACTICE

The connections between paradigms and mental models on the one hand and practical inquiry decisions and choices on the other will be discussed first abstractly and then in terms of what inquirers actually do.

What Are the Arguments in Theory?

Another strand of the Reichardt and Cook (1979) argument regarding the nature and role of philosophical paradigms in evaluation practice is to disconnect practical methodological decisions from philosophical assumptions. They argue that "the attributes of a paradigm are not inherently linked to either qualitative or quantitative methods. . . . [That is] paradigms are not the sole determinant of the choice of methods . . . [which] should also depend at least partly on the demands of the research situation at hand" (p. 16). They further argue that although the common association of particular methods with particular paradigmatic assumptions does reflect inquiry practice, it does not represent a necessary or determinant connection.

In contrast, Lincoln and Guba's (2000) arguments for the importance of philosophical purity (and thus paradigmatic incommensurability) are thoroughly intertwined with arguments for the special importance of paradigmatic assumptions in guiding, even directing inquiry practice. That is, philosophical purity is important precisely because social inquirers' practical decisions in the field are substantially framed and directed by their underlying ontological stances and epistemological beliefs. Methodology is bound to paradigm in this view. A realist ontology, for example, directs methods choices that emphasize accuracy of measurements of the external world. With a constructivist ontology, methods are chosen that emphasize the understanding of subjective and intersubjective meaningfulness.

Challenges to these extreme views include the following (Hammersley, 1992):

- The differences between different paradigms are not dichotomies or dualisms, but rather form continuous dimensions along which empirical inquiry can vary.

- Many "qualitative" inquirers hold a basically realist position about the social world, whereas many "quantitative" inquirers acknowledge that some of human action is constructed. So the interconnectedness of assumptions in a given paradigm is not inviolate.

- Research practice is much more complicated and disparate than what would be suggested by a paradigm-driven model, even acknowledging the existence of a plurality of paradigms.

Offering a perspective rooted in American pragmatism, Ken Howe (1988) presents a middle position, arguing that

> paradigms [should] bring themselves into some reasonable state of equilibrium with methods. . . . That is, rather than divorcing paradigms from the conduct of research (but nonetheless having them dictate what is to count as legitimate knowledge), [the pragmatist] can insist on a mutual adjustment between the two such that practice is neither static and unreflective nor subject to the one-way dictates of a wholly abstract paradigm." (p. 13)

Pragmatism is increasingly advanced as *the* appropriate paradigmatic partner for mixed methods social inquiry (Johnson & Onwuegbuzie, 2004; Teddlie & Tashakkori, 2003). A brief presentation of central tenets of pragmatism (according to John Dewey) will be offered in the next chapter, along with the reasons it is so attractive to mixed methodologists. Howe's middle-ground stance regarding the relationship between paradigms and practice well illustrates some of these reasons. Some engagement with pragmatism in practice will also be offered so that interested readers will not unreflectively embrace a pragmatic mental model for their mixed methods work.

What Do Social Inquirers Actually Do with Paradigms and Mental Models in Their Inquiry Practice?

There is scant empirical work on the actual influence of philosophical assumptions and other strands of inquirers' mental models on practice decisions, particularly in mixed methods contexts. Lois-ellin Datta (1994) reviewed evaluation studies identified as exemplars of qualitative and quantitative paradigms and found that these studies "seem actually to be mixed models" (p. 67), drawing on assumptions and characteristics of both traditions. So Datta observed that in practice, "already . . . we merge, combine, mix, and adapt, using the implicit standards in the theory to help establish explicit standards for practice" (p. 67). And Datta urged evaluators to consider adopting a new paradigm that better captures the actual mixing that goes on so that, pragmatically, paradigms and practice are more in harmony with and reciprocally supportive of one another. (Datta has long been a strong, articulate spokeswoman for a pragmatic framework for mixed methods social inquiry; see Datta, 1997a, 1997b, 2005.)

Katrin Niglas has conducted several thoughtful and useful studies on this topic within the domain of educational research. As background for this work, she reviewed other related studies of social inquiry practice. These studies yielded results similar to those of Datta, indicating that applied social inquiry practice could not be readily sorted into distinct, conceptually pure paradigmatic stances. Rather, practice was most commonly characterized by blends or mixes of paradigmatic positions, by the absence of clear or explicit relationships between philosophical beliefs and practice decisions, or by the absence of philosophy altogether.

In a preliminary empirical study, Niglas (1999) critically reviewed and analyzed a sample of forty-eight empirical studies from the *British Educational Research Journal* (1997–1999). For this analysis, Niglas extracted and classified six separate characteristics of each study in her sample: research aim, overall design, sampling type, data collection and analysis methods, validation methods, and types of claims. She endeavored to classify each as derived from either a qualitative or a quantitative paradigm, and she was particularly interested in assessing the paradigmatic coherence among these six aspects of inquiry practice. Among her interesting findings, she found that there was more clear mixing of data collection and analysis methods in the sample of studies reviewed than of inquiry purpose, overall design, or sampling. Moreover, a cluster analysis yielded four distinct clusters of studies: (1) eleven studies that were qualitative in all aspects; (2) sixteen studies that were quantitative in all aspects; (3) eleven studies that were based on qualitative designs (such as case study) and used nonrandom sampling methods, but also used primarily quantitative data handling methods; and (4) eight studies that were based on quantitative designs (such as experiments and surveys) that also incorporated some qualitative data and analysis from interviews and from open-ended survey items. That is, this study provided support that in practice educational researchers either use a single methodology and associated paradigmatic stance (aligned with a purist position, 59 percent of the studies) or a mixed methods design with one dominant methodology-paradigm and the inclusion of selected aspects of another (41 percent of the studies). More fundamentally, however, Niglas concluded that educational researchers make practice decisions primarily on the basis of the context, the purpose of the study, and the concrete problem at hand. (See Greene & Caracelli, 2003, for further discussion of this work.)

Niglas used a similar methodology in her dissertation study (Niglas, 2004), adding a seventh characteristic for analysis, that of data recording and representation methods, and a more elaborated analysis of the claims made by the researchers.

Niglas also attended carefully in this analysis to the different stages of the research study in which perspectives and techniques could be mixed. (This important issue regarding mixing in different stages of inquiry is revisited in Chapter Seven on mixed methods design.) Niglas's dissertation study used a sample of 145 educational research articles drawn from fifteen different European and North American journals (1999–2001). The results are more complex than the preliminary study—partly because Niglas used a larger sample; partly because her analytic frame itself was more complex, including action research and other paradigmatic stances in addition to traditionally "qualitative" and "quantitative" genres; *and* partly because the field of educational research itself has become more varied and diverse. Her analysis, in fact, yielded eight clusters of characteristics of empirical studies. The three largest clusters (about thirty studies each) were (1) studies that primarily used a quantitative survey design and methodology; (2) studies that primarily used a qualitative design and methodology, with little use of quantitative methods or numbers; and (3) studies that used a mix of designs with primarily qualitative methods. Niglas analyzed these clusters in multiple ways, with provocative and intriguing results, too numerous to report herein. Her overall conclusions include the following:

- "Mixed methods" empirical research in the field of education is quite common, although it takes a wide variety of forms, from mixing only different types of data collection techniques to mixing different kinds of inquiry designs and purposes.

- "The level of integration between qualitative and quantitative aspects [of educational research studies] remains relatively modest in most cases, especially the integration of different types of data at the stage of analysis. However, at the stage of interpretation, more extensive integration can be observed" (p. 148).

- An explicit rationale for the use of mixed methods is usually not offered in an empirical report. Using the typology of mixed methods purposes generated by Greene, Caracelli, and Graham (1989), Niglas's classification of the more implicit purposes for mixing indicated that complementarity was the most common, followed by expansion. The other three purposes identified by Greene et al. (1989)—triangulation, development, and initiation—were much more rare.

And more interpretively, integrating Niglas's own stances on these issues:

- The dichotomous nature of educational research—into qualitative and quantitative camps—is not characteristic of actual research practice, nor should it be. Rather, quantitative and qualitative methodologies themselves are not mutually exclusive, they do not represent incompatible paradigms, and they do not exhaust the range of paradigms available to educational researchers today. Others include critical theory, post-modernism, phenomenology, and hermeneutics.

- It is the concrete research problem and inquiry purpose, rather than philosophical position, that importantly determine the design and methods of a study. "Depending on the complexity of the problem, the design can be either qualitative, quantitative, or a combination of both" (p. 147).

▪ "The most burning practical question about the combined use of qualitative and quantitative approaches is its influence on the quality of educational research"—a question that remains incotmpletely answered by this study (p. 147).

A REFLECTIVE STANCE

So these are the contested spaces in which philosophy, perspective, and practice encounter one another—and either join together in a reciprocal, respectful, and mutually beneficial conversation or walk right by without noticing one another—or perhaps pretending not to notice. The stance presented in this book is that mental models inevitably influence practice choices, with or without the inquirer's intentional engagement and consideration. It is simply not possible to design and conduct a social inquiry study without some conceptualization of what is being studied, why, and how. The stance presented in this book is also one that favors an openness to conversation and dialogue between the more abstract assumptions and stances of mental models and the concrete challenges of particular practice decisions in particular inquiry contexts. I like Ken Howe's framing of this conversation as a "mutual adjustment" so that practice is "neither static nor unreflective nor subject to the one-way dictates of a wholly abstract paradigm." I believe that conscious attention to how the various strands of mental models influence inquiry decisions renders such decisions more thoughtful, reflective, intentional, and thereby more generative and defensible. Considering the preceding vignettes, if Susan Jones or Brenda Morales select their inquiry designs—of quasi-experimentation and case study, respectively—after thoughtful consideration of the assumptions and stances that underlie such choices—of how such design choices frame the knowledge claims to be generated in the study, of alternative designs that may respond to the inquiry purpose and context—then such choices are more likely to be defensible and strong than if designs are selected without such intentional reflection. And if Sam Johnson remains inattentive to his own biases and commitments and how they influence his HIV/AIDS evaluation study, the quality and credibility of his work may well be jeopardized.

Moreover, a reflective, thoughtful stance of intentional engagement with the premises, perspectives, stances, and commitments of one's mental model is especially important in mixed methods social inquiry. Otherwise, it can remain unclear just what is being mixed in a mixed methods study, and the potential benefits of mixing can remain underrealized.

Chapter Five further engages the "paradigm issue" in mixed methods social inquiry, specifically by presenting a set of stances on the role of paradigms in mixed methods practice, along with illustrations of each stance. The chapter continues to take up the third issue in Teddlie and Tashakkori's list of major unresolved issues and controversies in the mixed methods field, that of the "paradigmatic foundations" for mixed methods research, or what to do with paradigms when mixing methods.

As a segue to this chapter, I first present what I have come to call my mixed methods journey: a story of how I became interested in a mixed methods approach to social inquiry and, more profoundly, a mixed methods way of thinking. I believe that all readers of this book also have their own mixed methods stories, and that the telling of those stories can constitute one important step toward thoughtful awareness and understanding of one's own mental model and thus toward reflective and engaged mixed methods practice.

MY MIXED METHODS STORY

My mixed methods story begins in graduate school—not because it really began then, but because my consciousness of it began then—and continues with major episodes from my professional life as an evaluation practitioner and scholar. I believe there is also an important personal dimension to mixed methods stories, but that is more muted in this telling.

Graduate School, Early 1970s

My graduate program in educational psychology at Stanford University had a very strong methods component, but the methods were exclusively quantitative, featuring substantial coursework in educational measurement, in the logic of experimental design, and in statistics. I did take one course in educational anthropology with George Spindler. But the course was about content, about thinking anthropologically and cross-culturally about educational issues, not about method. *My memory of that time,* in the language I have learned since that time, was that I was striving to learn all I could about how to do methods right. John K. Smith calls this the proper methods properly applied. I understood at that time that if you could do this—apply the proper methods properly—you would get truth *and* tenure.

First Job, Mid- to Late 1970s

My first post-Ph.D. full-time job was back in the eastern part of the United States where I grew up. It was a soft-money job in what was then the Curriculum Research and Development Center at the University of Rhode Island. And it was a wonderful time to be a young applied research and evaluation professional. There were about twenty of us young Ph.D.s working hard together in this R&D center and playing hard together outside of work. A major portion of the work we did was evaluation of local educational programs funded by the federal government's Elementary and Secondary Education Act of 1965. I had been fortunate to study a bit about program evaluation with Lee Cronbach while in graduate school, but this work in New England was different because it was out in the real world, with real teachers and children. I didn't have any particular training in how to do this kind of evaluation inquiry. So I did what most evaluators at that time did—I used the methods that I knew for these local evaluation contexts. I tried to properly apply what I thought were proper methods. And I also tried to adhere to quite prescriptive state guidelines (framed by federal guidelines) about how I was to do these local educational evaluations.

For example, I evaluated Title I compensatory educational programs, which provided supplementary instruction in reading and or math to low-achieving students in eligible low-income schools. And I evaluated Title IVC innovative educational programs—like the Roger Williams Park Zoo Education Project, which provided curricular and field-based educational units to middle school students on the topics of zoo animals and zoos, and preservation of wetland areas. I evaluated these distinctively different projects with the same prescriptive state guidelines, which included, for example:

- An objectives-based evaluation philosophy. The evaluations were supposed to assess the extent to which programs reached their intended objectives.

- Requirements for pre-post, comparison group types of evaluation designs.

- Some openness to multiple kinds of methods, as in interviews with teachers, but a strong preference for quantitative methods, including required standardized assessments of intended outcomes.

- Three evaluation reports a year—implementation (fall), interim (spring), and final (at the end of the school year). These reports were intended to track both evaluation progress and program progress, as in assessment of instruments developed, activities implemented, and program progress toward objectives.

- Requirements for evaluators to provide, in each report, specific program recommendations for program improvement.

I followed these guidelines as diligently as I knew how, selecting the right kind of t-test for assessments of mean differences, being wary of growth scores, recalling the difference between random and fixed effects in my ANOVAs, worrying about whether the norms for a given test were appropriate for the children being served by a particular program, and so forth. And I imagine the work I did with my colleagues was adequate at the time.

But *in my memory of that time*, I felt that there was something very wrong with all of this evaluation activity. I felt there was a substantial mismatch between the evaluations I was doing and the important needs for information and insight in the local sites in which I was working. The work I was doing was for the state. And even though I shared all of my evaluation reports with the local sites as well, these reports seemed to have insufficient connections to the daily challenges and concerns experienced by the program people on site. And that bothered me.

Learning More About Evaluation, Late 1970s and 1980s

Spurred partly by this discomfort and also by the broader need to learn more about evaluation, as I was doing quite a bit of it, I engaged in the kinds of professional development activities most professionals pursue:

- I read journals and books.

- I sought out workshop opportunities, including one in Washington DC for "women evaluators," run by Michael Scriven and Jane David, as I recall.

▪ I joined a professional evaluation organization—at that time called ENET, or the Evaluation Network—oriented mostly toward evaluation practitioners.

▪ I sought out evaluators within my primary professional organization at that time— the American Educational Research Association (AERA)—through some participation in Division H about school-based evaluation and Division D about methods more generally.

From the vantage point of today, this time period of the late 1970s and 1980s was an explosive time for the field of evaluation. The public demand for evaluation was escalating, accompanied by increased scholarly attention. Others had been learning that the "proper methods" of experimentalist social science didn't always work in the field, and there was a proliferation of evaluative thinking and an expansive exploration of methodological theory. Amidst this dynamic and exciting discourse about evaluation, there was also quite a ferment about qualitative methods, both for evaluation and for educational and social research more generally. (The history presented in Chapter Three captures much of this ferment.)

My memory of that time is that I thoroughly enjoyed being an active listener of the discourse and beginning learner about qualitative methods. It was all very exciting, and it appealed to my 1960s-bred spirit of rebellion. It also potentially offered a response to the disquiet I had experienced in my early evaluation work: the worry that what I was doing was not meaningful to people on site.

The Generous Guidance and Encouragement of Egon Guba

During this period, I met Egon Guba, probably through AERA. I already knew his name as a leader in the advancement of qualitative methods in research and especially evaluation. Egon took some interest in me and strongly encouraged me to pursue serious learning of qualitative methods. He did this most powerfully by asking me to participate in a couple of conferences on qualitative methods.

The first was a small working conference held in June 1988 at Stanford University and run by Elliot Eisner and Buddy Peshkin. The papers presented in this conference became the book edited by Eisner and Peskhin, *Qualitative Inquiry in Education: The Continuing Debate*, published in 1990. A key highlight of this conference was Harry Wolcott's dramatic telling of the final chapter in his Brad trilogy.

The second conference in which Egon involved me was his "paradigm dialogue" conference, held in San Francisco in 1989. (The conference proceedings were edited by Egon and published in a 1990 book, *The Paradigm Dialog.*) This conference was, in an important sense, Egon's farewell to the field—he retired shortly thereafter. It was organized around three paradigms—post-positivism, constructionism, and critical theory. There was a keynote speaker for each paradigm—Denis Phillips, Yvonna Lincoln, and Tom Popkewitz, respectively. Then there were about ten issue papers, on such topics as criteria for judging quality, implementation, values, and ethics, presented by a selected speaker with one or two selected discussants. Egon asked me to do the issue paper on knowledge accumulation. I said I didn't know enough to do that. He assured me I did. I assured him I did not. He didn't back down, however, and I eventually agreed to do it, but only with enormous trepidation and anxiety and hours and hours and hours of work. But I did write and present the paper and was present at the conference.

And this was an enormously influential event in my own career trajectory. The conference was wonderfully dynamic and exciting, full of talk of realism and idealism, objectivity, and subjectivity, emic and etic perspectives. The tone at this conference certainly was one of healthy competition among these alternative ways of thinking about social science and evaluation, conversations that were neither acrimonious nor nasty. The issues engaged were ones I hadn't really studied in graduate school, because there was only one methodology to learn at that time. And I loved learning about these issues. I struggled to understand them in their philosophical form, but especially liked thinking about them in their practical form, in terms of how these new ways of thinking about inquiry, knowledge, and values could work in my own inquiry practice. I recall in particular that Buddy Peshkin served as an ethnographer at this conference and gave a presentation of his insights about the conference experience at the end of the two or three days. I mainly recall that he talked about the gap or disjuncture between the highbrow discourse of the presenters and the more common talk of the audiences. His examples were captivating and his thematic insights so very thoughtful. I wanted to be able to do that, too. I was becoming a qualitative convert.

The encouragement and guidance of Egon Guba were indeed pivotal in my career, for which I feel profoundly grateful and deeply indebted. I think we all routinely underestimate the importance of our mentors along the way.

Meanwhile, Teaching Qualitative Evaluation at Cornell

Meanwhile, in 1983, I had gotten a real job at Cornell University, teaching evaluation and, in particular, teaching qualitative approaches to evaluation. As all teachers know, there is no greater incentive and catalyst for one's own continued learning that having to teach something that you were not taught yourself. The learning curve for me was enormously accelerated at this time. And of singular importance, it was fueled by graduate student interest in, even enthusiasm for this exciting and seemingly revolutionary domain of qualitative inquiry. The classes I taught in qualitative evaluation methods were filled with a wondrous diversity of people from multiple social scientific fields, from multiple professional work experiences, and from multiple corners of the world. At that time, many Cornell graduate students—in human ecology, education, rural sociology, urban planning, international nutrition, and other applied fields—had returned to school to further develop their own capacity to change the world. Our collective learning experiences about qualitative methodologies often felt a bit revolutionary in and of themselves.

Experiencing the Great Qualitative-Quantitative Debate: Controversy and Conflict

How did I experience the controversy and conflict that surrounded the brash emergence of qualitative methods on the social scientific stage? In two main ways, I think, *from the vantage point of today.*

First, especially at the start but also recurrently throughout this time period of the 1980s and early 1990s, it felt like a battle, like a contest with winners and losers. This was partly because influential spokespeople like Egon Guba and Yvonna Lincoln helped shape it that way. Their writing and their talks strongly positioned their paradigm of constructionism as the best, as the truth, as superior to outdated ideas about objectivity, propositional knowledge, and realist assumptions about the social world. Theirs was the fourth generation of evaluation, superceding in an evolutionary way all preceding generations. Partly in reaction to this and partly out of true belief or fears rooted in the unknown, those champions of existing science repositioned their views as superior to all others. And so the battle was joined.

This battle was fueled by strong resistance among some participants to the very legitimacy of qualitative ways of knowing. It is one thing to argue about which among several legitimate alternatives is best. It is quite another to have to defend the very existence and thereby legitimacy of your own stance. This all took a very long time. And it took a lot of hard work. Especially as a qualitative newbie, I frequently struggled with the challenges of legitimating the assumptions and stances of interpretive and constructivist traditions. I wondered more than once what was really at stake in this battle.

Second, at the same time, some of my best friends were quantitative people. And my own intellectual roots were quantitative. This, combined with my value commitment to respecting multiple stances and perspectives, to accepting diversity and difference, generated for me a lingering chord of uncertainty about the ambitious promises of qualitative methods. I wasn't really sure that they were our salvation or that they could deliver on all of their promises. And, of course, at times this felt like I was breaking ranks with the true believers. At times, I kept my uncertainties to myself.

But then I began writing and talking about my uncertainties. I recall writing in one paper about the value and the limitations of contextualized qualitative stories (Greene, 1996). I suggested that such stories are valuable for their holistic and narrative portrayal of important human experiences but limited in voice and power on the policy stage, especially in evaluation contexts. Over a period of time, I came to more explicitly believe that—like all ways of knowing—interpretivism is partial and limited and needs other ways of knowing to help out. Over time, I began to think more seriously about how different ways of knowing might be able to help each other out.

These then were the seeds of my mixed methods thinking, which took root as early as the mid-1980s. And beginning with collaborative work at this time with colleagues at Cornell (Greene & McClintock, 1985; Greene et al., 1989), my more intensive engagement with mixed methods ideas began to grow and flourish.

Further Inspirations

The primary sources of nourishment for my ideas about mixed methods approaches to social inquiry over the past fifteen years or so have been threefold. First and quite simply, the increasing interest in and popularity of mixed methods social inquiry during the latter part of the twentieth century has provided me with multiple opportunities to develop, try out, and refine my ideas. Notably, I have been privileged to have been invited to give one- or two-day workshops in mixing methods in many forums in the United States and around the world, customarily to demanding audiences of practitioners. Not only have I received instant feedback on the merits of my own ideas about why and how to mix methods in applied social research and evaluation, but I have also learned and benefited considerably from ideas and experiences shared by workshop participants. Talented graduate students have also provided innovative field tests of some of my ideas over the years.

Second, my own field of research and practice in program and policy evaluation has provided constant motivation for my continued interest in mixed methods approaches to social inquiry. As the most applied of all social scientists—because our work takes place in consequential sites of life and work—evaluators are frequently among the first to adopt new concepts and technical advances in methodology. The idiosyncratic complexities of the contexts in which we work command all of our methodological inventiveness and creativity. So, as signaled by the quote from Lois-ellin Datta at the outset of Chapter Three on the history of mixed methods inquiry, evaluators have been mixing methods for decades, certainly throughout my professional engagement in the field. Being surrounded by mixes of all sorts in my own field of practice then further motivated my interest in helping theory catch up with practice. I wanted to promote thoughtful planning about mixing methods among evaluators. I wanted to provide concepts and ways of thinking that could help practicing evaluators systematically construct thoughtful rationales and thereby develop stronger and more powerful mixed methods designs. I wanted to help realize the generative potential of this way of thinking about evaluation and applied social research.

Third, and perhaps of greatest influence, I came to understand that there was a compelling value confluence between my developing ideas about mixing methods and my coming-of-age commitments to tolerance, acceptance, and respect for people of all kinds and colors and shapes. I came to realize that at its most profound, a mixed methods approach to social inquiry represents a potentially deep and meaningful engagement with different ways of knowing and being. As discussed at the end of Chapter Two on a mixed methods way of thinking, I came to believe that a mixed methods approach offers multiple avenues to meaningfully engage with difference and diversity. I came to believe that with a mixed methods approach I could position my work in service of values I cherish—values of tolerance, understanding, and acceptance.

So this is my mixed methods story. Please think about telling yours.

CHAPTER

STANCES ON MIXING PARADIGMS AND MENTAL MODELS WHILE MIXING METHODS

THIS PART of the journey gives form to the continuing controversies surrounding the nature of philosophical assumptions and stances relevant to social inquiry and especially their role in social inquiry practice. A set of alternative mixed methods stances on these issues is offered—representing the views of various participants in the ongoing mixed methods conversation. Each stance is also illustrated with a snapshot of a mixed methods empirical study. The traveler will thus be able to try on various mixed methods paradigm stances and assess each for goodness of fit, aesthetic grace, and practical utility.

▩ ▩ ▩

Previous chapters in this book have advanced the following argument regarding the philosophical and paradigmatic character of mixed methods inquiry. All social inquiry is conducted from *within* the inquirer's particular ways of seeing, hearing, and understanding the social world. These ways of sensemaking can be well captured in the construct of a mental model, which includes philosophical assumptions about the nature of the social world, the nature of the knowledge we can have about that world, and the methods that can meaningfully represent that knowledge, *as well as* the inquirer's own predispositions, beliefs, values, and practical or experiential wisdom. Further, mental models are inherently implicated in social inquiry; they constitute the framework or lens from within which we direct our inquirer's gaze and apply our inquiry science to the social world. And different mental models do present conflicting characteristics, assumptions, and beliefs, but these can be generative conflicts, meaningfully engaged through respectful dialogue. That is, there are no logical or inherent reasons why different mental models cannot be engaged within the same inquiry study. This is so even though different mental models are indeed connected to different methodological traditions. But these connections are loose, not tight; they arise because different methodologies are better matched to different mental models rather than because methods and paradigms are intrinsically bound one to another. So in any given inquiry context, the inquirer's methods choices remain open—not dictated by abstract assumptions. That is, practical inquiry decisions involve a mutual adjustment between the parameters and contours of mental models and the requirements and demands of inquiry contexts. In these important ways, social inquiry design is responsive to the practical context at hand.

This chapter situates this argument within the larger literature on the challenges of mixing paradigms while mixing methods, or what Teddlie and Tashakkori (2003) call the issue of the "paradigmatic foundations" of mixed methods social inquiry. The chapter revisits the two key issues discussed in the previous chapter—(1) the nature of a philosophical paradigm, mental model, or a set of assumptions that is relevant to social inquiry, and (2) the role of paradigms, mental models, or assumptions in making practice decisions—and presents various positions on these two issues that form five additional stances on "the paradigm issue" in mixed methods social inquiry (additional to the argument of this book). Elaborations and examples are offered for each stance, with particular attention to the last two. One of the last two is the stance advanced in this book, labeled the dialectic stance in this discussion. The other is probably the leading contender for a response to "the paradigm issue"—that being, to identify an alternative paradigm that in and of itself embraces a plurality of assumptions and methods.

VARIOUS STANCES ON MIXING PARADIGMS WHILE MIXING METHODS—AN OVERVIEW

We contend that epistemological and methodological pluralism should be promoted in educational research. . . . Today's research world is becoming increasingly interdisciplinary, complex, and dynamic; therefore, many researchers need to complement one method with another, and all researchers need a solid understanding of multiple

methods used by other scholars to facilitate communication, to promote collabora-
tion, and to provide superior research. (Johnson & Onwuegbuzie, 2004, p. 15)

Advocacy for a mixed methods approach to social inquiry is by definition a stance of advocacy for methodological pluralism. Less integral to a shared definition of mixed methods inquiry is a stance of advocacy for epistemological or, more broadly, paradigmatic pluralism. There are instead diverse stances on the wisdom and practicalities of mixing paradigms or mental models while mixing methods. As presented in Exhibit 5.1, these stances can be meaningfully differentiated by their different responses to the two issues taken up in the previous chapter: (1) the nature of a paradigm or mental model and (2) the role of paradigms or mental models in practical inquiry decisions. These two issues represent the two bullets under each stance presented in Exhibit 5.1. In this exhibit and the discussion that follows, the focus will be on social inquiry paradigms rather than more broadly on mental models. This is because the deliberations in the literature focus on paradigms. The reader is urged to keep in mind the broader construct of mental models while engaging with this discussion, as the logic is applicable to both formal philosophical paradigms and the mental models construct. It is also important to note that the six stances discussed in this chapter are neither completely independent of one another nor exhaustive of all possible stances. Rather, they represent the dominant arguments in the literature to date.

EXHIBIT 5.1. **Mixing Methods *and* Mixing Paradigms or Mental Models?**

Stance
- *What is the nature of a philosophical paradigm for social inquiry?*
- *What role do paradigms play in social research and evaluation practice?*

Purist stance
- Paradigms are integrally constituted by sets of interconnected philosophical assumptions (ontological, epistemological, methodological) that must be respected and preserved. The assumptive sets of different paradigms are incommensurable.
- Paradigmatic assumptions importantly guide and direct practical inquiry decisions. Because the assumptions of different paradigms are incompatible (incommensurable), it is not possible to mix paradigms in the same study.

A-paradigmatic stance
- Paradigms comprise philosophical assumptions and stances regarding reality, knowledge, methodology, and values that are logically independent and therefore can be mixed and matched in varied combinations.

- What matters most in guiding practical inquiry decisions are the practical characteristics and demands of the inquiry context and problem at hand, not abstract philosophical paradigms.

Substantive theory stance

- Paradigms comprise philosophical assumptions and stances regarding reality, knowledge, methodology, and values. Paradigms may well be embedded in or intertwined with substantive theories.
- What matters most in guiding practical inquiry decisions are the substantive issues and conceptual theories relevant to the study being conducted, not philosophical paradigms in and of themselves.

Complementary strengths stance

- Paradigms are constituted by sets of interconnected philosophical assumptions regarding reality, knowledge, methodology, and values that must be respected and preserved. The assumptive sets of different paradigms are not fundamentally incompatible but are different in important ways.
- Paradigmatic assumptions importantly guide and direct practical inquiry decisions, along with context and theory. Because the assumptions of different paradigms are different in important ways, methods implemented within different paradigms should be kept separate from one another. In this way, paradigmatic and methodological integrity can be maintained.

Dialectic stance

- Paradigms are constituted by sets of interconnected philosophical assumptions regarding reality, knowledge, methodology, and values. The assumptive sets of different paradigms are different in important ways, but paradigms themselves are historical and social constructions and so are not inviolate or sacrosanct.
- Paradigmatic assumptions importantly guide and direct practical inquiry decisions, along with context and theory. Important paradigm differences should be respectfully and intentionally used together to engage meaningfully with difference and, through the tensions created by juxtaposing different paradigms, to achieve dialectical discovery of enhanced, reframed, or new understandings.

Alternative paradigms stance

- Paradigms comprise sets of various philosophical assumptions regarding reality, knowledge, methodology, and values. Historical philosophical incommensurabilities among paradigms are reconcilable through new, emergent paradigms, such as contemporary pragmatism, scientific or critical realism, or transformation-emancipation.
- Traditional inquiry paradigms are no longer relevant to practice. What should guide mixed method practice, along with contextual and theoretical demands, is a new paradigm (for example, pragmatism) that actively embraces and promotes the mixing of methods.

Source: Greene and Caracelli, 1997a; Teddlie and Tashakkori, 2003.

The Purist Stance

The purist stance (labeled so initially by Rossman & Wilson, 1985, and then used by Greene, Caracelli, & Graham, 1989) is advanced by proponents of various paradigms. These proponents argue that paradigms are constituted by sets of interconnected or interlocking philosophical assumptions that form an integral whole that must be respected and preserved. Some assumptions are shared across paradigms—for example, the value-ladenness of inquiry—but each set of paradigmatic assumptions must be maintained as a set to preserve paradigmatic integrity. Moreover, the assumptions of some different paradigms are contradictory and thereby incommensurable. To take ontology as an example, the post-positivist assumption that there is a social reality that can be objectively known (mind-independent) is incommensurable with the constructivist assumption that meaningfulness in human experience is socially constructed and therefore subjectively interpreted (mind-dependent). Furthermore, paradigms substantially direct and guide practical inquiry decisions; that is, purists maintain that it is *because* of the assumed valuing of linear causal knowledge in science that post-positivists often choose experimental or quasi-experimental inquiry designs. It is *because* of the assumed interpreted character of human experience that constructionists often choose up-close methods like on-site observations and personal interviews. It is *because* of the assumed coequal status of practitioner knowledge and expert knowledge that participatory action researchers choose collaborative inquiry processes for their work. The assumptions of philosophical paradigms are thus consciously invoked when making practical inquiry decisions.

In recent times, the purist stance was advanced perhaps most vehemently in the midst of the qualitative-quantitative debate (see Chapter Three) by vocal leaders of the qualitative camp, notably Egon Guba and Yvonna Lincoln (Guba 1985; Lincoln & Guba, 1985, 2000; see also J. K. Smith, 1983). This is understandable, as Guba, Lincoln, and others were battling precisely for the legitimacy of constructionist and interpretivist *paradigms,* which they defined as interconnected ontological, epistemological, and methodological assumptions (assumptions about the nature of the social world, social knowledge, and how to best generate it). After all, the great debate was not chiefly about method, but about these underlying philosophical assumptions or logics of justification (again, see Chapter Three). To construe a paradigm otherwise was to trivialize the issues at hand and, more important, to threaten the tenuous legitimacy of paradigms associated with qualitative methodological traditions. So according to purists one can mix methods but only *within* a given paradigm. (See also Cook, 2002, 2004, and Raudenbush, 2005, for more contemporary arguments for a purist position within a post-positivist paradigm.)

FOR EXAMPLE

Illustrating a Purist Stance

A mixed methods study of the "dynamics" of caregiving for the elderly illustrates a mix of methods within a single philosophical framework or mental model (Sanchez-Ayendez, 1998). (My thanks to members of my mixed methods graduate class in the spring of 2006 for locating this and other examples featured in this chapter.)

This "qualitative study" sought to generate "an in-depth understanding of the circumstances in which Puerto Rican middle-aged female caregivers carry out the tasks relevant to informal support" (p. 76). The focus of the study was on instrumental tasks. The author used several standardized quantitative instruments (such as the General Well-Being Schedule) to develop descriptive profiles of the elderly and their caregivers in the study sample. Interviews with the caregivers then included structured and open-ended questions to gather information regarding instrumental caregiving tasks and the interactive dynamics associated with them. One set of results was presented by task cluster—for example, daily tasks (like cooking), routine nondaily tasks (like shopping or doctors' appointments), and health emergencies—and included significant quotes and mini-stories from the respondents. A second set of results focused on the stresses and supports experienced by caregivers in their role. This set included some frequencies for selected responses (for example, how many caregivers had support from another family member and who that was) as well as respondent quotes. The discussion of the results underscored the holistic character of the caregivers' lives within which their work as a caregiver created challenges and stress, as well as the "situational and subjective dimensions" of the caregivers' perceptions and understandings of their work. "Directing attention to the process and context of caregiving adds a holistic dimension to the situation of elderly individuals who are sick or disabled" (p. 95). This is the language of an interpretive paradigm or mental model. An interview with the author would be needed to assert with more confidence that this is indeed an interpretive, qualitative study. The form of the study, the presentation of the results, and the language used in interpreting them, however, all point to an interpretive philosophical framework. As such, this appears to be a mixed methods study within a purist paradigmatic stance.

The A-Paradigmatic Stance

The a-paradigmatic stance (labeled so by Teddlie & Tashakkori, 2003) represents almost the opposite of the purist stance. The label of this stance suggests its core premise—that paradigms are not centrally important to good inquiry practice.

My practical (and controversial) view is that one can learn to be a good interviewer or observer, and learn to make sense of the resulting data, without first engaging in deep epistemological reflection and philosophical study. . . . [One can] simply conduct

interviews and gather observational data to answer concrete program and organiza-
tional questions without working explicitly with a particular theoretical, paradigmatic,
or philosophical perspective . . . without making a paradigmatic or philosophical
pledge of allegiance. (Patton, 2002, pp. 69, 145)

In this stance, paradigms are viewed as abstract conceptual ideas that can usefully inform inquirers' methodological development and understandings, but only in a general way. Paradigms help to *describe* inquiry practice; they do not *prescribe* it as suggested by the purists. And paradigms themselves are not sacrosanct or inviolate. Rather, the varied assumptions and stances that paradigms comprise can be mixed and matched in multiple combinations as appropriate to the context (Reichardt & Cook, 1979, and see the discussion on this in Chapter Four).

What most influentially informs practical inquiry decisions for proponents of this stance are the particular characteristics and demands of the inquiry context. For researchers, inquiry purpose, questions, and sample characteristics may be most influential. For evaluators, the nature of the evaluation contract and the information needs of various stakeholders are commonly important shapers of evaluation design and methods. In the evaluation field, this a-paradigmatic point of view has been most thoroughly articulated in the form of a "utilization-focused evaluation theory" by Michael Patton (2000).

From my observations of the field, I would venture the perhaps controversial hypothesis that much (even most) mixed methods research and evaluation is either purist or a-paradigmatic in implementation. Methods are mixed, even thoughtfully mixed, but all within just one philosophical framework or, perhaps even more commonly, the one mental model of the inquirer. Conscious attention to this model, or not, is what differentiates the purist from the a-paradigmatic inquirer. These two stances are highly defensible in theory and well substantiated by their adherents. However, from the perspective presented in this book—a perspective well captured in the idea of a mixed methods way of thinking—these two stances may represent missed opportunities for generative and more insightful understanding in our social inquiry practice.

FOR EXAMPLE

Illustrating an A-Paradigmatic Stance

A mixed methods study of the challenges in home visitation for families in child abuse and neglect situations illustrates the a-paradigmatic stance (LeCroy & Whitaker, 2005). This study sought a "better understanding of difficult situations that confront home visitors to identify specific skills and competencies that can be used for training" (p. 1005) and used a sequential mix of qualitative focus groups followed by a structured quantitative inventory. Specifically, twenty focus groups of five to eight home visitors each (n = 114) were conducted at an Arizona statewide meeting of the Healthy Families program. Using trained facilitators, groups were instructed to "make a list of difficult or challenging [home visiting] situations you have encountered, situations in which you were not sure what to do, situations that did not go well" (pp. 1005–1006). From the large pool of situations generated by the focus groups, the researchers constructed an inventory of seventy-seven problem situations, along with Likert response scales of frequency and difficulty. The inventory was administered by mail to another sample of Healthy Family home visitors, of whom ninety-one (90 percent) responded. The inventory results were analyzed descriptively and with principal components factor analysis to explore possible dimensions underlying respondents' ratings of difficulty.

In the published article, the results focused primarily on data from the inventory, with an emphasis on the characteristics of home visiting situations rated most frequent and most difficult and their possible underlying dimensions. Examples of the most difficult situations are "helping parents who threaten to commit suicide" and "working in the homes during the summer heat." The discussion emphasized training implications. For example, "the frequency ratings . . . provide a very direct agenda for training, for example, working with teenage mothers, knowing what activities to do during a home visit, working with families that are not motivated . . ." (p. 1009). And "the factor analysis also suggests a way of conceptualizing an overall training effort" (p. 1009).

The authors of this study did not invoke paradigmatic assumptions in their presentation of their work. Instead, this work appears to be framed and guided by a mental model that (1) is rooted in a realist ontology or the assumption that the social world exists independent of our constructions or interpretations of it, but also (2) attends to and appreciates the complexity of most human contexts or situations; (3) values the different roles and contributions of different kinds of methods and data, both qualitative and quantitative; and (4) values practitioner perspectives and experiences. This study sought to better understand the particular challenges of home visiting *in particular contexts* by working from the perspectives and experiences of those closest to the phenomena being studied. This is a form of contextual responsiveness and thus well illustrates the a-paradigmatic mixed methods stance.

The Substantive Theory Stance

The third stance in Exhibit 5.1 originated as part of the mixed methods conversation primarily from the field of evaluation. It is associated with an approach to evaluation that privileges the substantive theory of the program being evaluated, rather than the methods to be used (Bickman, 1987, 1990; Chen, 1990; Chen & Rossi, 1983; Pawson & Tilly, 1997; Rogers, Hacsi, Petrosino, & Huebner, 2000; Weiss, 1998). Van der Knaap (2004) in fact presents an argument that a theory-oriented approach to evaluation can potentially "reconcil[e] positivist and constructivist approaches to evaluation" (p. 28). For the traditionally method-driven field of evaluation, an emphasis on substantive theory is a significant departure from business as usual. For other fields of social inquiry, the contours and character of the substantive issues at hand probably typically influence practice decisions, at least in part.

The argument in evaluation is that evaluations should contribute primarily to conceptual and practical knowledge regarding how best to address our social problems (House, 1994). Evaluators should concentrate on understanding the meaningfulness and effectiveness of a given program design and implementation in a given context, toward better understanding of that programmatic response to that social problem and, over time, better understanding of how best to address that social problem. One valuable way to do this is to frame evaluation studies using theories of the program being studied. These program theories then become the guiding framework for evaluation design and method choices, and the evaluation becomes theory-oriented rather than method-driven.

In this stance, paradigms do not feature prominently. That is, of course, the point—a point also shared by the a-paradigmatic stance discussed previously. What does feature prominently are the conceptual and substantive theories relevant to what is being studied; for example, critical factors contributing to childhood obesity, important correlates of the spread of HIV/AIDS, meaningful incentives for youth of color to engage in school learning, non-profit organizational characteristics associated with sustainability. Perhaps in this stance key features of paradigms are interwoven with or even embedded in the relevant substantive theories. A theory that attributes school success or failure primarily to the individual student and the student's family may embrace very different paradigmatic assumptions from a theory that attributes school performance to the structural and economic regimes of government policies.

The importance of this stance for a mixed methods argument is that methods are subservient to concepts in theories. In particular, data are not analyzed and aggregated by method; rather, data analysis is framed and organized by concept or theory. In an evaluation study, for example, results are presented not for each method separately, but by evaluation question or by key program component. Again, for the traditionally method-driven field of evaluation, this is a significant departure.

FOR EXAMPLE

Illustrating a Substantive Theory Stance

An intentional use of this mixed methods paradigmatic stance is evident in an evaluation of a middle school "program intended to integrate active learning strategies, computer access, and interdisciplinary instruction into regular classroom activities" (Cooksy, Gill, & Kelly, 2001, p. 121). In this program, small groups of students work at activities such as individual tasks at computers, collaborative hands-on tasks at exploration stations, or writing tasks at text stations. Students rotate through the various stations, thus engaging the material in a variety of ways. This program was piloted in one school for two years, accompanied by a formative evaluation, and then expanded to two other schools and evaluated on its outcomes in years three and four.

For the outcomes evaluation, the evaluators developed a program theory in the form of a logic model from document review and interviews, and then iteratively refined the model in consultation with various program stakeholders. Logic models portray key elements of a program—typically including resources, activities, and both short-term and longer-term outcomes—that collectively offer a representation of how the program is supposed to operate. In this logic model, for example, teacher activities included "train students in cooperative learning, station rotation, and computer use" and "develop appropriate (authentic) assessments." Initial student outcomes included "self-direction" and "computer skills."

The authors highlighted the value of the logic model in this evaluation by tracking the short-term student outcome of computer skills, which was located in the model as a link between program activities and the longer-term outcome of student learning. The program's logic model "shows that improved computer skills depended first on teachers' incorporation of computers into class assignments and second on students' access to computers. The sources of evidence about these two activities were surveys of the teachers and students" (p. 124). In school A, teachers "consistently reported frequent use of the computers in the learning activities and to support lesson objectives," and students in school A who were in the program being evaluated were "more likely to report regular use of computers" (p. 126) than their control group peers. In school B, teachers reported less frequent use of computers, and almost equal numbers of school B students in the program reported increased access to computers as reported decreased access. With this pattern, the evaluators expected to find stronger evidence of increased computer skills in school A compared with school B.

The authors then observed that within each school, the various data sources on students' computer skills actually showed divergence among themselves and with predictions based on teacher implementation and student access. Illustrating good mixed methods thinking, the evaluators sought various explanations for these patterns of divergence, including unsound measurement, inflated teacher responses (perhaps due to a positive program bias), and measures that actually tapped into different perspectives (such as from students and from parents). In summary, the evaluators reflect as follows:

> Juxtaposing the results from the different sources highlighted the inconsistent reports about computer skills from the students, teachers, and parents within and across schools. Similarly, examining the outcome data in light of what the data on program implementation predicted revealed a mismatch between the expected pattern and the data. In combination with the lack of convergence across the data sources, the inability to match the pattern of outcomes relative to the schools' implementation reinforced our conclusion that a [program] effect on computer skills had not been observed. (p. 127)

The language throughout this evaluation study is about concepts, patterns, predictions, not about the nature of knowledge or the social world. As such, this evaluation study offers a window into the substantive theory paradigmatic stance in action.

Another example of the substantive theory stance integrated standardized assessments and open-ended interviewing with GIS in an effort to develop a spatial, ecodevelopmental portrayal of substance use among urban youth (Mason, Cheung, & Walker, 2004). The guiding framework for this study—in which various data sources were integrated—is the authors' ecodevelopmental model, which (like Bronfenbrenner's original ecological model) has concentric rings of environmental activities and influences surrounding the youth at the center. Distinctive features of this model in this study include its GIS data linkages and geographical representations and its emphasis on the youth's own social networks.

The Complementary Strengths Stance

The fourth paradigmatic stance in Exhibit 5.1 is labeled the *complementary strengths stance* by Teddlie and Tashakkori (2003). This stance is rooted in an early and influential mixed methods book by John Brewer and Albert Hunter (1989)—revealingly entitled *Multimethod Research* rather than *Mixed Methods Research*. The "fundamental strategy [of multimethod research] is to attack a research problem with an arsenal of methods that have nonoverlapping weaknesses in addition to their complementary strengths" (p. 17). While privileging convergence across different methods with offsetting weaknesses biases and thus a triangulation framework for mixed methods inquiry, the authors also note the value of divergent findings as "signal[ing] the need to analyze a research problem further" (p. 17). Brewer and Hunter further emphasize the importance in multimethod research of implementing any given method well; that is, with quality and integrity so that it will yield the data it is best designed to generate. For example, laboratory experiments are designed to provide precise causal data with limited external validity, whereas surveys yield relational data with good generalizability. The particular strengths of each method must be preserved in multimethod research, or its potential for comparisons across diverse data sets—each of defensible quality—will be undermined.

Janice Morse (2003) elaborates on a complementary strengths stance by distinguishing between mixing methods in a single project or study and mixing methods across studies in an overall program of research. Like Brewer and Hunter, Morse is concerned about threats to methodological integrity that may be posed by mixes of methods: "We must ... remain aware that the ad hoc mixing of strategies or methods (i.e., 'muddling methods' [Stern, 1994]) may be a serious threat to validity as methodological assumptions are violated" (p. 191). She contends that a single study or project must have a single "theoretical drive," defined as "the overall direction of the project as determined from the original questions or purpose and is primarily inductive or deductive" (p. 190). So when a study with an overall inductive theoretical drive includes quantitative methods, these "imported strategies are supplemental" to the major qualitative methodology and are used primarily to help interpret or illustrate the qualitative findings. And qualitative methods in an overall deductive study would play a similar role. Across studies within a program of research, different kinds of methodologies may be dominant. Also called *multimethod research* by Morse, this is the use of different research methodologies for individual studies, "each conducted rigorously and complete in itself in one project. The results are then triangulated to form a comprehensive whole" (p. 190). (See also the discussion on Morse's ideas in Chapter Seven on mixed methods design.)

In sum, what distinguishes the mixed methods complementary strengths stance is a recognition of the important role of paradigms in framing and guiding inquiry practice, along with a respect for the importance of maintaining the integrity of any given methodological tradition in order to generate defensible results that well honor the strengths of that tradition. Different authors recommend different strategies for how best to accomplish this. The issue of methodological integrity is, of course, a critical one that will be revisited in Chapter Nine.

FOR EXAMPLE

Illustrating a Complementary Strengths Stance

An excellent example of the complementary strengths stance in action is the set of interconnected studies conducted by Eckert (1987) on the displacement of low-income seniors living in one city's downtown hotels by economic development and gentrification. Grounded in ethnographic inquiry, this planned sequential set of studies blended both qualitative and quantitative research in order to "preserve the insights and understandings derived from qualitative/experiential approaches while enhancing the ability to replicate, verify, and generalize findings" (p. 242). The inquiry was schematically represented as a spiral that incorporated three main stages, moving from contextual ethnographic description toward nomothetic and generalizable explanation.

In the first stage (which lasted four years), the researcher pursued an ethnographic understanding of how older adults living on fixed incomes in single room occupancy hotels adjust and survive in a changing urban environment. The researcher held a job as a desk clerk in a downtown hotel, which allowed him to develop trust with the elderly residents and an understanding of the rhythms, joys, and challenges of their daily life experiences. From this phase, important themes in these seniors' lives were identified; for example, the challenges of procuring adequate health care and nutritious diets. Eckert was also able to develop and administer a questionnaire about these important thematic issues to a broader representative sample of residents in that hotel.

> The questionnaires offered us hard data about the categories and ideas that had turned up in the participant observation. None of the quantitative material we obtained by means of survey research could have been obtained by observation alone, although the questions or their suitability could not have been determined without the observations. One needs both. (p. 250)

Stage 2 of this research involved hypothesis testing and explanation, specifically investigating the stresses experienced by seniors as they were forced to relocate from their downtown hotel to elsewhere, due to redevelopment of the area (deemed "blighted" by city planners). A quasi-experimental design was used to compare older adults who were forced to move with a matched group in contiguous hotels who were not forced to move. The short-term outcomes measured in stage 2 did not demonstrate any negative health effects of forced relocation. Eckert, however, wondered about longer-term effects.

These were pursued in stage 3, which essentially extended the comparative design of stage 2 over an additional two-year period, plus supplemented these methods with a small ethnographic component to better understand the experiences and effects of relocation on the ground. Interestingly, no longer-term ill effects of relocation were found either.

This is an exemplary mixed methods study illustrative of a complementary strengths paradigm stance precisely *because* of the respect demonstrated for the different ways of knowing typified by different paradigms and methodological traditions. Further, this respect was enacted in a sequential design in which the different methods were implemented with substantial fidelity to their own assumptive framework. And although some communication across methods was inevitable, the designed intent was to implement each methodology separately and thus with intrinsic integrity.

The Dialectic Stance

The mixed methods paradigm stance favored by this author is the dialectic stance. I recognize and accept the legitimacy of all other stances and even employ some of these myself in my inquiry practice. In fact, a high-priority issue for the mixed methods field is to delineate features of inquiry contexts that are best matched to various mixed methods paradigm stances, along with the broader question of when to even employ a mixed methods rather than a monomethod approach (Datta, 1997b).

I choose to advance the dialectic stance over the others primarily for its generative potential (Greene, 2005c; Greene, Benjamin, & Goodyear, 2001; Greene & Caracelli, 1997a, 1997b). I view the mixing of methods overall as a methodological strategy that can yield better understanding of the phenomena being studied than can a single method, as all methods each offer but one perspective, one partial view. And I believe that better understanding takes its most important form as generative insights, which are in turn best attained through a respectful conversation among different ways of seeing and knowing. Our rich tradition of philosophical paradigms and even richer array of multiple mental models offer many different ways of seeing and knowing, many different conversational partners. A mixed methods dialectic stance seeks

> *Understanding that is woven from strands of particularity* and *generality,* contextual complexity and *patterned regularity, inside* and *outside perspectives, the whole* and its constituent parts, *change* and *stability, equity* and *excellence,* and so forth. That is, *[it] seeks not so much convergence as insight . . . the generation of important understandings and discernments through the juxtaposition of different lenses, perspectives, and stances; in a good mixed methods study, difference is constitutive and fundamentally generative.* (Greene, 2005c, p. 208, emphases in original)

Charles Ragin (1987) offered a parallel dialogic framework for conducting comparative research that integrates distinct traditions of variable-oriented and case-oriented research in the same study. Arguing that "the nature of the dialogue that develops between theoretical ideas and data analysis [and thus evidence] is shaped in part by the nature of the methods of data analysis used" (p. 165), Ragin proposed an expanded dialogue that includes both causal regularity and contextual complexity. Ragin further proposed a particular form of Boolean algebra as the analytic framework for such a dialogue between ideas and evidence, as a way to address large numbers of cases without forsaking complexity. (See also the software developed by Ragin for this Boolean algebraic approach and his work on fuzzy set analysis, http://www.u.arizona.edu/~cragin/cragin/publications.shtml).

As noted, I also advance a dialectic stance because it enables a meaningful engagement with difference and thus promotes values of tolerance, acceptance, and equity. I believe that values are inextricably interwoven with methodologies, and I seek to position my work in service of the public good, advancing values consonant with a strong democracy (Greene, 2005b, and see Chapter One). In this view, that is, mixed methods inquiry is not just a methodological advance, but also a sociopolitical one. (See Greene, Benjamin, & Goodyear, 2001; Greene, 2002; and Kushner, 2002, for a dialogue on these issues.)

FOR EXAMPLE

Illustrating a Dialectic Stance

The commitments of participatory action research (PAR) as advocated by Stephen Kemmis and Robin McTaggart (2000) are parallel to those of the mixed methods dialectic stance and thus serve well to illustrate the dialectic stance in action. In fact, Kemmis and McTaggart present their perspective on PAR as a "contribution to going beyond the 'paradigm wars' that have bedeviled social research over much of the past century" (p. 573). Their argument is rich and complex, and the reader is encouraged to explore it in depth. For illustrative purposes, two facets of the Kemmis and McTaggart PAR framework will be presented here.

First, PAR is fundamentally conceptualized as a social change-oriented dialogue among the commonsense understandings of participants in a social context who are dissatisfied with the way things are and want to change them, alongside the outside understandings of social theorists and researchers.

The participant perspective poses a substantial challenge to social theory: to articulate "common" sense in a way that will be regarded as authentic and compelling by participants themselves, without converting participants to the imposed perspective of a specialist social theorist. . . . The criterion of authenticity involves a dialectic sometimes described in terms of "the melting of horizons" (Gadamer, 1975)—seeing things intersubjectively, from one's own point of view and from the point of view of others (from the inside and the outside). (pp. 573–574)

Second, Kemmis and McTaggart center their PAR framework around five different conceptualizations of practice (agentic human action). The first four are differentiated by underlying perspectives that emphasize the individual or the social/collective and by their assumed stances of objectivity or subjectivity (external or internal) in conceptualizing phenomena and methods. With a 2 × 2 framework, these four conceptualizations of practice, their location in the 2 × 2 framework (in italics), and their associated methodological traditions and illustrative methods are as follows:

1. Practice as individual behavior; the individual performances, events, and effects that constitute practice as it is viewed from the outside *(individual-objective;* quantitative, correlational-experimental methodologies; tests, psychometric measures)

2. Practice as social and systems behavior; the wider social and material conditions and interactions that constitute practice as it is viewed from the outside *(social-objective;* quantitative, correlational-experimental methodologies; systems analysis)

3. Practice as intentional action; the intentions, meanings, and values that constitute practice as it is viewed from the internal perspective of the actor *(individual-subjective;* qualitative, interpretive methodologies; clinical analysis, journals, diaries)

4. Practice as socially structured; the language, discourses, and traditions that constitute practice as it is viewed from the inside, the internal social perspective of members of a discourse community *(social-subjective;* qualitative, interpretive methodologies; historical analysis, discourse analysis)

Kemmis and McTaggart then present a fifth view of practice and its associated methodologies as a political, reflexive, dialectic endeavor. In this fifth view, it is understood "that to study practice is to change it, [so] the process of studying it is also 'political'" (p. 578). Moreover, this kind of inquiry is inherently reflexive—"it is a process of enlightenment about the standpoint from which one studies practice as well as about the practice itself" (p. 578).

This view of practice and its study is also inherently dialectic. This view of practice challenges the dichotomies or dualisms that separate the first four views from one another. . . . It attempts to see each of these dimensions not in terms of polar opposites, but in terms of the mutuality and relationship between these different aspects of things . . . to be understood dialectically . . . as mutually opposed (and often contradictory) but mutually necessary aspects of human, social, and historical reality, in which each aspect helps to constitute the other. (p. 578)

Practice in this fifth view is understood as socially and historically constituted, and as reconstituted by human agency and social action. And critical methodologies—like PAR—accompany this view of practice. In PAR, the participant perspective is privileged because "participant change is the *sine qua non* of social change" (p. 590).

In sum, as advanced by Kemmis and McTaggart, PAR recognizes and legitimizes difference and diversity (of perspective, action, and methodological tradition alike) and intentionally seeks to engage with such diversity in a dialectic, dialogic process toward mutually constituted understanding. In these ways, this conceptualization of PAR is a strong example of the assumptions, stances, and commitments underlying a mixed methods dialectic paradigm stance.

The Brazilian Amazon land use study featured in Interlude One in this book (by John Sydenstricker-Neto, 2004) is a noteworthy empirical example of a mixed methods study with a dialectic paradigm stance.

The Alternative Paradigm Stance

The final mixed methods paradigm stance is arguably the most popular amongst theorists in this domain. This stance perceives paradigms in ways similar to the other stances and, like the complementary strengths and dialectic stances, allocates a role to paradigms in influencing practice decisions (alongside contextual and theoretical considerations). Distinctively, proponents of this stance seek to respond to the challenges of mixing paradigms while mixing methods by embracing an alternative, more "emergent" paradigm that inherently welcomes or even requires a mix of methods, but that is not troubled by issues of incommensurable philosophical assumptions or stances. An alternative paradigm, that is, offers its own internal coherence and integrity and so does not present the tensions and challenges that can accompany the joint use of two more traditional paradigms (like post-positivism and social constructionism or realism and critical feminism).

Among the alternative paradigms championed for mixed methods social inquiry, the most popular is some form of *pragmatism* (advanced by Datta, 1997b; Howe, 1985, 1988, 2003; Johnson & Onwuegbuzie, 2004; Tashakkori & Teddlie, 1998; and Teddlie & Tashakkori, 2003, among others). Also promoted as mixed methods alternative paradigms are some form of *scientific realism* (House, 1994; Maxwell,

2004a; Niglas, 2004; Pawson & Tilly, 1997) and a transformative or *emancipatory paradigm* for social inquiry (Mertens, 1999, 2003). In the following discussion, each of these alternatives will be briefly elaborated, with emphases matched to their prevalence in the mixed methods conversation.

On Pragmatism Pragmatism is a distinctively American philosophical tradition with roots in "the writings of three American thinkers: the natural scientist and philosopher Charles Sanders Pierce (1839–1914), the psychologist and philosopher William James (1842–1910), and the philosopher, psychologist, and educationalist John Dewey (1859–1952)" (Biesta & Burbules, 2003, pp. 3–4). Important contributions were also made by George Herbert Mead and, more recently, neopragmatists like Richard Rorty. A significant challenge in discussing key stances of pragmatism is that there is not one pragmatism but many, stemming from the different disciplinary roots of the original pragmatists and from the different topics they engaged in their work.

Johnson and Onwuegbuzie (2004), in an argument expressly for the use of pragmatism as *the* mixed methods paradigm, present a generic or synthesized portrait of this philosophical tradition. They suggest that the project of pragmatism has been to find a middle ground between philosophical dogmatisms and skepticism and to find a workable solution (sometimes including outright rejection) to many longstanding philosophical dualisms about which agreement has not been historically forthcoming.

The characteristics of pragmatism offered by these authors include the following:

- Recognizes the existence and importance of the natural or physical world as well as the emergent social and psychological world that includes language, culture, human institutions, and subjective thoughts.
- Places high regard for the reality of and influence of the inner world of human experience in action.
- [Views] knowledge . . . as being both constructed and based on the reality of the world we experience and live in.
- Replaces the historically popular epistemic distinction between subject and external object with the naturalistic and process-oriented organism-environment transaction.
- Justification comes in the form of what Dewey called "warranted assertability."
- [Views] theories instrumentally (they become true and they are true to different degrees based on how well they currently work; workability is judged especially on the criteria of predictability and applicability).
- Views current truth, meaning, and knowledge as tentative and as changing over time. What we obtain on a daily basis in research should be viewed as provisional truths.
- Capital "T" Truth . . . is what will be the "final opinion" perhaps at the end of history.

- Prefers action to philosophizing.

- Takes an explicitly value-oriented approach to research that is derived from cultural values; specifically endorses shared values such as democracy, freedom, equality and progress. (Table 1, p. 18)

Pragmatism thus offers "an immediate and useful middle position philosophically and methodologically"; its primary method maxim or rule is translated into inquiry practice as "choose the combination or mixture of methods and procedures that works best for answering your research questions" (p. 17).

A more particular (and very thoughtful and useful) portrait of Deweyan pragmatism (especially as connected to educational research) is offered by philosophers Gert Biesta and Nicholas Burbules (2003). John Dewey's ideas about social inquiry are rooted in his transactional or relational view of knowledge or understanding. The meaning of human experience, that is, resides neither exclusively in the objective real world nor exclusively in the internal mind of the knower, but rather in their interaction or transaction. Moreover, the truth of this meaning is enacted in the consequences of the interaction itself. Truth or knowledge is thus contextual, temporal, and related to action. In other words, action is constitutive of truth, meaning, and knowledge. And inquiry is initiated by a felt difficulty, a perceived indeterminacy, an imbalance between organism and environment. Everyday inquiry, just like more disciplined and well-planned scientific inquiry, is undertaken to pursue and learn about or resolve this indeterminacy or unease. Distinctive to scientific inquiry is that the actions and inferences made are embedded in a conceptual network. Moreover, Dewey rejected the fact-value distinction and embraced the major tenets of liberal democracy as prerequisite to social science. Finally, Dewey agreed that inquiry methods must fit the questions posed, but more profoundly, he averred that methods also define the question just as the question defines the methods, that methods and questions are mutually constitutive (Burbules, personal communication, March 2006).

And in the field of evaluation, Datta (1997b) offered a pragmatic basis for mixed methods evaluation studies:

> I propose for our field that "pragmatic" means the essential criteria for making design decisions are practical, contextually responsive, and consequential. "Practical" implies a basis in one's experience of what does and does not work. "Contextually responsive" involves understanding the demands, opportunities, and constraints of the situation in which the evaluation will take place. "Consequential" in this discussion, [as] defined by pragmatic theory, . . . [means] that the truth of a statement consists of its practical consequences, particularly the statement's agreement with subsequent experience. (p. 34, emphases in original)

The attractiveness of pragmatism as a paradigm for mixed methods social inquiry is evident in its rejection of historical dualisms, its acceptance of both realist and constructivist strands of knowledge, and its practical, consequential character. However, the enactment of this paradigm in and for mixed methods inquiry remains a continuing and important challenge. To approach mixed methods inquiry pragmatically does *not* mean to ignore or set to one side philosophical assumptions and stances when making practical methods decisions. For that is the a-paradigmatic stance. Rather, a pragmatic paradigm signals attention to transactions and interactions; to the consequential, contextual, and dynamic nature of character of knowledge; to knowledge as action; to the intertwinement of values with inquiry; and so forth. Just how these philosophical commitments get enacted in methodological decisions and interpretive inferences is a matter requiring further conceptual and practical development.

On Scientific Realism

Realism provides a philosophical stance that is compatible with the essential characteristics of both qualitative and quantitative research, and can facilitate communication and cooperation between the two. (Maxwell, 2004a, p. 1)

In support of this promotion of realism for mixed methods inquiry, Maxwell first argued for an interactive relationship between philosophy and practice, much like the argument presented in this book (Chapter Four). Maxwell then noted that, like pragmatism, there are many different forms of and labels for realism as a philosophical stance, but that all share a view that the real world exists independently of our perceiving or knowing it.

Key features of realism as discussed by Maxwell include the following:

- Theoretical concepts refer to actual features and properties of the real world, rather than the positivist view that they are logical constructions from observational data.

- Social inquirers cannot attain complete "objective" knowledge of this real world, because all theories are grounded in a particular perspective and world view. So "there can be more than one scientifically correct way of understanding reality in terms of conceptual schemes with different objects and categories of objects" (Lakoff, 1987, p. 265, as cited in Maxwell, 2004a, p. 2).

- Mental phenomena, such as emotions, beliefs, and values, are part of reality, not separate from it, and can, for example, be part of the causal explanation for an observed event.

- Causality is intrinsic to the world or to our understanding of it. Causality, however, does not consist of recurring regularities or general laws, but rather real causal mechanisms and processes that can (in principle) be directly observed as manifest in particular contexts. Causality, that is, is context-dependent.

With these features, Maxwell argues, realism provides space for both traditionally qualitative and quantitative ways of thinking and understanding. For example, the acknowledgment of mental phenomena as real, combined with "the process-oriented approach to causality, recognizes the importance of *meaning,* as well as of physical and behavioral phenomena, as having explanatory significance" (p. 5, emphasis in original).

Like pragmatism, scientific realism presents stances that make space for key tenets of both traditionally qualitative and quantitative methodologies. In particular, these stances embrace knowledge that is of the real world and simultaneously contextual, perspectival, and constructed.

On Emancipation A "transformative-emancipatory" paradigm for mixed method inquiry has been persistently advocated by Donna Mertens, whose research and evaluation engages the life worlds of people who are deaf or hearing impaired. Mertens (1999, 2003) passionately promotes a form of social inquiry that serves the interests of those on the margins of society and invokes the inherent value dimensions of inquiry in support of this stance.

> *Transformative scholars assume that knowledge is not neutral but is influenced by human interests, that all knowledge reflects the power and social relationships within society, and that an important purpose of knowledge construction is to help people improve society. (Mertens, 1999, p. 4)*

Mertens's work displaces method as the central nexus of inquiry decision making and replaces method with the critical importance of values and politics, as they are implicated in particular inquiry stances, assumptions, questions, and methodologies. Mertens's work thus signals attention to the sociopolitical location of social inquiry in society (Greene, 2005b). And in a mixed methods context, Mertens's stance serves to foreground value consciousness in inquiry (an idea to which I will return in the next chapter).

REPRISE

There remain diverse ideas about whether or not and how to mix paradigms while mixing methods in mixed methods social inquiry. These ideas are importantly, though not exhaustively, differentiated by different conceptualizations of the nature of philosophical social science paradigms and especially by different stances on the role of paradigms in actual inquiry decision making. For the latter, the critical difference is whether and to what extent philosophical assumptions and stances influence and guide practical inquiry decisions. Stances that allocate a minor role to paradigms in guiding practice include the a-paradigmatic stance and the substantive theory stance. For these, characteristics and demands of the context or the concepts being studied, respectively, are the most important influences on practice decisions such as methods choices. Stances in which paradigms *do* constitute an important influence on practice decisions include those of the purists, who eschew the sensibility of mixed-paradigm inquiry because of incommensurable assumptions; the complementary strengths proponents who focus on maintaining the integrity of each paradigm by keeping their methods separate; the dialectic advocates, who promote the importance of respectful dialogue among different sets of assumptions and perspectives; and those advocating an alternative paradigm, who perceive such a paradigm as not troubling these paradigmatic issues.

In mixed methods inquiry practice, the first step is to identify one's stance on these issues. Just what is to be mixed in the study at hand, and why or with what justification? This stance then influences in a guiding, not deterministic way the remainder of the practical decisions involved in planning and conducting mixed methods social inquiry. It is to these practical decisions that I now turn.

INTERLUDE

AN ILLUSTRATION OF A MIXED METHODS WAY OF THINKING

JOHN SYDENSTRICKER-NETO'S doctoral dissertation, "Land-Cover Change and Social Organization in Brazilian Amazonia" (2004), and his paper "Population and Deforestation in Brazilian Amazonia" (2006) offer an exemplary illustration of conducting social inquiry with a mixed methods way of thinking. Situated in the field of rural sociology, this ambitious study incorporated multiple and diverse epistemological traditions, disciplinary perspectives, inquiry methodologies, and research instruments and analysis strategies. Moreover, many of these dimensions of diversity were positioned in interactive dialogue, one with the other, presenting repeated opportunities for generative analysis and insight. Snapshots from this study follow, freely using the words of the author (with his approval). The interested reader is referred to the full study for details.

■ ■ ■

STUDY PURPOSE

The primary purpose of Sydenstricker-Neto's dissertation was to get beyond simple population-increase explanations of tropical deforestation to a better understanding of the human socioeconomic and biophysical causes driving deforestation in the Brazilian Amazon, as well as their interactions. The study was conducted in an area of the western Brazilian Amazon called Machadinho D'Oeste, in the state of Rondonia. Machadinho D'Oeste was one of a number of areas of the Brazilian Amazon opened to controlled colonization under government policy in the 1980s. Controlled colonization practices included demarcating land parcels to fit the terrain, establishing relatively small parcels to encourage settlement while safeguarding mandatory forest preserves, and building an infrastructure that included a feeder road connected to all land parcels and basic public services. Machadinho D'Oeste was selected for this study in large part because previous data on land use for this area showed distinctive patterns of change, compared with other colonization communities in the Amazon, early on toward more sustainable land use practices and then a return to significant conversion of forest to agricultural use. In the words of Sydenstricker-Neto (2004),

> My major objective was to identify to what extent historically grounded local social relations and specific conditions of natural resource systems had jointly shaped the ways in which settlers used their agricultural parcels and common-forest reserves. Methodologically, I was interested in linking socio-demographic information and Geographical Information Systems (GIS) analysis to qualitative data on local institutions [specifically, local farmer cooperatives] in order to quantify changes in the landscape and highlight the importance of institutions and organizations in mediating human population-environment relationships.... Conceptually, my research establishes a dialogue between largely independent fields (population studies and environmental sociology) and issues (land use and land-cover change and agricultural decision making processes) ... [thus offering] a stronger perspective than one derived from a single discipline. (pp. 5–7, emphases added)

This statement of inquiry intent clearly reveals substantial commitments to multiplism and to dialogic engagement with difference of perspective.

MIXED METHODS RESEARCH DESIGN

The mixed methods design of this study intentionally resisted the compartmentalized, reductionist character of knowledge development in the twentieth century and was framed by the following multiplistic conceptual stances:

- The perspectives of environmental science, which is an inherently interdisciplinary field located at the intersection of disciplines in the biophysical sciences, the social sciences, and the humanities.

■ A fundamental assumption of "conjoint constitution," whereby nature and society give rise to one another. "Although I acknowledge that there is a biophysical reality that constrains human actions, this biophysical reality means nothing until it is socially defined or constructed by real actors" (Sydenstricker-Neto, 2004, p. 94).

■ An assumption that all forms of knowledge, including scientific knowledge, are partial and thus that local and practical knowledge must also be legitimized. "A full account of the environment by western society can only be accomplished by overcoming the alienation of the separation of abstract knowledge (i.e., scientific and managerial) and practical knowledge" (Sydenstricker-Neto, 2004, p. 92). In this study, the local land knowledge of long-time Amazonian residents—the rubber tappers, nut collectors, and subsistence farmers—was of special value.

■ A strong mixed methods way of thinking. "The mixed-method research approach is a promising means to [generate] *better understanding* of complex problems. In addition, it has the potential to offer more venues to produce outcomes that are more meaningful to larger audiences, including the subjects themselves and other local stakeholders" (Sydenstricker-Neto, 2004, pp. 92–93, emphasis added).

Framed by these multiplistic conceptual stances, Sydenstricker-Neto's mixed methods design was also self-consciously multiplistic and intentionally integrative.

■ This design incorporated both realist and constructivist epistemologies. "Assuming *conjoint constitution* of society-environment relationships, . . . I am interested in the human and physical dimensions of these relationships" (Sydenstricker-Neto, 2004, p. 94).

■ As noted, Sydenstricker-Neto's design also incorporated perspectives and concepts from multiple disciplines: sociology, population studies, crop and soil sciences, environmental information science.

■ The assumptions and stances of both quantitative and qualitative research methodologies were included in this research design. In particular, Sydenstricker-Neto identified the importance of studying physical traces as well as social constructions, causality as well as meaning, and distanced analysis of regularities as well as contextualized understanding of local meaning (from Greene and Caracelli, 1997a).

■ The research design included multiple and diverse data gathering techniques; specifically, land cover maps from satellite imagery, GIS, household surveys, and qualitative interviews with settlers.

From the outset, this research design was further framed as interactive and dialogic, not only including multiple and diverse perspectives but also actively seeking conversation among them. "A conversation is better than an isolated thinking process, and conversation is far more likely to provide solid findings and intriguing insights" (Sydenstricker-Neto, 2004, p. 96). In the language of mixed methods, Sydenstricker-Neto stated that the design mixed methods for purposes of *triangulation* and *complementarity,* although I would add *initiation* to his list (see Chapter Six).

MIXED METHODS ANALYSIS

Sydenstricker-Neto's inquiry purposes were substantially supported by his use of fuzzy sets analysis for the multiple data sets in this study. Fuzzy sets analysis belongs to the statistical family of clustering-type analyses. It is particularly useful for analyzing data representing complex constructs with multiple dimensions, data representing transitions or continua rather than discrete categories, or data that are heterogeneous in form. The boundary between a meadow and a forest is usually fuzzy rather than a clear line. Similarly, the role of a farmer is complicated by his or her family, social, and political relationships. Fuzzy sets analyses honors complexities of this kind (Sydenstricker-Neto, 2004, p. 115).

Sydenstricker-Neto used a "Grade of Membership" form of fuzzy sets analysis in his dissertation to better understand the complex, contingent, and dynamic relationships among all the constructs in his study and the nature and extent of land deforestation over time in Machadinho D'Oeste. The four primary types of farmers identified in his analysis were forest farmer, transition farmer, diversified farmer, and rancher/coffee farmer.

SAMPLE RESULTS

Again, the primary question driving this study was, who was likely to deforest and why? Machadinho D'Oeste was selected for study precisely because there were dramatic changes in the land cover use in this area over the 1986–1999 period. A region "predominantly covered by primary forests at the beginning of the settlement process was deforested and pasture and coffee trees became the predominant agropastoral systems" (2006, p. 10).

The fuzzy sets analysis on the demographics of variations in land use over time revealed a complex portrait of who is likely to deforest, a portrait that extends well beyond simple population-increase explanations of deforestation. One part of this portrait conveys different relationships between labor needs and land uses of pasture versus crops. Specifically, pasture for livestock requires significantly less labor than farming for crops, after the initial investment. Moreover, labor demands vary substantially across different kinds of crops and types of soil. Another factor of importance in this relationship is the contributions of off-farm employment.

These and many other complex contingent findings gave rise to the following kinds of conclusions from this exemplary study:

■ The land-use dynamics ... identified in the study area are complex, but in a general sense, farmers have moved from an initial emphasis on subsistence crops to monoculture of coffee and pastureland.

■ Population matters not solely in terms of population size, but more importantly, in terms of how individuals relate to the natural environment and the activities they perform within a particular context. In this sense mediating factors such as cultural background, rural experience, managerial skills, and integration into the regional and local cultural context are important to assess how human beings are able to consciously regulate and modulate their relationship with their biophysical environment. (2004, pp. 313–314)

Thinking in a mixed methods way is a defining characteristic of this exceptional and socially significant dissertation study.

PART

2

PRACTICING MIXED METHODS SOCIAL INQUIRY

Part Two addresses practical topics in mixed methods inquiry. These include purposes for mixing methods, mixed methods designs, mixed methods data analysis, criteria for judging the quality of mixed methods studies, and writing up and reporting mixed methods work. The author's own ideas about mixed methods practice are presented alongside the ideas of other contributors to the development of the mixed methods field. Examples are also liberally used to illustrate and substantiate the ideas presented. Guidelines for mixed methods practice are still in the development stage, and considerable opportunities remain for contributions from thoughtful and creative inquirers.

CHAPTER

MIXING METHODS
ON PURPOSE

WITH THIS chapter, the journey now moves into the domain of mixed methods practice, accompanied by a backpack carrying the inquirer's reflective stances on the nature and role of philosophy in social inquiry practice. This practical part of the journey begins with an engagement with the various purposes for which an inquirer can mix methods. That is, just as social inquiry practice itself is grounded in the purpose and questions for that study, mixed methods design and practice is anchored in the identification of particular purposes for mixing. Five primary purposes for mixing are identified and illustrated: triangulation, complementarity, development, initiation, and expansion. The traveler will develop an understanding of each and thereby begin to assemble his or her mixed methods toolkit.

■ ■ ■

The character and form of social inquiry are firmly rooted in substantive purpose. Social inquiry today has multiple legitimate purposes, from building generalizable theory to generating contextual understanding, and from catalyzing organizational development to voicing social critique (see Chapter Two). Framed in a broad acceptance of the important role of mixed methods approaches to social inquiry, Newman,

Ridenour, Newman, and DeMarco (2003) offer a "roughly hewn, tentative, fluid, and flexible" (p. 169) list of purposes for social inquiry, displayed in Table 6.1. These authors argue that

> There is a link between understanding the purpose of one's research and selecting the appropriate methods to investigate the questions that are derived from that purpose. We argue that there is an iterative process between considering the research purpose and the research question. [From] this iterative process . . . decisions about methods are made. [Further] we make the case that when the purpose is complex (as it often is), it is necessary to have multiple questions, and this frequently necessitates the use of mixed methods. (p. 169)

TABLE 6.1.   A "Roughly Hewn" List of Inquiry Purposes.

General Purpose	Examples
Predict.	Build general laws.
Add to the knowledge base.	Confirm findings.
	Replicate others' work.
	Reinterpret previously collected data.
	Clarify structural and ideological connections between important social processes.
Have a personal, social, institutional, or organizational impact.	Deconstruct or reconstruct power structures.
	Refute claims.
	Set priorities.
	Resist authority.
	Influence change.
	Improve practice.
Measure change.	Measure consequences of practice.
	Test treatment effects.
Understand complex phenomena.	Understand culture.
	Understand change.
	Understand people.

(Table 6.1 continued)

Test new ideas.	Test innovations.
	Test hypotheses.
	Test new solutions.
Generate new ideas.	Generate hypotheses.
	Generate theory.
	Uncover relationships.
	Uncover culture.
Inform constituencies.	Inform the public.
	Heighten awareness.
	Hear from those who are affected by the treatment or program.
Examine the past.	Acknowledge past misunderstandings.
	Reexamine tacit understandings.
	Examine social and historical origins of current social problems.

Source: Newman et al., 2003.

I fully and enthusiastically support these authors' emphasis on the root importance of inquiry purpose and questions. A study does *not* begin with design or method, but rather with a well-defined and well-justified purpose and a clearly delineated set of inquiry questions (Chelimsky, 2007). One does *not* initiate a study by proclaiming, "I want to do an ethnography," or "I want to do a randomized experiment," or "I want to do a mixed methods study." Rather, social inquiry begins with a substantive intention or purpose and a substantive set of questions. Methodology is ever the servant of purpose, never the master. And because mixed methods purposes are *about methodology*, it is critical to think about identifying and selecting the reasons for mixing methods (or mixed methods purposes) *in service to* the broader substantive purpose and questions being pursued in the study. The question to address about choosing mixed methods purposes is, What form of "better understanding" will serve the substantive purpose and questions of the overall study best?

MIXING METHODS FOR BETTER UNDERSTANDING

As presaged in Chapter Two, the overall broad purpose for mixing methods in social inquiry is to develop a *better understanding* of the phenomena being studied. The fundamental claim being made here is that a mix of methods will generate a better understanding than will a single method alone. This claim, of course, is subject to empirical investigation. Tom Weisner's collection of studies of middle childhood offers examples of mixed methods studies supporting this claim (Weisner, 2005). Yet Lois-Ellin Datta (1997b) cautions us to remember that sometimes a monomethod study will serve the inquiry purpose just as well as or even better than a mixed methods study, likely at lesser cost. Continued research and reflection are needed regarding the contextual, substantive, and political conditions under which a mixed methods study, compared to a monomethod study, would serve the overall inquiry purposes best.

Also from Chapter Two, better understanding within a mixed methods framework can take various forms:

1.   Getting it right, enhancing the validity or credibility of our findings.

2.   Doing our work better, generating understandings that are broader, deeper, more inclusive, and that more centrally honor the complexity and contingency of human phenomena.

3.   Unsettling the settled, probing the contested, challenging the given, engaging multiple, often discordant perspectives and lenses.

4.   Foregrounding the political and value dimensions of our work, to not just illuminate them but also to engage with each other about our differences, to advance our dialogues.

Different mixed methods purposes—that is, different forms of "better understanding"—are connected to different inquiry questions, different combinations of methods, and different approaches to mixed methods analysis. These connections are pursued in subsequent chapters; this chapter presents more specific purposes for mixing methods, along with multiple examples. The chapter then describes and illustrates the practical procedures involved in identifying purposes for mixing methods and finally relates mixed methods purposes to mixed methods paradigm stances (from Chapter Five).

PURPOSES FOR MIXING METHODS

My own sustained engagement with the emerging field of mixed methods social inquiry began with a review of a sample of mixed methods evaluation studies that I conducted with two colleagues, Valerie Caracelli and Wendy Graham, in the late 1980s. The idea of mixing methods was a faint smudge on the horizon as the great qualitative-quantitative debate was beginning to wind down. We had read what conceptual material related to mixing methods that we could find—including, for example, classic references on the concept of triangulation and Thomas Cook's elegant treatise on "post-positivist critical multiplism" (1985), discussed in Chapter Two—and then we were eager to turn to practice. We wanted to describe, analyze, and learn from the state of mixed methods practice in our field of evaluation. So we selected a sample of fifty-seven mixed methods evaluation studies—studies that used at least one quantitative method designed to represent social phenomena numerically and one qualitative method designed to represent social phenomena textually—and systematically reviewed each one for its descriptions of mixed methods purpose, design, data analysis, and utilization, as well as information on study context, management, and resources. In this review, we focused significantly on mixed methods purpose and design, as directed from our theoretical readings, although we also recorded information on the other review components. A full description of this study can be found in Greene, Caracelli, and Graham (1989).

The set of five purposes for mixing methods that emerged from this study was grounded in both the theoretical literature and the empirical evaluation practice reviewed. That is, the mixed methods purposes suggested by the theoretical literature were substantially confirmed by the evaluation studies reviewed. Moreover, this set of mixed methods purposes has held up well in the ensuing decades, offering a meaningful range of reasons and possibilities for mixing different kinds of methods in one social inquiry study. These five mixed methods purposes are described and illustrated next.

The illustrations come from a hypothetical scenario involving an evaluation of a nutrition education program implemented in all middle schools of an urban school district. The district serves a very diverse set of urban communities, including significant socioeconomic and racial and ethnic diversity. Called *Eat Right!* the program is part of a multifaceted policy and programmatic response to the disturbing increase in the incidence of childhood obesity in the United States over the past ten years (Institute of Medicine, 2005, 2006). The *Eat Right!* program (1) provides preteens with information about the benefits of good nutrition and the health risks of diets heavy in fried food, soft drinks, fat, and sugar, and (2) offers more healthy food choices to middle school students in their school cafeteria. The educational strands of the program include video and print materials featuring well-known athletes, hip-hop singers, and writers, notably from communities of color. These educational strands are implemented in health, science, and physical educational classes. The cafeteria changes include eliminating soft drinks and offering fruit drinks (with minimal sugar), milk, and water instead; offering only one fried food at each lunch; and adding a salad bar with low-calorie, low-fat dressing. *Eat Right!* aims to increase middle school students' knowledge about healthy diets and to encourage and enable them to choose healthy foods for themselves at lunch.

The discussion now presents five distinct purposes for mixing methods, derived from Greene et al. (1989), and illustrates each using this hypothetical evaluation scenario.

Mixing Methods for Purposes of Triangulation

In its classic sense, triangulation seeks convergence, corroboration, or correspondence of results from multiple methods. The classic rationale for triangulation is to increase the validity of construct and inquiry inferences by using methods with offsetting biases, thereby counteracting irrelevant sources of variation and misinformation or error. In a mixed methods study with a triangulation intent, different methods are used to measure the *same phenomenon*. If the results provide consistent or convergent information, then confidence in inquiry inferences is increased. So mixing methods for purposes of triangulation may be particularly important for inquiry constructs of high leverage or importance in a given context.

In the *Eat Right!* evaluation context, program outcomes are likely to be constructs of high importance, especially in today's climate of high accountability, and therefore good candidates for multiple measurement. For the outcome of increased nutrition knowledge, the evaluator could use a pre-post structured knowledge test as well as semi-structured individual or group interviews. Test data represent student responses to particular bits of nutrition knowledge, and the interviews could gather students' knowledge about parallel but broader principles of healthy eating. (The interviews could not be completely open or unstructured, as the evaluator must ensure that they are measuring the *same* conceptualization of nutrition knowledge as the knowledge test. Triangulation is not possible across assessments of different constructs.) And for the outcome of choosing healthier foods for lunch in the school cafeteria, the evaluator might consider some mix of direct observation, a self-report survey, or even analysis of leftover and disposed-of food from a sample of lunchtimes. Each of these methods captures a different lens or perspective on the focal phenomenon of healthy eating.

The question often arises—as in the Trend study of housing vouchers presented in Chapter Two—what if one mixes methods for purposes of triangulation, but the results don't converge? In Thomas Cook's words, well then, you have an "empirical puzzle" that warrants further examination, probing, and analysis. Interesting empirical puzzles are actually sought after in a mixed methods study with an *initiation* intent, as discussed shortly, because they can lead to unexpected and highly valuable insights. Again, the insights generated by Trend's further probing and analysis of the discrepant results of the administrative and observation data for one site well illustrate this generative potential of mixed methods inquiry.

The concept and allure of triangulation have featured prominently in the mixed methods conversation, both historically and presently (see Chapter Three). Some of the thoughtful discussions on triangulation incorporate possibilities of nonconvergence of results within the triangulation framework. Mathison (1988), for example, discusses three possible patterns of results attained from the use of different methods in a triangulation study: results that do converge, results that are only partially consistent, and results that are actually contradictory. In the emerging theories about mixed methods inquiry, these other patterns of results can be usefully connected to other mixed methods purposes. Moreover, different mixed methods purposes call for different mixed methods designs, as discussed in the next chapter. So I find it more conceptually valuable to retain the classic conceptualization of triangulation as convergence for purposes of enhanced validity and credibility of inference, and I will do so throughout this book.

Mixing Methods for Purposes of Complementarity

The second purpose for mixing methods is one of the most common in practice: mixing methods for purposes of complementarity. In our original review of fifty-seven mixed methods evaluation studies, one-third of the studies had a complementarity mixed methods purpose. With this purpose, a mixed methods study seeks broader, deeper, and more comprehensive social understandings by using methods that tap into different facets or dimensions of the *same complex phenomenon*. In a complementarity mixed methods study, results from the different methods serve to elaborate, enhance, deepen, and broaden the overall interpretations and inferences from the study. It is because most social phenomena are complex and multifaceted that a complementarity mixed methods purpose fits many inquiry contexts.

In the *Eat Right!* evaluation context, a number of phenomena could benefit from a complementary mix of methods. The evaluator could assess the quality and mean-ingfulness of the implementation of the educational components of the program from both student and teacher perspectives, using surveys, interviews, or both for each perspective. Having data on how both students and teachers experienced the program provides a more complete and comprehensive understanding of its imple-mentation. The evaluator could also assess the intended program outcome of choosing healthy foods for lunch through a combination of direct observation and student group interviews. If this mix were identified for purposes of triangulation, as discussed earlier, the two methods must measure the *same* conceptualization of the phenomenon of interest (choosing healthy foods for lunch). For a complementarity purpose, however, methods are intentionally chosen or designed to measure differ-ent facets of the same complex phenomenon. In this example, direct observation may record actual food choices made, while student interviews may engage peer influences on such food choices. Together, these two sets of data provide a more comprehensive and complete account of this intended program outcome.

In practice, the patterns of results from a mix of methods designed to be comple-mentary may range from convergence (as in triangulation) to divergence (as in initiation), even though an overlapping or interlocking pattern is the one intended. These different patterns of results are not inherently problematic, nor do they violate the intended purpose of complementarity. Mixed methods *practice* is ever so much more complicated and challenging than mixed methods *theory*. So mixed methods purposes—along with other components of practice—can evolve and change during the course of the study. Such evolution is likely to reflect unanticipated insights and perceptions that indeed contribute to better understanding.

Mixing Methods for Purposes of Development

Rooted in the classic ideas of sociologist Sam Sieber (1973) and evaluator Doren Madey (1982) (see Chapter Three), a third purpose for mixing methods is development. In a mixed methods development study, the results of one method are used to inform the development of the other method, where development is broadly construed to include sampling and implementation, as well as actual instrument construction. By definition, methods in a development mixed methods study are implemented sequentially. Most often, both methods would be assessing *a set of constructs or phenomena* (for example, attitudes and beliefs about immigration policies and practices). And the second method may assess all of the constructs assessed in the first method, or a subset of them (for example, responses to hypothetical immigration scenarios). The mixed methods development rationale aims for better understanding via capitalizing on inherent method strengths.

In the *Eat Right!* evaluation context, the evaluator might enact a development purpose by first using a questionnaire to assess student perceptions of the value and meaningfulness of their experiences in the program. Then the results of the questionnaire could be used to purposefully select a sample of extremes—students with substantially higher than average and substantially lower than average positive program perceptions—for individual interviews designed to gather in-depth information about students' program experiences. The questionnaire results could also inform the particular questions asked in the interviews; for example, issues on which there was considerable variation in student response or consistently negative responses. In some mixed methods development studies, findings and interpretations could be significantly enriched by returning to the results of the first method, after the second method is implemented, and conducting some kind of integrated analysis of both sets of data together. This would constitute a complementarity mixed methods intent and is currently an underutilized mixed methods design option.

The basic idea of development—of using the results of one method to inform the development of another—is not unique to mixed methods social inquiry, nor is it an innovative idea. Social scientists in many fields quite routinely use some form of qualitative method to learn more about a context—salient events, relational norms, linguistic idiosyncrasies—in order to develop or adapt a questionnaire that is well suited to that context. And using the results of a quantitative analysis to identify individuals or cases for further qualitative study is also common practice in many corners of the social science community. Similarly, some other concepts in the emerging theories about mixed methodology represent time-honored traditions in social science, perhaps most notably triangulation. In these cases, the unique contributions of these emerging mixed methods theories then are the collection, assembly, and orchestration of these ideas, along with the generation of new ideas, within an overall conceptual framework attuned to the particular parameters and possibilities of mixing (Caracelli & Greene, 1993, 1997).

Mixing Methods for Purposes of Initiation

Fourth, the mixed methods purpose of initiation represents the most generative of the purposes for mixing, as it evokes paradox, contradiction, divergence—all in the service of fresh insights, new perspectives, original understandings (Greene, 2005c). With initiation, different methods are implemented to assess various facets of the *same complex phenomenon*, much like complementarity, but the intended result is indeed divergence or dissonance. Initiation is the planned incarnation of Tom Cook's "empirical puzzle"—a puzzle that warrants further investigative analysis, which in turn can lead to important insights and new learnings. Further, should such a puzzle arise in a study with a different purpose for mixing—say, triangulation or complementarity—it would be wholly consistent with a *mixed methods way of thinking* (Chapter Two) to actively pursue this puzzle rather than interpret it as a failure to attain convergence or consonance. Some of the empirical classics in the mixed methods literature well illustrate this generative value of mixed methods initiation.

The generative potential of a mixed methods study with an initiation intent is likely to be enhanced by identifying methods that are significantly different from one another in stance, form, and perspective. Our *Eat Right!* evaluator, for example, could endeavor to better understand the context in which these middle school students are making food choices, both in and out of school. The evaluator could mix student self-reports of what they choose to eat for lunch in the school cafeteria, as well as what food they choose or are served during the rest of the day, with community assessments of the number and type of grocery stores, fast-food restaurants, and other food establishments in the students' home neighborhoods. This broadened lens is likely to offer a complex portrait of the food landscape for these students, including peaks and valleys of both dissonance and consonance. As another example of initiation, the evaluator could attend to different ethnic and cultural traditions regarding healthy diets by using one method based in mainstream American culture and another method rooted in contemporary subcultures in the United States, including Mexican-, African-, and Asian-American. Interesting points of convergence and divergence are likely to emerge from such a juxtaposition of cultural beliefs and practices about healthy diets.

Mixing Methods for Purposes of Expansion

Finally, methods can be mixed in social inquiry for purposes of expanding the scope and range of the study. In an *expansion* mixed methods study, different methods are used to assess *different phenomena*. So the scope of the study is expanded by extending methods choices to more than one methodological tradition, thus enabling selection of the most appropriate method for each construct within an expanded set of study foci.

In our initial review of fifty-seven mixed methods evaluation studies, expansion was the most prevalent of all mixed methods purposes, characterizing nearly half of the studies. This is not surprising as a very common evaluation design of that era was the use of quantitative methods to assess program outcomes and qualitative methods to assess program implementation. This was the classic early expansion design in the field of evaluation, signaling evaluators' eagerness to incorporate newly learned qualitative traditions and methods into their work. A more sophisticated expansion design would be to use a mix of different methods for assessing more features of both program implementation and program outcomes.

In the *Eat Right!* program evaluation, the evaluator could assess student knowledge gains with a standardized pre-post test of nutrition knowledge, possible changes in lunchroom norms via a modest ethnographic inquiry component, and parental awareness of the program through a random selection of families for phone interviews. Each method assesses a different phenomenon; collectively, they expand the range of the study well beyond the reach of a single method or methodological tradition.

AN ILLUSTRATION OF MIXED METHODS PURPOSES IN PRACTICE

An evaluation study by Mark Waysman and Riki Savaya (1997) well illustrates these varied purposes for mixing methods. Because it also well illustrates different dimensions of mixed methods design, I will return to this example in Chapter Seven.

In the 1990s, Waysman and Savaya (1997) conducted an evaluation of the work of a nonprofit agency in Israel that provided technical assistance to other nonprofit community-based organizations. SHATIL was founded in 1982 by the New Israel Fund to provide technical assistance to the organizations supported by the Fund, numbering approximately four hundred. At that time, these funded organizations worked for social change in varied domains, including human rights, social and economic development for the poor, Jewish-Arab relationships, and religious pluralism and tolerance. The organizations were staffed by people from a great diversity of ethnic, cultural, and religious backgrounds. SHATIL provided direct assistance in five areas: organizational consultation, fundraising and finance, advocacy, media and public relations, and volunteer recruitment and management. SHATIL also provided indirect assistance in the form of professional development and workshops for groups of organizations, support for organizational collaborations, and maintenance of specialized libraries and data sets of benefit to client organizations.

The evaluation was initiated by SHATIL after ten years of activity. SHATIL was interested in gathering feedback from client organizations as a way to look ahead and engage in some prospective planning. SHATIL raised funds for the evaluation from the Ford Foundation in the United States. The evaluation had four objectives:

1. To map the characteristics of organizations that apply to SHATIL;
2. To map the services provided to these organizations;
3. To assess the perceived contribution of SHATIL to the development and goal attainment of these organizations; and
4. To evaluate the satisfaction of these organizations with the services provided by SHATIL. (Waysman and Savaya, 1997, p. 229)

Key evaluation challenges included the diversity of organizations served and especially the diversity of services provided to these organizations by SHATIL. Further, while SHATIL was interested in "narrative descriptions of how clients perceive their experiences with SHATIL, [the funder] required 'hard data' about outcomes" (p. 229).

The evaluation was designed in three phases that progressed from the general to the specific, "both in sources of information and in types of information solicited" (p. 229).

> The first phase employed [qualitative] open-ended methods (focus group and personal interviews) to elicit general information about SHATIL, its clients and their concerns. The following phase was based on a survey questionnaire, whose items were more specific and focused. In the final phase (a second round of focus groups), the information sought was even more specific and focused on one particular issue (sources of satisfaction and dissatisfaction). The data in each phase [were] used in planning the following phase. (pp. 229–230)

Further details about the methods used in each phase will be provided in the Chapter Seven discussion of mixed method design dimensions. The present discussion will now turn to the various mixed methods purposes incorporated into this evaluation study, relying extensively on the words of the authors.

> The main aim of using mixed-methods in this study was expansion, which occurs when researchers mix methods in order to extend the scope, breadth and range of inquiry. . . . Different methods are employed to learn about different phenomena within the same study, thereby expanding its reach. The different methods are chosen based on their respective fit for studying the phenomena in question. . . . The use of mixed methods in this study enabled us to capture the richness and diversity of the program and to provide SHATIL with the different types of knowledge that they sought (narrative description as well as statistical analysis) in a way that no single method could possibly have done.

> Worth noting here is that different methods were adopted not only to evaluate different components of the study . . . but also to examine different aspects within components. For example, we examined two different process variables: amount of services received and critical turning points in the consultation process. We chose to measure amount of services quantitatively—by counting hours—using existing data from SHATIL's management information system. . . . In contrast, we felt that the best way to study critical turning points in the consultation process was via open-ended questions that were included in both the focus groups and the survey questionnaire. This mixture of methods thus enabled us to expand the number of process variables that the study covered.

> The second major reason for employing mixed methods in this study was development. This entails the sequential use of data from one method to plan and devise the use of another method. . . . For example, participants in the first round of focus groups were asked to specify which consultant behaviors and characteristics had, in their experience, helped or hindered the consultation process. They mentioned a number of traits, such as task versus process orientation, degree to which consultant

blocks or encourages open discussion, and degree to which s/he promotes autonomy versus dependency. The survey instrument in the following stage incorporated a quantitative semantic differential measure with items formulated to cover these constructs that had emerged in the qualitative group interview.

We also employed mixed methods in this evaluation for purposes of . . . complementarity . . . which refers to the added complexity and detail that ensue from combining methods. . . . The second round of focus groups with most and least satisfied clients provided descriptive information about sources of satisfaction and dissatisfaction, which helped to interpret the findings obtained from the statistical analysis of the survey.

Although the use of mixed methods was not planned for the purposes of corroboration [triangulation] or initiation, it seems in retrospect that these benefits were also realized here, at least to some degree. . . . For instance [for corroboration], one of the major aims of the study was to learn about client organizations' degree of satisfaction with SAHTIL services. In the first round of focus groups, clients expressed a high degree of satisfaction with SHATIL staff and services. They emphasized the emotional nurturing provided by SHATIL staff, their consistent availability, and the benefits derived from the instrumental assistance provided by SHATIL. Findings from the quantitative survey corroborated this picture: 72% of clients [responding] rated their overall satisfaction with SHATIL as high.

On the other hand, some of the [first round] focus group participants expressed feelings of being patronized by SHATIL staff. . . . Findings from the quantitative measure, however, revealed that only a small minority of clients [responding] (15%) shared this sentiment. If we had included only the qualitative component, we might have overestimated the prevalence of this finding. . . .

[Related to mixing methods for purposes of initiation, in] the first round of focus groups . . . participants raised several issues that neither the evaluators nor the staff of SHATIL had thought to address in the study. One critical issue that emerged unexpectedly . . . pertained to the lack of clarity regarding eligibility for services. . . . It was thus decided to explore this issue further by including relevant items in the survey questionnaire, whose findings subsequently confirmed the existence of a problem in this area. These results resonated strongly among SHATIL staff, who were not aware of the problem, and several meetings were held to develop procedures to cope with this issue. . . . Had we used quantitative measures exclusively, we would have missed these important issues, some of which were of utmost relevance to SHATIL. . . .

[Also] as noted earlier, the qualitative and quantitative components of this study raised contradictory findings regarding paternalistic behavior on the part of SHATIL staff. . . . This inconsistency forced us to reconcile these apparent contradictions by raising a new research question: can we characterize the organizations for whom this issue is

of concern? Further examination of the data did, in fact, reveal that the problem had been raised primarily by minority organizations (Arabs and Ethiopians). In response to this finding, SHATIL initiated a search for ways to increase the cultural sensitivity of service delivery. (pp. 233–235, emphasis in original)

This reflective discussion by Waysman and Savaya on the mixed methods purposes of their evaluation study attends to both planned and unplanned-but-actualized purposes for mixing methods. In this way, this discussion models strong and effective mixed methods thinking. In applied social inquiry, plans sometimes go awry and more often do not fully anticipate all the events that actually unfold. The Waysman and Savaya discussion focuses on the particular constructs and issues they were endeavoring to understand, as in client *satisfaction* with SHATIL services, and how and why they might mix methods to better understand these constructs and issues. In these ways, this discussion also models strong and useful practical thinking regarding the planning of mixed methods purposes and subsequent methods choices. This point is elaborated in the section that follows.

PRACTICAL PROCEDURES FOR THINKING ABOUT AND IDENTIFYING MIXED METHODS PURPOSES

The practice of social inquiry is substantially more complicated, contingent, and organic than any theory of methodology could ever hope to prescribe. And this is especially true for theories of mixing methods in social inquiry. Most practical social inquiry studies have multiple questions or hypotheses, each involving multiple constructs or variables, or issues or concerns to be addressed. So does one mix methods for different questions or hypotheses, different constructs or issues, or what? And what about overall inquiry design, as in survey or quasi-experiment or action research or case study? Does one mix at this level of methodology, or is mixing centered on the assessment and understanding of particular constructs or issues or concerns?

These are questions with as yet uncertain answers, questions that are more fully engaged in the next chapter on mixed methods design. At this point, various participants in the mixed methods conversation offer different and distinctive views on just what is being triangulated with a mixed methods purpose of triangulation, or just what is being expanded with an expansion purpose, as well as just what is being mixed in a mixed methods study.

The guidance offered in this book focuses on mixing methods around the assessment or measurement of particular constructs or variables, or issues or concerns, or in some cases around the inquiry questions being posed. There are several reasons underlying this perspective. First, this perspective maintains and reinforces the idea that methods choices *follow* substantive decisions, that methods are positioned *in service to* the substantive questions of interest in a given context. It is only after an overall inquiry purpose is identified—say, to *explain changes* in middle school students' lunch choices accompanying the implementation of the *Eat Right!* program—and after the particular constructs or variables of interest have been identified—say, calorie and nutritional content of food chosen and students' reasons for choosing foods at lunch—that the inquirer considers methods choices. In this context, the inquirer may productively choose a mix of observational, unobtrusive, and interview methods. Second, one of the most generative possibilities in mixed methods inquiry is the troubling of assumed or taken-for-granted meanings of a given construct—for example, what constitutes a healthy diet for children and youth—with dissonant data from another source or perspective. Healthy diets from the perspective of a nutrition expert are likely to be quite different from what young people themselves think is healthy, and this may well vary by ethnic subculture in the United States today. This dissonance can offer highly generative and meaningful opportunities for better understanding and, in turn, more thoughtful and effective action in the context at hand.

Third, by focusing on the mixing of methods around the assessment of key inquiry constructs, attention is drawn conceptually to the paradigmatic and mental models that could accompany each method choice, and thereby to the issues related to mixed methods paradigmatic stances discussed in Chapter Five. So in making decisions about the purposes for mixing methods around the assessment of a given construct and then about the particular methods to mix, the inquirer also engages the more abstract question of mixing paradigms along with mixing methods. At the same time, by focusing the mixing of methods around the assessment of key inquiry constructs, attention is drawn practically to the more concrete issues of sampling, analysis, and quality criteria. Placing the focus on deciding how to measure the inquiry constructs of interest thus simultaneously engages the more abstract questions of philosophical assumptions and conceptual stances *and* the more concrete decisions about actual data gathering and analysis.

Fourth and finally, beyond these conceptual reasons, there is the practicality of considering and making mixed methods decisions. At this stage in the development of the field of mixed methods social inquiry, it is most straightforward and easiest to focus the mixing on the assessment of the key constructs and issues being studied in a given context. This is not to reject the value of mixing at other stages in the inquiry. As discussed more fully in Chapter Seven, several contributors to the mixed methods conversation have offered thoughtful ideas about mixing inquiry designs and even inquiry purposes that go beyond the mixing of methods for data gathering, analysis, and interpretation (*and their accompanying mental models*). From a practical view, I would maintain, however, that the mixing of methods for assessing inquiry constructs and issues of interest—and the associated sampling, analysis, and interpretive mixes invoked—constitute the most basic, straightforward, and again, generative approach to choosing what to mix and why.

These ideas can be illustrated with an example from the SHATIL evaluation. Waysman and Savaya were especially interested in the *satisfaction* of client organizations with the services provided by SHATIL. This construct of satisfaction was measured in all three phases of the evaluation. In the first phase, qualitative focus group interviews with a purposeful sample (aiming for diversity) of representatives from client organizations yielded information on the "perceptions and experiences from a broad range of SHATIL's clients regarding service delivery, unmet needs, and areas of concern" (p. 231). This information thus contributed to the contextual definition and understanding of the construct of client satisfaction in this evaluation context. The use of qualitative methods in phase I represents the authors' choice of the mixed methods purpose of expansion. The authors then engaged a mixed methods development purpose when they used the information generated in phase I to construct the questionnaire used in phase II. This questionnaire was administered to all client organizations, yielding a more structured assessment of client satisfaction. Then, again with a mixed method development purpose, the authors chose questionnaire respondents with extremely high and extremely low satisfaction scores on the questionnaire and conducted two follow-up focus groups in phase III, specifically pursuing the factors related to satisfaction and dissatisfaction for these two groups.

MIXED METHODS PURPOSES AND STANCES ON MIXING PARADIGMS WHILE MIXING METHODS

The final entry in this chapter on mixed methods purposes addresses the connections between such purposes and the various stances on mixing paradigms or mental models while mixing methods that were discussed in Chapter Five. Struggling with connections of this kind is an important part of the development of any theory of methodology. A stronger, more coherent, and more useful methodological theory comprises interconnected and integrated parts (Greene, 2006).

Although there is no one-to-one correspondence between stances on mixing paradigms or mental models and mixed methods purposes, there are some logical alignments and connections. There are presented in Table 6.2. A review of this table provokes

TABLE 6.2.   **Connections Between Mixed Methods Paradigm Stances and Purposes.**

Mixed Methods Paradigm Stances	Logically Compatible Mixed Methods Purposes
Purist stance ■ Different paradigms have incommensurable assumptions. ■ Paradigms guide and direct practical decisions.	*Within one paradigm*, all purposes except initiation are compatible. Because it is not possible to mix paradigms while mixing methods, initiation is not a good fit to a purist stance

(continued)

(Table 6.2 continued)

A-paradigmatic stance	All purposes are compatible and could constitute a good fit, depending on the context.
■ Paradigm attributes can be easily mixed and matched.	
■ Context, not paradigms, guides practical decisions.	
Substantive theory stance	*Within one substantive theory*, all purposes except initiation could be a good fit.
■ Paradigms are importantly different but not incommensurable.	
■ But substantive theory, not paradigms, guides practical decisions.	
Complementary strengths stance	Triangulation and expansion are the best fit because methods, and accompanying paradigms, need to be kept separate.
■ Paradigms are importantly different but not incommensurable.	
■ Paradigms, context, and theory all guide practical decisions, but paradigms should be kept separate.	Complementarity and development could also be compatible.
Dialectic stance	Initiation is the best fit.
■ Paradigms are importantly different but not incommensurable.	Complementarity and development could also be compatible.
■ Paradigms, context, and theory all guide practical decisions, and paradigms should engage in dialogue.	
Alternative paradigm stance	This depends on the characteristics of the alternative paradigm being used.
■ Old paradigms should give way to new ones that embrace multiple methods.	
■ New paradigms, context, and theory all guide practical decisions.	

several important reflections. First, further work on the connections between paradigm stance and mixed methods purpose is needed, as the alignments suggested in Table 6.2 remain quite rough. Second, to fulfill its strong generative potential, the mixed methods purpose of initiation requires some important mixing of underlying paradigmatic assumptions, or conceptual ideas and perspectives, or both. Absent such mixes, an initiation mix is more likely to be disappointing. And third, compatibility and fit are also importantly influenced by context, as suggested by several of the contingent entries in this table.

The discussion now turns to issues of mixed methods designs. As will be evident by the discussion in Chapter Seven, the planning of a mixed methods study is just as iterative as the planning and design of most other social inquiry studies. Identifying purposes for mixing methods and developing a design that fulfills such purposes— including choices of specific methods, samples, analyses, quality criteria, and interpretation and reporting strategies to employ—both involve an iterative process of negotiation, review, and refinement.

CHAPTER

DESIGNING MIXED METHODS STUDIES

THE PRACTICAL part of this mixed methods journey continues. In this chapter, the traveler will visit the relatively well developed territory of mixed methods design. Distinctively, this territory is quite crowded with multiple ideas for different kinds of mixed methods designs, each offering a useful framework. The traveler will visit various design frameworks and develop an understanding of the particular character of each, as well as the commonalities and differences among them. To aid understanding, illustrations of selected designs will also be offered. The traveler's toolkit will be significantly expanded upon leaving this territory of mixed methods design.

■ ■ ■

The design of a mixed methods study follows directly from the identified purpose for mixing, because different purposes call for different *mixes* of methods, different *priorities* or weights allocated to the different methods, different *interactions* among the methods during the course of the study, and different *sequences* of implementation. These are the primary dimensions of mixed methods design that have emerged as important thus far in the developing theories of mixed methods social inquiry.

In this chapter, I will discuss these dimensions of mixed methods design, present their connections to mixed methods purposes and paradigm stances, and illustrate their applications in inquiry practice. Because, in my thinking, types of mixed methods designs follow on from the identified purposes for mixing, different mixed methods designs will be portrayed as closely linked to their respective mixed methods purposes. In addition, I will briefly describe selected other formulations of mixed methods design alternatives championed by other contributors to the mixed methods conversation.

Prior to this discussion of different types of mixed methods designs, I will present two other perspectives and sets of ideas on the nature and potential of mixed methods design. These perspectives relate to broader, more macro design issues and represent important continuing challenges for the field. Specifically, these broader issues are (1) the challenges of mixing methods at different stages of the inquiry process, as most thoughtfully engaged by Abbas Tashakkori and Charles Teddlie, and (2) the merits and feasibility of mixing methods within a single inquiry study or across studies within an integrated program of research, as engaged by Janice Morse and others.

MIXING METHODS AT DIFFERENT STAGES OF SOCIAL INQUIRY: MIXED METHODS AND MIXED MODEL DESIGNS

This discussion outlines the evolution of thinking by Abbas Tashakkori and Charles Teddlie about mixed methods design typologies and their associated thinking regarding what are the critical design dimensions for mixed methods inquiry and what are meaningful variants of mixed methods design. This story not only relates important information about mixing at different stages of inquiry, but also provides a glimpse of the rapid pace at which the field has evolved in recent years.

Beginning with their 1998 book *Mixed Methodology: Combining Qualitative and Quantitative Approaches,* Tashakkori and Teddlie have advanced important ideas about the mixing of methods and methodologies at different stages of the inquiry process. Rooted in their embracement of the end of the paradigm wars and their adoption of a pragmatic orientation for social inquiry, these theorists have turned their lens on the big picture of social inquiry design, with a bounded focus on traditional quantitative and qualitative inquiry traditions. Their work has differentiated the mixing of these two broad inquiry traditions at the level of overall design (such as survey, quasi-experiment, or case study) from the mixing of more specific techniques of data gathering and analysis characteristically but not inherently linked to different inquiry traditions (such as structured, standardized, theory-driven, quantitative techniques, contrasted with unstructured, contextual, emergent, qualitative techniques). Mixing at the level of overall design was until recently called *mixed model social inquiry* by Tashakkori and Teddlie. This overall design level primarily refers to inquiry purpose and questions and engages differences like a broad orientation to exploration or confirmation for the study. Mixing at the level of data gathering and analysis technique was until recently called *mixed methods inquiry* by these authors; it refers to the mixing only of different kinds of data gathering and analysis methods (qualitative and quantitative).

As elaborated in the following discussion, Tashakkori and Teddlie's perspectives conceptualize method as separate or at least separable from philosophical paradigm or mental model. Thus they have perceived the need to discuss mixed *model* designs, which feature the mixing of paradigms and broad inquiry orientations and purposes, in addition to mixed *method* designs, which in their formulation do not. In this book, I have adopted the stance that method cannot be divorced from the inquirer's assumptions about the world and about knowledge, the inquirer's theoretical predispositions, professional experience, and so forth. Rather, I believe that method is always implemented from *within* a particular assumptive framework. So when one mixes methods, one may also mix paradigmatic and mental model assumptions as well as broad features of inquiry methodology. This explanation of our different perspectives notwithstanding, Tashakkori and Teddlie's concentration on different stages of inquiry remains valuable.

In their 1998 book, these authors offered a typology of mixed model designs that incorporated three distinct stages of inquiry and the possibility of mixing at each stage. Rooted in evaluation theorist Michael Patton's earlier ideas about mixed methodology (1980), these three stages are:

1. Type of investigation, including the formulation of inquiry questions or hypotheses—exploratory versus confirmatory. Exploratory studies pose questions and usually precede confirmatory studies, which test hypotheses.

2. Data collection operations, including design, measurement techniques, sampling, and data quality criteria and procedures—qualitative versus quantitative.

3. Data analysis and inference—qualitative versus statistical.

> A 2×2×2 cross-classification of these [three stages] leads to eight types of models for conducting research. . . . Two of the eight resulting types of studies are the traditional qualitative and quantitative models. The other six categories are mixed model studies, combining components of the qualitative-quantitative distinction across different stages of the research process. (Tashakkori and Teddlie, 1998, p. 56)

For example, one mixed model features a confirmatory intent and qualitative data operations and analysis. Another, noted as "rare," features an exploratory intent and qualitative analysis of quantitative data (with prior "qualitizing" of the quantitative data).

Finally, more complex mixed model designs, called *multiple mixed model designs* by Tashakkori and Teddlie, feature mixing *within* one or more stages of inquiry. These studies, that is, could combine both an exploratory and confirmatory intent, both qualitative and quantitative data collection operations, both qualitative and statistical analysis and inference. In many ways, the discussion in the present book focuses on these more complex mixed model studies, as my focus is on mixing different ways of gathering, analyzing, representing, and thus knowing human phenomena. And in critical ways, Tashakkori and Teddlie's emphasis on the prior importance of the purpose of the inquiry—"the preeminence of the research question over considerations of either paradigm or method" (p. 167)—echoes my own convictions that methodological decisions are always made in service to substance (Chapter Six).

In the introductory (Teddlie & Tashakkori, 2003) and concluding (Tashakkori & Teddlie, 2003b) chapters of the ambitious *Handbook of Mixed Methods,* these authors refine and expand their earlier thinking about mixed methods and especially mixed model designs. They distinguish between monostrand and multistrand mixed model studies. Monostrand studies are the eight models generated in the 1998 matrix formed by crossing the three stages of inquiry. In these studies, the mixing happens across stages of inquiry such that one stage is of a different inquiry genre than the other two. Multistrand mixed model studies—acknowledged by Tashakkori and Teddlie as actually more common than monostrand studies in both theory and practice and clearly the emphasis in this book—involve "multiple types of questions . . . and both types of data and data analysis techniques. The inferences that are made on the basis of the results are both subjectivist/constructivist . . . [and] objectivist . . . in approach. This type of design may be sequential or parallel," meaning the methods are implemented one after the other or at the same time (Teddlie & Tashakkori, 2003, p. 30).

Teddlie and Tashakkori (2003) further identify more specific subtypes of multi-strand mixed model designs, based on (1) whether or not the overall orientation, purpose, and questions of the study are mixed; (2) whether or not methods for data collection, analysis, and inferencing are mixed; and (3) which procedure for mixing is used—concurrent implementation, sequential implementation, or conversion of one data type into another. And they reemphasize that a mixed model design requires mixing in more than one stage of inquiry, whereas a mixed methods design mixes only during the methods stage. For example, in a sequential mixed model design, one type of study is conducted as the first strand (say, a survey). Then the results of that strand are used to generate purposes and questions for the second strand, which involves a study of a different type (say, a case study). Inferences from both strands together contribute to overall meta-inferences from the study. Finally, "fully integrated mixed model designs are the most advanced, and most dynamic of all mixed model designs. . . . In this type of study, multiple approach questions are asked and answered through the collection and analysis of both QUAL and QUAN data" (p. 689). In the *Handbook* final chapter, these design ideas are very usefully illustrated with diagrams that help the reader differentiate one from another.

The latest update on mixed methods and mixed model designs from these authors (Teddlie & Tashakkori, 2006) offers still further refinements on their thinking and situates mixed methods studies in a "general typology of research designs." Notably, they drop their prior distinction between mixed methods and mixed model studies, arguing that "newer conceptualizations of mixed methods research all recognize the fact that a study is not considered mixed if there is no integration across stages" (p. 14). And they point out that the definition of mixed methods research adopted for the new *Journal of Mixed Methods Research* also emphasizes the importance of integration. For this journal, "mixed methods research is defined as research in which the investigator collects and analyzes data, integrates the findings, and draws inferences using both qualitative and quantitative approaches or methods in a single study or program of inquiry" (p. 15). In this regard, these authors coin the label *quasi-mixed design* for studies that lack this important integration across inquiry stages. Second, Teddlie and Tashakkori focus their latest design typology on four major dimensions:

1.   The number of methodological approaches used, distinguishing between mono-method and mixed methods designs (and thus situating mixed methods inquiry in a more general typology of inquiry design)

2.   The number of strands or phases in the inquiry design, distinguishing between monostrand and multistrand designs

3.   The type of implementation process—concurrent, sequential, or conversion

4.   The stage of integration

An example of a mixed methods design in this typology is a *concurrent mixed design*, in which "there are at least two relatively independent strands: one with QUAL questions and data collection and analysis techniques and the other with QUAN questions and data collection and analysis techniques. Inferences made on the basis of the results from each strand are synthesized to form meta-inferences at the end of the study" (p. 20). This and other mixed methods designs are also illustrated in this paper with examples from the field.

The work of Tashakkori and Teddlie has centered around the development of a meaningful and useful *typology* for designing mixed methods studies. They have argued, generally convincingly, for the value of mixed methods design typologies for guiding practice, legitimizing the field, generating possibilities, and serving as useful pedagogical tools (Tashakkori & Teddlie, 2003b; Teddlie & Tashakkori, 2006). Typologies are organized conceptual categorizations of possibilities that are generated by cross-classifying key dimensions of interest. In my view, the most important features of a typology are the dimensions used to create it. And in this regard, the work of Tashakkori and Teddlie has contributed generative ideas and possibilities to the mixed methods field. Their work has singled out key dimensions of difference in mixed methods inquiry and creatively engaged such dimensions in the generation of various mixed methods design typologies. They have made the further point that an exhaustive typology of mixed methods designs is not possible, due significantly to the frequent mutation of a planned design into other diverse forms. For example, as noted in the previous chapter, a mixed methods study developed for purposes of complementarity could readily generate results that do provide, in a complementary fashion, an enriched understanding of a complex phenomenon (as intended), alongside results that converge on particular facets of this phenomenon as well as results that are more dissonant and divergent (not as intended). As observed by Maxwell and Loomis, "the actual diversity in mixed methods studies is far greater than any typology can adequately encompass" (2003, p. 244). These observations notwithstanding, the typology development of Tashakkori and Teddlie constitutes an important contribution to the ongoing development of mixed methods thinking and practice.

As discussed further in the following discussion, my own thinking about mixed methods design shares considerable intellectual space with that of Tashakkori and Teddlie, but also contains some differences. As noted already, one difference is that in my view, method is always implemented from *within* a particular assumptive framework. This is not to say that methods are wedded to particular paradigms or inquiry traditions (see chapters Four and Five), but rather that an inquirer's own interpretive understanding of the social world and of the theoretical and practical intent of the study inevitably color the ways in which methods are implemented and data understood. Self-conscious attention to these assumptive frameworks (paradigms, mental models) is engaged at the outset of a mixed methods study when the inquirer decides which paradigmatic stance makes the most sense for that study (Chapter Five). This idea of paradigmatic stance is aligned with Tashakkori and Teddlie's design dimension of "number of methodological approaches used," but constitutes a more elaborated conceptualization of what it may mean to mix methodological approaches or paradigms or mental models when one conducts a mixed methods study. A second difference between my design thinking and that of Tashakkori and Teddlie is that I intentionally seek to provide space for multiple different paradigms and methodological approaches, whereas these authors concentrate on broad quantitative and qualitative traditions. Finally, although we all agree that methods decisions are made in service of *substantive* purpose, I perceive a stronger link between an intended *purpose for mixing* and mixed method design decisions. There is certainly ample space in the contemporary mixed methods conversation for these complementary yet distinct sets of ideas.

MIXING METHODS WITHIN A SINGLE STUDY OR ACROSS STUDIES IN A PROGRAM OF RESEARCH

Our early empirical study of fifty-seven mixed methods evaluation studies (Greene et al., 1989) yielded a number of key dimensions that distinguish various mixed methods designs in practice, one of which was whether the methods were mixed within a single study or across studies in a coordinated program of research. (The other dimensions that surfaced in this review will be further discussed later in this chapter.) In some important ways, this design dimension stands apart from the others in character and in underlying rationales for one position or another.

As presented in Chapter Five in discussing the "complementary strengths paradigm stance" for mixed methods studies, several contributors to the mixed methods literature have argued that the mixing of methods and associated assumptive stances can be risky to the integrity of any given method and thus the quality of the data obtained from that method (Brewer & Hunter, 1989). These authors have argued that therefore methods must be kept carefully separated from one another to preserve the distinctive strengths of each one.

Janice Morse (2003) shares this concern about methodological integrity and argues that to preserve such integrity requires that any given study has only *one* "theoretical drive," defined as "the overall direction of the project as determined from the original questions or purpose and is primarily inductive or deductive" (p. 190). So in a study with an inductive drive, qualitative data would be likely primary and quantitative data supplemental, serving only to illustrate or support the inductive inferences attained. For a study with a deductive drive, the reverse would be true. Then different drives could be used across studies in the same program of research and meta-inferences developed from them collectively. But a given study cannot mix primary drives or purposes; specifically, argues Morse, a given study cannot be both inductive and deductive in intent. This stance is importantly different from that presented in this book and from that presented by Tashakkori and Teddlie (see also Yin, 2006). These latter theorists distinguish a major mixed methods design dimension as the "number of methodological approaches used." And a primary argument of this book is that some of the greatest potential of mixed methods inquiry is the generative possibilities that accompany the mixing of different ways of knowing, perceiving, and understanding. So this design dimension of mixing within or across studies remains strongly contested in the field. The remaining discussion of mixed methods designs will focus on the mixing of methods *within a given study,* as that is more consonant with the premises of this book.

DIMENSIONS OF DIFFERENCE IN MIXED METHODS DESIGN

In addition to the five particular and interesting mixed methods purposes discussed in Chapter Six, our empirical review of mixed methods evaluation studies (Greene et al., 1989) also generated seven design dimensions along which this sample of studies took distinctive form. These dimensions, which we called *characteristics* or *elements* but conceptualized as continua or dimensions, and our original descriptions of them follow (from Greene et al., 1989). As is evident, our focus at that time was on the mixing of qualitative and quantitative methods and traditions, although this was more informed by practice than intentionally framed by theory.

1. *Paradigms.* The design characteristic labeled *paradigms* refers to the degree to which the different method types are implemented within the same or different paradigms. We recognize that any given pair of methods either is or is not implemented within the same paradigm, rendering this design characteristic dichotomous. Evaluation practice, however, commonly includes multiple methods of both types. [So this characteristic should be considered] holistically, representing the degree to which the whole set of methods is conceptualized, designed, and implemented with the same or different epistemological frameworks.

2. *Phenomena.* The term *phenomena* refers to the degree to which the qualitative and quantitative methods are intended to assess totally different phenomena or exactly the same phenomenon.

3. *Methods.* The methods characteristic represents the degree to which the qualitative and quantitative methods selected for a given study are similar to or different from one another in form, assumptions, strengths, and limitations or biases.

4. *Status.* This characteristic represents the degree to which a study's qualitative and quantitative methods have equally important or central roles vis-à-vis the study's overall objectives. . . . [That is, status refers to] the relative weight and influence of the qualitative and quantitative methods with respect to their frequency and their centrality to study objectives.

5. *Implementation: Independence.* The degree to which the qualitative and quantitative methods are conceptualized, designed, and implemented interactively or independently can be viewed on a continuum.

6. *Implementation: Timing.* [This refers to whether the different methods are implemented concurrently or sequentially.] Although we represent this characteristic as a continuum, we again recognize that a given pair of methods is typically implemented concurrently or sequentially, not in between. Yet, a short quantitative method could be paired with a longer qualitative method, or pre-post tests could be implemented before and after participant observation. . . . Variation on this design element also arises from the use of multiple methods within a mixed set.

7. *Study.* The final design characteristic labeled *study* is essentially categorical. The empirical research . . . encompassed [either] one study or more than one study. (pp. 262–264)

Like the initial set of purposes, these design dimensions continue to be relevant to mixed methods discussions. Different participants in these discussions use different labels for these dimensions and identify different ones as most important. Some of these design dimensions have been reallocated to other parts of mixed methods thinking and emerging theory. And a few other dimensions of importance to mixed methods design have been added over the years, notably the "number of strands or phases" included in Teddlie and Tashakkori's most recent design typology (2006). Yet for the most part this initial set of design dimensions that can usefully differentiate one kind of mixed methods design from another has been remarkably resilient.

In my own thinking, different mixed methods designs appear to be most centrally distinguished by the design dimensions of (1) the intended independence or interaction among different methods during the process of a study, and (2) status (called *dominance* in John Creswell's design types). A mixed methods study in which the various methods remain independent from one another is very different from a study in which the various methods are intentionally interactive during the course of the study's implementation. And a mixed methods study with one primary and one supplementary methodology (or sets of methods) is quite different from a study in which the various methodologies or sets of methods are granted relatively equal weight and status in the study. With respect to the other five design dimensions from our original empirical review, in my thinking the *paradigms* dimension is now incorporated into the idea of varying mixed method paradigmatic stances presented in Chapter Five, and the *phenomena* dimension is actually well captured by variations in mixed method purposes discussed in Chapter Six. The *timing* of the implementation of different sets of methods is often linked to purpose, determined by practical considerations, or of little consequence to the overall study. For example, timing in a mixed methods study with a development purpose is necessarily sequential, whereas timing in a mixed methods study with a triangulation purpose is necessarily concurrent. So this design dimension continues to usefully describe different mixed methods designs but less usefully helps an inquirer thoughtfully consider design options of consequence. And as noted earlier, the mixing in one *study* or across a set of studies is a distinct design element that is accompanied by its own continuing debate.

That leaves the design dimension of *methods,* referring to "the degree to which the qualitative and quantitative methods selected for a given study are similar to or different from one another in form, assumptions, strengths, and limitations or biases" (Greene et al., 1989, p. 262). In some important ways, this design dimension has not received the attention it merits, even though the opportunity to compensate for inherent method weaknesses, capitalize on inherent method strengths, and offset inevitable method biases was a strong and compelling initial rationale for the mixing of methods in social inquiry (Cook, 1985; Mark & Shotland, 1987b), and remains so for some theorists today (Onwuegbuzie & Johnson, 2006). This dimension of mixed methods design could give important guidance on what particular kinds of methods to select in a given inquiry context. Yet not enough is known about methodological strengths and weaknesses, propensities and biases. And these are not only technical concerns, as in social desirability biases in survey responses or overestimates of pre-post gains due to regression to the mean. These are also contextual and political concerns, as in the varying credibility of some forms of data among different audiences for social inquiry and the differential capacity of different methods to meaningfully capture and represent the interests and perspectives of different members of a social context. Especially lacking is good empirical research on many of these issues. May I encourage the mixed methods community to take up this challenge of learning more about methodological strengths and weaknesses through empirical study alongside conceptual analysis?

In the next section, I present my ideas about designing mixed methods studies, focusing on the two key design dimensions of interaction-independence and status but also carrying along the popular design dimension of sequence and, again, directly connecting these design ideas to mixed methods purpose. In some important ways, my ideas about mixed methods purposes represent the broad macro level of design intention and rationale.

COMPONENT AND INTEGRATED MIXED METHODS DESIGNS

As noted previously, in my thinking, the most salient and critical dimensions of mixed methods design are (1) whether the methods chosen are implemented relatively independently from one another and connected or mixed only at the level of inference *or* the methods are implemented in planned interaction one with the other throughout the course of the study, and (2) whether the methods are intended to be of relatively equal weight in a study *or* one (set) is considered primary and the other secondary. Sequencing of methods (concurrent or sequential) is also relevant to mixed methods design distinctions, but again more descriptively and linked closely to the intended purpose for mixing. These key design dimensions do not form a meaningful or practically useful typology in my view, but rather constitute two broad clusters, based on the independent-interactive design dimension of difference, which my colleague Valerie Caracelli and I have called component and integrated designs, respectively (Caracelli & Greene, 1997).

> *In component designs, the methods are implemented as discrete aspects of the overall inquiry and remain distinct throughout the inquiry. The combining of different method components occurs at the level of interpretation and conclusion rather than at prior stages of data collection or analysis. . . .*
>
> *[Integrated designs] characteristically attain a greater integration of the different method types. The methods can be mixed in ways that integrate elements of disparate paradigms and have the potential to produce significantly more insightful, even dialectically transformed, understandings of the phenomenon under investigation.* (Caracelli & Greene, 1997, pp. 22–23)

Metaphorically, component designs bring different methods into common action or harmony, yet the methods remain distinctly identifiable throughout the study, whereas in integrated designs the different methods are blended or united into a whole. Component designs are high school bands, integrated designs are exquisite symphony orchestras. Component designs are tossed salads, integrated designs are cream soups. Component designs bring into the same family purebred dogs like standard poodles or Labrador retrievers, integrated designs favor intentional mixed breeds like labradoodles (http://labradoodle-dogs.net/) or yorkiepoos (http://www.mixedbreedpups.com/yorkiepoo.htm).

Each cluster of mixed methods design is more fully described in the following section, along with illustrative examples. A complete listing of all possible designs in each cluster is not possible, because, as discussed previously in this chapter and in Chapter Six, mixed methods practice is considerably more varied than any design framework could comprehensively describe. In particular, in mixed methods theories, design clusters and typologies focus on the mixing of two different kinds (or sets) of methods for purposes of assessing one or more discrete constructs. Yet like much social inquiry, most mixed methods practice entails multiple sets of methods, each assessing multiple constructs. This discrepancy between the simplicity of mixed methods theory and the complexities of social inquiry practice is further pursued through examples later in this chapter.

Component Designs

Mixed methods studies in which different types of methods generally remain separate and are discretely identifiable throughout the study—that is, component designs—are arguably more common in practice than mixed methods studies with intentional blending or merging of methods, data, and inference. It is quite common today for applied social inquirers to use a variety of methods in an empirical study, analyze the data from each independently, develop a set of conclusions or inferences that represent each method and data set, and then at the end of the study endeavor to make some linkages or connections among the various sets of results. The kind of linkage made often reflects the purpose for mixing. Yet making such linkages effectively and defensibly remains a nontrivial task and thus an important area for further work in the mixed methods field.

For example, qualitative data are often intentionally used to help "explain" quantitative findings. To illustrate, an educational researcher studying organizational correlates of the achievement gap may conduct ethnographic classroom observations of purposefully selected interactions among students and between teachers and students as a way to identify additional classroom-level factors of possible importance. The researcher wishes to use these qualitative data to help explain the results of her regression analysis, which assessed the relationship of multiple organizational factors at the district, school, and classroom level to student achievement. How can defensible explanations be generated when the data come from different samples and represent different lenses? In another common example, program evaluators often use qualitative methods to assess the quality of program implementation and quantitative methods to assess the magnitude of program outcomes, and they also wish to use the implementation data to help understand and explain the outcome results. How can evaluators meaningfully and defensibly connect implementation and outcome data when the data take different forms and represent different phenomena?

This challenge of linking or connecting the results from different methods is likely a combination of an analytic challenge and an interpretive challenge. Analytically, some of the ideas presented in Chapter Eight on mixed methods data analysis may be relevant. Interpretively, the challenges of defensibility and warrant of inference remain, to which some of the ideas in Chapter Nine on quality criteria for mixed methods studies may pertain.

Back to component designs: there are two well-established examples of component mixed methods designs and other less well-established possibilities. These possibilities are imagined by categorizing the key characteristics of the well established designs, as presented in Table 7.1, and then envisioning the remaining possibilities. Such imaginings are one value of typologies.

Convergence. The use of two or more different methods to measure the same phenomenon for purposes of convergence represents the classic mixed methods purpose of triangulation. This design may most useful when a study includes critical constructs or phenomena that require inferences of nearly unquestioned quality. Key outcomes in an evaluation study can require multiple measurement for just such

TABLE 7.1. **Component Mixed Methods Design Examples.**

Example of Component Design	Relevant Mixed Methods Purpose	Phenomena Assessed with the Different Methods	Status of Methods	Sequence of Imple- mentation	Linking Task
Conver- gence	Triangula- tion	Same	Equal	Concurrent	Comparison of results
Extension	Expansion	Different	Variable	Variable	None or connection of results

reasons. The strongest convergence design requires not just separation but indepen- dence of method, one from the other. With independence, convergence in results can- not be attributed to one method possibly influencing the other during the course of the study. The strongest convergence design also includes methods of relatively equal weight and methods that are implemented close enough in time to each other that the phenomenon being assessed does not change. The linking or connective task in a design intended for triangulation purposes is one of comparison—that is, comparing the results of one method to the results of another method and assessing the nature and degree of convergence. In a classic mixed methods article, Todd Jick observed in a now well-quoted commentary:

> It is a delicate exercise to decide whether or not results have converged. In theory, a multiple confirmation of findings may appear routine. If there is congruence, it pre- sumably is apparent. In practice, though, there are few guidelines for systematically ordering eclectic data in order to determine congruence or validity. For example, should all components of a multimethod approach be weighted equally, that is, is all the evidence equally useful? If not, then it is not clear on what basis the data should be weighted, aside from personal preference. Given the differing nature of multi- method results, the determination [of convergence] is likely to be subjective. (Jick, 1983, p. 142)

A classic mixed methods study by Gretchen Rossman and Bruce Wilson (1985) provides excellent examples of convergence and triangulation in action. The study involved a three-year evaluation of regional educational service agencies (RESAs), which operated regionally to provide services to groups of school districts not avail- able to each district separately. Data collection methods included surveys and interviews of school and RESA personnel and analysis of documents. The methods appeared to be of relatively equal weight and implemented at the same time. Two analyses seeking "convergence in argument" are shared by the authors. The first, "qualitative converging with quantitative," focused on the perceived helpfulness of the RESAs by local school personnel. The quantitative survey data from school administrators were used to identify RESAs at both extremes of perceived helpfulness and the qualitative interview data from these same administrators then reviewed to assess convergence. "Farmland" was most positively rated on the survey and was characterized in the interviews as "extremely helpful, innovative, and entrepreneurial" (p. 635). "Rural-Industrial" was most negatively rated on the survey and was described in the interviews as "not much help and as not having any curriculum service" (p. 635).

> *Thus, interview data were used to corroborate the idea that the two RESAs were perceived quite differently. In this case, the quantitative data drove the selection of agencies for [follow-up qualitative analysis] and built the initial argument about variation in service orientation. Qualitative data were then used to show convergence with the initial quantitative data—to corroborate through another method that variation existed. (p. 635)*

The second convergence analysis in this study illustrated "quantitative converging with qualitative" results. This analysis focused on the primary role adopted by the RESAs being evaluated. A document analysis of agency mission statements yielded roles that included two types of assistance and one of enforcement—general assistance through multiple services, focused assistance through training and knowledge dissemination, and regulation or enforcement of state policy. This qualitative categorization was then corroborated through analysis of survey data from employees in each agency. The survey "probed the extent to which [employees] played eleven different roles (designed to reflect the differences between assistance and enforcement)" (p. 636). Factor analyses of these data, followed by bivariate plots of each agency on the two resulting factors, "yielded data that corroborated findings generated through qualitative methods" (p. 636). Rossman and Wilson's creative and thoughtful mixed method analytic work remains exemplary today.

Extension. The use of different methods to assess different phenomena represents the mixed methods purpose of expansion. In this purpose, a mixed method lens extends methods choices to more than one methodological tradition, thus enabling selection of the most appropriate method for each construct in an expanded set of study foci. The specifics of this design are contextually and practically determined, rather than guided by methodological considerations related to the mix of methods. As noted earlier, there can be an interesting analytic challenge of connection in this design—finding ways to link the results of one method with those of a different method. So although common in practice, the extension mixed methods study does not present or offer particular opportunities for a mixed methods way of thinking.

Integrated Designs

Integrated mixed methods designs, in which the methods intentionally interact with one another during the course of study, offer more varied and differentiated design possibilities. Like the linking challenge in component designs, the interaction challenge in integrated designs is undertheorized and understudied. Yet the particular ways in which samples, instruments, data sets, and analyses may "interact" or "have a conversation" with one another during the conduct of a study constitutes the very heart of integrative mixed methods inquiry. Thus, in addition to the mixed methods classics and the excellent empirical examples that are beginning to appear in both mixed methodological and substantive forums, continued conceptual work on this challenge is needed.

Examples of integrative mixed methods designs are offered next and tabulated in Table 7.2. Because in integrated designs the methods are always assessing the same phenomenon (though often both different and overlapping facets of this phenomenon), this column is excluded from Table 7.2.

TABLE 7.2. **Integrated Mixed Methods Design Examples.**

Example of Integrated Design	Relevant Mixed Methods Purposes	Status of Methods	Sequence of Implementation	Integrative Task
Iteration	Development	Preferably equal	Sequential	Data representation
Blending	Complementarity Initiation	Preferably equal	Concurrent	Joint analysis or connection during analysis
Nesting or embedding	Complementarity Initiation	One method primary	Concurrent	Joint analysis or connection during analysis
Mixing for reasons of substance or values	Complementarity Initiation	Preferably equal	Variable	Joint analysis, comparison or connection during analysis

Iteration. A mixed methods study in which the results of one method are used to inform the development of another (including instrumentation, sample selection, and implementation) represents long-standing inquiry practice in multiple methodological traditions, now brought under the mixed methods umbrella. In an iterative design, the methods are by definition implemented sequentially and are preferably—though not necessarily—of equal weight. The preference for parity in method influence reflects my bias toward the generative and dialogic possibilities in mixed methods inquiry, which are best enacted in spaces with equity of perspective and voice. But iterative designs may just as effectively meet the needs of a given context with one primary and one supplementary method. An excellent example of an iterative design, which included three stages over a period of several years, is the Eckert (1987) study of the displacement of low-income elderly residents of single room occupancy hotels by gentrification that was presented in Chapter Five. This study was initiated with a four-year ethnographic stage, followed by two stages of quasi-experimental comparison of seniors forced to move with those who lived and remained in nearby hotels.

The integrative task in an iterative design is to represent the results of one method in ways that meaningfully inform the desired development of another. For example, in the Eckert study, the extensive results of the ethnography needed to be represented in thematic ways that captured important or vulnerable facets of the seniors' daily lives that could be threatened by relocation; for example, eating a nutritious diet. These themes then constituted the starting point for the development of more structured instruments that could measure these facets of seniors' lives in the next quasi-experimental phase, pre-post and longer-term follow-up.

Blending. A very common mixed methods design in practice is the use of two or more different methods to assess varied facets of the same complex phenomenon, representing the mixed methods purposes of complementarity or initiation. Again, the methods are preferably (in my view) of generally equal weight in the study and are implemented concurrently so that the phenomenon of interest does not change across methods. And the integrative task is one of joint analysis or connection between data of different kinds during the analysis process.

The Rossman and Wilson (1985) evaluation of RESAs cited earlier offers an interesting example of a blended design for purposes of complementarity, involving the surveys and interviews they conducted with school personnel. Recall that these two methods appeared to be of relatively equal status in the study and were implemented at the same time. The blended part of this mix of methods involved the assessment of how the RESAs delivered services to local educators.

Analysis of interviews with district administrators identified five different service delivery modes: long-term project assistance, workshops, brief interactions, telephone contacts, and use of the resource center. How contacts are made is important to service agencies. However, further elaboration is needed to understand to what groups services should be targeted. To answer that we made use of quantitative data. (Rossman and Wilson, 1985, p. 637, emphasis added)

Analysis of the survey data explored how frequently teachers and administrators used each of these service delivery modes.

> *We found that administrators received considerably more services from their RESA than did teachers. Most dramatically, administrators were in touch with RESA personnel via the telephone over ten times as often as teachers. . . . Teachers apparently did not have the same informational needs, although we had anticipated much higher teacher use of workshops and resource centers. (p. 637)*

In this example, then, the interviews identified different types of service delivery modes and the survey contributed the frequency of use of each mode by local administrators compared to teachers. Together, these data offered a more complete portrait of RESA service delivery and use than either could alone. This same study further illustrates a blended design implemented for the mixed methods purpose of initiation, which Rossman and Wilson describe as "the analytic function that turns ideas around" (p. 637).

I have used the Rossman and Wilson evaluation study to illustrate both a convergence and a blended design. And both designs have been illustrated with the same set of methods—document analysis as well as interviews and surveys (with both RESA and school personnel). This study thus provides an excellent example of how mixed methods practice characteristically happens; specifically, how a given set of methods can in fact be mixed for more than one purpose. This is primarily because each method is measuring multiple constructs and the mix happens at the level of construct or phenomenon. The convergence example focused on the constructs of the perceived helpfulness of the RESA by local educators and the primary role adopted by each RESA (assistance or enforcement). The blended example focused on the construct of RESA service delivery. The methods used thus assessed all of these constructs and others, permitting multiple purposes for mixing and multiple design types—all with the same set of methods. Clearly, not all mixed methods purposes can be fulfilled with the same mix of methods, as some purposes require method independence and others method interaction, and some require sequential and others concurrent method implementation. But many mixed methods purposes can be fulfilled with the same mix of methods. Finally, this evaluation study preceded much of the conceptual work in mixed methods inquiry by a good ten years. Thus it is likely that the evaluators engaged these various mixed methods purposes through thoughtful and creative analyses, rather than by intentional design. The educational value of their work remains enduring nonetheless.

Embedding or Nesting. A somewhat rare but potentially generative integrative mixed methods design involves the embedding or nesting of a supplementary or secondary method in the design and implementation of the study's primary methodology or set of methods. *Distinctively in this design, the secondary method follows or adheres to key parameters of the primary method—for example, sampling or designed controls—rather than following the parameters usually associated with this secondary method.* This design can serve mixed methods purposes of complementarity or initiation. And like the blended design, the integrative challenge is one of joint analysis or connection between differing data sets during the process of analysis.

Another classic mixed methods study illustrates this embedded or nested design, with a mixed methods purpose of initiation. Maxwell, Bashook, and Sandlow (1986) embedded ethnographic observation methods in an experimental evaluation of the outcomes of physicians' participation in one hospital's medical care evaluation (MCE) committees. These committees were charged with regularly reviewing patient records against explicit criteria for the treatment of particular diseases. The committees aimed to identify instances in which the quality of care provided in the hospital could be improved.

In the quasi-experimental design, some MCEs were selected to participate in an educational program developed to improve the functioning of MCEs. A set of matched control MCEs was also identified. Multiple quantitative measures— including knowledge tests, clinical case recall interviews, and analysis of patient records—were used to assess knowledge and performance outcomes for physicians in both experimental and control MCEs. In addition, ethnographic observations were conducted of both experimental and matched control MCEs, *following the sampling parameters of the quasi-experiment rather than the characteristic purposive sampling associated with ethnography.* The observations focused on documenting the committees' functioning and learning. (See also Gibson-Davis & Duncan, 2005, for an example of ethnographic methods implemented in tandem with a randomized experimental design, and another example of the ethnographic methods using the sampling parameters of the experiment.) The quantitative measures demonstrated significant positive effects for the experimental MCEs, results that were illuminated and enhanced by the ethnographic data.

Specifically, the authors of this study intentionally joined critical features *of meaning and understanding* (from the ethnographic methods) with *causal explanation* (from the quasi-experimental design), thus well illustrating an initiation intent. And the ethnographic data indicated that the knowledge and performance changes yielded by the quantitative measures came from an unanticipated causal process (again, well illustrating the generative potential of the mixed methods purpose of initiation). The design of the study assumed that participation in the revised MCEs would directly increase physicians' knowledge regarding diagnosis and treatment. Instead, the ethnographic data revealed that the program's effects were achieved indirectly by increasing the physicians' confidence in applying knowledge that they already possessed.

Mixing for Reasons of Substance or Values. Finally, there are integrated mixed methods designs that use a mix of methods for particular forms of "better understanding" (the overall purpose or rationale for mixing methods) that are directly tied to the substantive or ideological framework being employed in the study. In previous work, we called the former of these designs *holistic,* in which "the mixed methods tension invoked by juxtaposing different inquiry facets [representing different methodological traditions] is transferred to a substantive framework, which then becomes the structure within which integration occurs" (Caracelli & Greene, 1997, p. 27). Examples of such substantive frameworks include a social science theory, a program theory in an evaluation study, and a concept map.

Mixing methods for more values-based or ideological reasons has been commonly called a *transformative* mixed methods design, following the "transformative paradigm" advanced by Donna Mertens for mixed methods inquiry (Mertens, 2003). In this design, "the rationale for mixing methods ha[s] less to do with methodology and more to do with values or ideology . . . [for example, mixing methods] to represent pluralistic interests, voices, and perspectives, and through this representation, both to challenge and transform entrenched positions through the dialog that the . . . inquiry fostered" (Caracelli & Greene, 1997, p. 29).

Reprise

As suggested by this discussion, the process of developing a thoughtful and appropriate mixed methods design is less a process of following a formula or a set of prescriptive guidelines and more an artful crafting of the kind of mix that will best fulfill the intended purposes for mixing within the practical resources and contexts at hand. Key dimensions of difference in mixed methods designs include the planned independence or interaction among the methods and data sets during the course of the study and the equal or unequal status and prominence accorded to each method or set of methods. Design is importantly anchored in mixed methods purpose—which stems directly from overall inquiry purpose—and is shaped by context and resources. To reiterate two other important aspects of designing mixed methods studies, first, a selected mixed methods purpose—and associated design—for a given inquiry may not always be fulfilled. Intended triangulation may become complementarity or even initiation, as results may diverge instead of converge. Intended complementarity may become either triangulation (in cases of convergence) or initiation (in cases of divergence), or even both for different phenomena. This is not inherently problematic, but likely engages the generative potential of mixed methods inquiry. And second, mixed methods practice is very much more complicated than theory. Theory suggests simplistic mixing of two or more methods for one purpose. Yet because our methods assess multiple phenomena, one mix of methods may be designed for multiple purposes. This is illustrated in the following discussion by revisiting the SHATIL evaluation that was introduced in Chapter Six, as well as the RESA evaluation used as examples in this chapter. Prior to this illustration, other authors' formulations of mixed methods designs will be briefly presented.

OTHER FORMULATIONS OF MIXED METHODS DESIGN

Ideas about mixed methods design have constituted the busiest site of creative development in the mixed methods theoretical literature. The ideas of Tashakkori and Teddlie and of Morse were presented at the beginning of this chapter. Snapshots of three additional prominent mixed methods design frameworks follow.

The Interactive Design Approach

Joseph Maxwell (Maxwell, 1996; Maxwell & Loomis, 2003) has offered a different way of thinking about and approaching the design of mixed methods studies. Rather than focusing on "types" of and typologies for mixed methods designs, Maxwell presents an interactive approach that engages all of the primary components of inquiry design (inquiry purposes, conceptual framework, inquiry questions, validity strategies, and methods) in a networked or weblike association rather than a linear or cyclical sequence. This approach also employs

> a distinction between two approaches to explanation, which we call variance theory and process theory, [evoking] somewhat different definitions of these two types of research [quantitative and qualitative, respectively] from those found in most other works, and thus it leads to a somewhat different idea of what mixed methods research consists of. (Maxwell & Loomis, 2003, p. 243, emphasis in original)

Maxwell presents his ideas as complementary to rather than competitive with others in the field.

At the center of Maxwell's interactive framework for designing social inquiry, including mixed methods studies, are the inquiry questions. The inquiry questions "function as the hub or heart of the design because they form the component that is most directly linked to the other four. The [inquiry] questions need to inform, and be responsive to, all of the other components of the design" (p. 246). The process of design then involves the iterative development of the inquiry questions, in interaction with the overall inquiry purposes and conceptual framework *and* in interaction with the planned data gathering and analysis methods and validation criteria and strategies. Maxwell and Loomis offer thoughtful discussion of the paradigm issue in their formulation of mixed methods design, as well as highly instructive analyses of existing designs using the interactive framework. They conclude by citing five particular advantages or contributions of the interactive approach to mixed methods design, including the following:

- The interactive design model that we have presented can be a valuable tool in understanding the integration of qualitative and quantitative approaches and elements in a particular study. . . .

- There is considerable value in a detailed understanding of how qualitative and quantitative methods are actually integrated in particular studies. For example, the degree of integration of qualitative and quantitative elements in the conceptual framework, analysis, or validity components of a study might not correspond to the integration of data collection methods. . . .

- [Finally], the design model that we have presented is a tool for designing or analyzing an actual study rather than a template for designing a particular *type* of study. In a sense, we are presenting a more qualitative approach to mixed methods design, emphasizing particularity, context, holistic understanding, and the process by which a particular combination of qualitative and quantitative elements plays out in practice, in contrast to a more quantitative approach based on categorization and comparison. As with qualitative and quantitative approaches in general, we advocate an integration of the two approaches. (pp. 267–269, emphasis in original)

A Typology of Mixed Methods Design that Focuses on Sequencing and Status of Methods

The work of John Creswell (Creswell, 2002; Creswell, Plano Clark, Gutmann, & Hanson, 2003) has focused on the development of a mixed methods design typology that is anchored in the design dimensions of (1) sequence of implementation—sequential or concurrent—and (2) the priority given to one method or set of methods versus methods of equal status. Attention is also given to the stage of mixing and the presence of an explicit "theoretical perspective." These dimensions form six major types of mixed methods designs in Creswell's typology, as follows:

1. Sequential explanatory design, "characterized by the collection and analysis of quantitative data followed by the collection and analysis of qualitative data. Priority is typically given to the quantitative data, and the two methods are integrated during the interpretation phase of the study" (Creswell et al., 2003, p. 223). In this design, the qualitative data function to help explain and interpret the findings of a primarily quantitative study.

2. Sequential exploratory design, "characterized by an initial phase of qualitative data collection and analysis followed by a phase of quantitative data collection and analysis . . . [with] priority given to the qualitative aspect of the study [and] the findings . . . integrated during the interpretation phase. . . . The primary focus of this design is to explore a phenomenon" (p. 227).

3. Sequential transformative design, in which one method precedes the other, priority may be given to either method, and the results are integrated during interpretation. This design is guided primarily by a theoretical perspective, "whether it be a conceptual framework, a specific ideology, or advocacy" (p. 228).

4. Concurrent triangulation design, which has the same attributes as the convergence design for purposes of triangulation described earlier.

5. Concurrent nested design, similar to the preceding discussion of an embedded or nested design, prescribes the nesting of one method within a study dominated by another method.

6. Concurrent transformative design, which is guided primarily by the inquirer's use of a specific theoretical perspective, as in the sequential transformative design presented earlier.

Extended-Term Mixed-Method (ETMM) Evaluation Designs

As an example of continued developments in the mixed methods field, Madhabi Chatterji (2005) proposed a design for evaluation studies that responds to contemporary pressures for rigorous evidence from experimental studies while simultaneously attending meaningfully to the contextual and temporal dimensions of social phenomena. Dubbed the extended-term mixed-method (ETMM) design, this alternative rests fundamentally on the assumed importance of:

> a temporal factor to be considered in gaining understandings of programs as they develop and take hold in organizational or community settings. . . . In-depth and often site-specific studies of context variables, along with systematic examinations of program inputs and processes as potential moderators and intervening factors, are a necessary prerequisite to both designing and implementing sound field experiments geared toward answering causal questions on program impact. (Chatterji, 2005, p. 15, emphasis in original)

Chatterji then outlines five principles of the ETMM design and presents a generally convincing argument for its value, especially in policy-oriented evaluation studies.

ILLUSTRATIONS OF MIXED METHODS DESIGNS IN PRACTICE

Two studies described previously are revisited in this section with an eye to the particularities of their mixed methods designs.

The SHATIL Evaluation (Continued)

Design features of the SHATIL evaluation conducted by Mark Waysman and Riki Savaya (1997) well illustrate the core ideas in this chapter. To reiterate descriptive information about this evaluation study from Chapter Six, SHATIL was founded in 1982 by the New Israel Fund to provide technical assistance to the approximately 400 organizations supported by this fund. At that time, these funded organizations worked for social change in varied domains, including human rights, social and economic development for the poor, Jewish-Arab relationships, and religious pluralism and tolerance. SHATIL provided direct assistance in five areas—organizational consultation, fundraising and finance, advocacy, media and public relations, and volunteer recruitment and management—as well as indirect assistance in such forms as professional development and information dissemination.

The evaluation was initiated by SHATIL about ten years after its founding in order to gather feedback from client organizations as input to prospective planning. The evaluation had four objectives:

1. To map the characteristics of organizations that apply to SHATIL;
2. To map the services provided to these organizations;

3. To assess the perceived contribution of SHATIL to the development and goal attainment of these organizations; and

4. To evaluate the satisfaction of these organizations with the services provided by SHATIL. (Waysman & Savaya, 1997, p. 229)

The three phases of the evaluation, progressing from the general to the specific, included the following aims and methods.

1. Phase I "used an open-ended, qualitative learning approach to examine the program's aims, the characteristics of the client organizations, and their needs and experiences. It consisted of two parts: (1) structured personal interviews with senior SHATIL staff, and (2) a series of four focus groups with representatives of organizations that received assistance from SHATIL" (p. 230).

2. For Phase II, a modular questionnaire was developed and administered to all client organizations based on the information gathered in Phase I. The questionnaire assessed client perceptions of SHATIL's services in general, as well their perceptions of the particular services they received.

3. Phase III returned to qualitative methods to assess in more depth particular sources of client satisfaction and dissatisfaction with SHATIL's services. Staff from organizations who responded to the Phase II survey and indicated extremely high or low satisfaction with SHATIL were invited to participate in one of two follow-up focus groups (representing high and low satisfaction).

Table 7.3 offers one matrix portrayal of the methods used and some of the constructs measured in this three-phase evaluation study.

In Table 7.3, method mixes are apparent for several constructs using the same set of methods (the initial client focus groups and the client questionnaire), notably client experiences in applying to SHATIL, client unmet needs, and especially client satisfaction with SHATIL's services. In the design framework presented in this chapter, these mixes best represent the integrated designs of *iteration*, whereby the results of one set of methods (Phase I staff interviews and client focus groups) inform the development of another method (Phase II client questionnaire), and *blending*, whereby different methods tap into different facets of the same complex phenomenon (such as client satisfaction). As noted in the Chapter Six discussion of this evaluation study, additional subfeatures of the design were intended to represent other mixed methods purposes.

The RESA Evaluation

The three-year evaluation of the regional educational service agencies (RESAs) by Rossman and Wilson (1985), cited previously, also well illustrates the use of one set of mixed methods in different design configurations, for different mixed methods purposes. RESAs operated regionally to provide services to groups of school districts not

TABLE 7.3. **Mixed Methods Design Features of the SHATIL Evaluation.**

Construct Assessed	Phase I Staff Interviews	Phase I Client Focus Groups	Phase II Client Modular Questionnaire	Phase III Client Focus Groups
Specific components and goals of SHATIL services	X			
Client experiences in applying to and working with SHATIL		X	X	
Client satisfaction with SHATIL service delivery		X	X	X
Client unmet needs and areas of concern		X	X	

available to each district separately. Table 7.4 offers one portrayal of the various methods used in this evaluation and a selection of the constructs measured, drawing from the examples presented in this chapter. In these examples, the first two constructs were assessed with a convergence design and the third with a blending design.

CONNECTING MIXED METHODS DESIGNS TO MIXED METHODS PARADIGM STANCES AND MIXED METHODS PURPOSES

The final entry in this design chapter revisits the prior practical steps in planning and implementing mixed methods inquiry—identifying a meaningful stance on mixing paradigms or mental models in the context at hand (Chapter Five) and identifying appropriate purposes for mixing methods for that study (Chapter Six)—and offers logical links to mixed methods design in Table 7.5. As observed at the end of Chapter Six, struggling with connections of this kind is an important part of the development of any theory of methodology. A stronger, more coherent, and more useful methodological theory comprises interconnected and integrated parts (Greene, 2006).

TABLE 7.4. **Mixed Methods Design Features of the RESA Evaluation.**

Construct Assessed	Document Review	Interviews with School Personnel	Surveys for School Personnel	Interviews with RESA Staff	Surveys for RESA Staff
Perceived helpfulness of RESAs by school personnel		X (administrators)	X (administrators)		
Primary RESA role (assistance or enforcement)	X				X
RESA service delivery mode		X (administrators)	X (administrators, teachers)		

And like the discussion concluding Chapter Six, this portrayal of logical links among the different steps in mixed methods social inquiry provokes further reflections. One, for several constellations of mixed methods paradigm stance and mixed methods purpose, a variety of both component and integrated designs would be compatible. And for the others, there is a stronger logical connection to one broad cluster of mixed methods designs than the other. But these are logical connections, not prescriptive dictates for practice. Two, mixed methods design decisions—even in the presence of a philosophically strong paradigm stance—are *at least* as importantly influenced by overall inquiry purpose, by the substantive character of the phenomena being studied, and by critical features of the context as they are by the assumptions of the paradigm(s) being invoked. And three, this portrayal clearly reinforces the contingent, contextual, and artful character of crafting thoughtful and defensible mixed methods designs. The theoretical ideas presented in these chapters offer sets of conceptual oars for guiding a mixed method, but the rower remains the artist.

TABLE 7.5. **Connecting Mixed Methods Designs to Mixed Methods Paradigm Stances and Mixed Methods Purposes.**

Mixed Methods Paradigm Stances	Logically Compatible Mixed Methods Purposes	Logically Compatible Mixed Methods Designs
Purist stance ■ Different paradigms have incommensurable assumptions. ■ Paradigms guide and direct practical decisions.	*Within one paradigm*, all purposes except initiation are compatible. Because it is not possible to mix paradigms while mixing methods, initiation is not a good fit to a purist stance.	*Within one paradigm,* most designs are possible.
A-paradigmatic stance ■ Paradigm attributes can be easily mixed and matched. ■ Context, not paradigms, guides practical decisions.	All purposes are compatible and could constitute a good fit, depending on the context.	Component designs Integrated designs
Substantive theory stance ■ Paradigms are importantly different but not incommensurable. ■ But substantive theory, not paradigms, guides practical decisions.	*Within one substantive theory*, all purposes except initiation could be a good fit.	Integrated designs are likely a better fit than component designs.
Complementary strengths stance ■ Paradigms are importantly different but not incommensurable. ■ Paradigms, context, and theory all guide practical decisions, but paradigms should be kept separate.	Triangulation and expansion are the best fit because methods, and accompanying paradigms, need to be kept separate. Complementarity and development could also be compatible.	Components designs are likely a better fit than integrated designs.

(Table 7.5 continued)

Dialectic stance	Initiation is the best fit.	Integrated designs
▪ Paradigms are importantly different but not incommensurable.	Complementarity and development could also be compatible.	
▪ Paradigms, context, and theory all guide practical decisions, and paradigms should engage in dialogue.		
Alternative paradigm stance	This depends on the characteristics of the alternative paradigm being used.	Component designs
▪ Old paradigms should give way to new ones that embrace multiple methods.		Integrated designs
▪ New paradigms, context, and theory all guide practical decisions.		

INTERLUDE

2

MIXED METHODS PURPOSES AND DESIGNS IN ACTION

Moving to Opportunity (MTO) is an ongoing federal demonstration project (initiated in 1994) that provided families living in high-poverty public housing projects with rent subsidy vouchers that could help them move to better neighborhoods. For the experimental group, the voucher could be used only in a community where the poverty rate was less than 10 percent. The experimental group also received housing and relocation counseling. A comparison group was offered Section 8 vouchers that they could use anywhere, and no counseling. A control group continued whatever housing assistance they already had. The vouchers and counseling were offered to some families but not others through a randomized lottery, thus creating a field experiment. This "design provides a unique opportunity to definitively measure and to understand the impacts of a change in neighborhood on the social well-being of low-income families" (http://www.nber.org/~kling/mto/). An excerpt from the ongoing study of MTO in one of its five urban sites (Boston) well illustrates the complexity and variety of mixed methods purposes and designs in practice. This work also dramatically underscores the valuable contributions made possible by mixing methodological perspectives and techniques in the same inquiry project.

Jeffrey Kling, Jeffrey Liebman, and Lawrence Katz (2005) describe the first several years of their mixed methods inquiry in Boston with the provocative title, "Bullets don't got no name: Consequences of fear in the ghetto." This presentation is included

138

in Tom Weisner's (2005) edited book of mixed methods inquiry in the domain of child development. Broadly, this inquiry project included qualitative methods of direct observation of the operation of the MTO program in Boston and in-depth interviews with housing counselors and with samples of both program and comparison group participants. The primary quantitative methods were a baseline survey administered to all program enrollees, a follow-up survey administered to all families in the study about two years after program enrollment, and an analysis of administrative data on employment and welfare status. The story recounted in the "Bullets don't got no name" write-up describes four ways in which the authors say that "qualitative fieldwork had a profound effect on our MTO research" (p. 244). I will use the mixed methods language of purpose and design presented in chapters Six and Seven to describe this study and then illustratively share some of the ways in which the qualitative fieldwork contributed "profoundly" to the study.

OVERALL MIXED METHODS PURPOSES AND DESIGN

As is customary in social inquiry today, Kling, Liebman, and Katz do not begin their write-up with an explicit statement of paradigmatic beliefs or of the mental models guiding this important empirical study. Yet, as argued throughout this book, social inquiry always proceeds within the assumptive frameworks of the inquirers. And in a mixed methods context, it is important to assess if philosophical assumptions and stances within a mental model are also being mixed, along with techniques from different methodological traditions. For just what is being mixed in a mixed methods study is interlaced with mixed methods purposes and designs. That is, an understanding of the mixed methods purposes and design dimensions employed in a given study requires some understanding of underlying mixed methods paradigmatic stance.

So what is the mixed methods paradigm stance adopted for this early study of MTO in Boston? Based on a careful reading of the written account of this study available *and* on hearing firsthand a presentation of an earlier version of this paper by the lead author, I believe the researchers conducting this study understood, appreciated, and accepted the distinctive character of quantitative and qualitative methodologies. In particular, I believe they understood and valued the inherent contextuality, particularity, and experiential nature of qualitative data, alongside the potential of quantitative data to offer generalizable results and findings. This was especially evident in the narrative and storied character of the qualitative interview guides and resulting data and in the careful econometric estimates of actual treatment-control group differences in outcomes in the quantitative data. That said, I am not sure if the researchers in this study actually mixed paradigms or mental models. I believe that the most likely mixed methods paradigmatic stance used in this study was a substantive theory stance. With this stance, the methods and analytic decisions are guided primarily by the characteristics and contours of what is being studied—in this case, changes in low-income families' lives afforded by moving to a better community—rather than by the assumptive stances of a philosophical paradigm or mental model. This supposition that these authors' methodological decisions were guided primarily by their conceptual agenda is supported by the emphasis placed in this write-up on the development of "an overall conceptual framework for thinking about the mechanisms through which changes in outcomes due to moves out of high-poverty areas might occur" (p. 244).

The overall design of this study was an *integrated* mixed methods design in which the different methods were of relatively equal weight and were implemented in intentional interaction with one another during the course of the study. The design further involved a sequential and iterative implementation of the different methods for the multiple mixed methods purposes of complementarity, initiation, and development. The *blended* (interactive) character of the design served the mixed methods purposes of complementarity and initiation, and the *iterative* character of the mixed methods design served the mixed methods purpose of development. And again, the underlying driver of this work was the quest for more a complete, elaborated, and nuanced conceptual understanding of the phenomenon and especially the consequences of relocation, along with policy lessons of importance.

More specifically, the study began with a baseline survey of all enrollees in MTO in Boston, which assessed their current living situation and employment, their reasons for wanting to move, and their connections to their neighborhood among other issues. Next, qualitative field work was undertaken to better understand program implementation in context; to "further explore issues, such as the importance of drugs and gangs, highlighted in the Baseline Survey and previous literature; . . . [and] to listen carefully to the stories of MTO families in order to develop new themes for our research that we had not anticipated in advance" (p. 248). The qualitative fieldwork at this stage of the study included onsite observations, extended interviews with the experimental group counselors, and personal interviews with a stratified random sample of twelve participants from the experimental group and the comparison group. (Noteworthy here is the use of the sampling logic of quantitative methodology to select individuals for in-depth qualitative interviews. This mixed methods idea of applying the framework and logic of one methodology to some aspect of a different methodology—an aspect like sampling or analysis—is discussed in both chapters Seven and Eight.) The use of the baseline survey to help *develop* priority questions for the qualitative interviews is evident in this methodological description—as is the *initiation* intent to develop new themes not anticipated in advance.

Following completion of the interviews, Kling et al. developed a structured survey instrument that comprised the basis for the study's quantitative analysis. The results of the interviews, say the authors, importantly "caused us to refocus our quantitative data collection strategy on a substantially different set of outcomes" (p. 244) from those initially planned, again well illustrating a development agenda. The outcomes initially planned were those familiar to labor economists—the employment patterns and earnings of MTO adults and the school experiences of MTO children. Yet of often dramatic salience to MTO parents in the interviews were concerns about safety and health, especially the safety of their children amidst daily crime and violence. So the study's main survey was refocused to include these other dimensions of daily life, well illustrating a complementarity agenda.

MIXED METHODS CONTRIBUTIONS TO THE MTO STUDY

Examples of the understandings attained in this study from its mix of methods are offered below. Readers are encouraged to read for themselves this account, and others from the MTO program of research, to better appreciate the powerful contributions of both stories and statistics.

Inclusion of a Broader, More Comprehensive Set of Outcomes

As noted earlier, this study assessed a broad set of possible outcomes of relocation, extending beyond those often studied by economists to those of salience to program participants (and reflecting such other disciplines as community and child development). Interestingly, the largest program effects were demonstrated for the outcomes related to health and safety. If these had not been added to the study, the MTO program might have been judged a failure, when in fact dramatic improvements in some families' well-being were accomplished through their MTO participation. In turn, without the survey, the generalizable importance of these health and safety outcomes for families moving out of high-poverty communities would not have been demonstrated.

Development of a Broader, More Comprehensive Conceptual Framework for Understanding Relocation

The need to live life "on the watch" captures key strands of the nuanced conceptual framework generated in this study to help explain the salient consequences of moving out of a high-poverty community. The interviews with MTO mothers yielded powerful descriptions of the fear for their children's safety that they experienced on a daily basis in their original home community. These mothers did not perceive the violence in their community as directed at them, but they were terrified that their children would be hurt simply by being in the wrong place at the wrong time. This fear engendered a vigilance on the part of their mothers such that "their entire daily routine was focused on keeping their children safe" (p. 244). Clearly then, moving to a community with a much less intense incidence of violence relieved some MTO mothers, who moved out from under the enormous responsibility of keeping their children safe every minute of every day, which opened up spaces in their lives for other things, like engaging with their children's school and education more fully.

And the fullness, complexities, and contextuality of this conceptual framework very well fulfills the ambition of integrated mixed methods designs to generate a more comprehensive understanding and account of the human phenomena being studied. (See further information on this study at www.jcpr.org/wp/wpprofile.cfm?id=247.)

CHAPTER

MIXED METHODS DATA ANALYSIS

THE MIXED METHODS traveler will visit the territory of mixed methods data analysis in this chapter. This territory presents many creative ideas for analyses that integrate different kinds of empirical data, most of which continue to be contributed by practitioners. So the conceptual territory of mixed methods data analysis itself still remains under development. Thus the traveler through this territory will sample from the rich storehouse of mixed methods analyses in practice and ideally be inspired to contribute his or her own creative work to this emerging site of mixed methods development.

■ ■ ■

The analysis strands of social inquiry are the heart of the investigative and interpretive process. Whether analysis is guided and assisted by statistical models and sophisticated software or by a sorting of narrative content and inductive reorganization of data collected, the meanings of the data are interlaced throughout the analytic process. These meanings, however, are not so much readily apparent in analytic results as they are inferred and interpreted by the inquirer as he or she engages in the work of data analysis. That is, statements of inquiry conclusions, interpretations, or warranted assertions arise from the mind of the inquirer, not directly from the output of a statistical or thematic analysis. Inference and interpretation are fundamentally human cognitive processes.

So it is with mixed methods data analysis and, in particular, with the mixing part of mixed methods data analysis. Such mixing can be aided by analytic frameworks, procedures, strategies, and even software, as the work of Pat Bazeley—to be described later in this chapter—enticingly illustrates. Yet the mix itself—in particular, the interpretations of the meanings of the mix—reside in the cognitive processing of the inquirer. As such, the mixing part of mixed methods social inquiry will always defy complete codification and will always resist inflexible prescriptions (Miles and Huberman, 1994).

Nevertheless, the mixed methods field remains ripe for further conceptual work on the challenges of analyzing, in well-planned and meaningful ways, multiple data sets of different form, content, and character. These challenges are especially important for integrated designs that intentionally incorporate a back-and-forth conversation among diverse methods and data sets. The mixed methods field can also continue to benefit from the creative thinking of diverse social inquirers in the form in exemplars of empirical mixed methods analytic work. Excellent exemplars exist; several will be shared in this chapter. And in the time-honored tradition of learning from case examples, these exemplars are highly instructive. They offer windows into numerous and distinctive analytic possibilities and potentialities. And further, they well illustrate how a mix of methods generated understandings and inferences that would not have been possible in a monomethod study.

This chapter first presents some ways of thinking about mixed methods data analysis, ways that are consonant both with the inherent cognitive character of data interpretation and inferencing and with the mixed methods way of thinking that is the signature message of this book (see Chapter Two). Then, extant work on approaches to mixed methods data analysis is presented in a framework that focuses on the particular analytic phases and processes that constitute important opportunities for mixing. Various forms of mixing are also discussed. The chapter concludes with three exemplary and highly instructive cases of creative mixed methods analysis.

The discussion in this chapter concentrates on analysis in integrated designs, as these require meaningful mixing during the conduct of the analysis, and as strategies and procedures for integrative analyses remain underdeveloped. The ideas in their general form are also relevant to component designs, especially to the nontrivial challenge of connecting results and conclusions from two or more different methodologies. But the mix for component designs is only at this stage of conclusions and inferences and thus presents fewer challenges.

THINKING ABOUT MIXED METHODS DATA ANALYSIS

These thoughts represent several key principles that guide my own thinking about, planning for, and conducting mixed methods data analyses:

- Decisions about analytic strategies and procedures in a mixed methods study are importantly connected to, but not dictated by prior methodological decisions. That is, the inquirer's identified mixed methods paradigm stance, purposes for mixing, and design dimensions for a particular study characteristically indicate broad analytic directions, but rarely specify particular analytic procedures or strategies.

■ Mixed methods analysis for component designs proceeds more or less *independently* for each method or set of methods, following the procedures of each methodological tradition. Then the mixing or linking or connecting happens at the inquiry stage of interpretation and inferencing. In contrast, a hallmark characteristic of integrated mixed methods designs is the intentional *interaction* among different sets of data during the study, especially during the analysis stage. Just how that interaction takes place represents an opportunity for creative ideas and imaginative thinking.

■ Interactive mixed methods analyses are highly iterative and are best undertaken with a spirit of adventure.

■ Not every creative idea for interactive analyses will generate sensible or meaningful results. As in all social inquiry analyses, some routes undertaken with hopeful excitement turn out to be dead ends.

■ Interactive analyses should include planned stopping points at which the inquirer intentionally looks for ways in which one analysis could inform another. These stopping points are best planned during the analytic phases that are most opportune for mixed analysis work. These phases are discussed in the next section.

■ Convergence, consistency, and corroboration are overrated in social inquiry. The interactive mixed methods analyst looks just as keenly for instances of divergence and dissonance, as these may represent important nodes for further and highly generative analytic work.

■ Challenges to data quality and integrity can arise in interactive mixed methods data analysis, as the data themselves become changed, even transformed into other forms and frames. The discussion in Chapter Nine takes up these challenges but does not fully address them, as issues of data quality in mixed methods work are just beginning to be addressed.

MIXED METHODS DATA ANALYSIS STRATEGIES

In all forms of social inquiry, data analysis serves to (1) reduce and organize the raw data into a manageable form that enables comprehensive descriptive reporting, as well as defensible further analyses; (2) assess patterns of interrelationships, connections, or trends, as well as differences, in the data; and (3) support and validate conclusions and inferences. The primary activities or phases of data analysis characteristically include some or all of the following:

1. Data cleaning—The data set is reviewed for valid responses, methodological soundness, and indicators of variability and range. This phase can also include

psychometric analyses related to instrument and data quality. Data considered suspect or not defensible are deleted or set aside for further review at a later time.

2. Data reduction—The raw data are analyzed and reduced to descriptive form. This form could consist of frequencies, descriptive statistics, factors, case summaries, descriptive themes, or other reduced displays of descriptive information.

3. Data transformation—In this phase, quantitative data may be standardized, scaled, factor analyzed, or transformed into log linear form; qualitative data may be transformed into critical incidents, chronological narratives, or other forms of displays; and symbolic data (for example, photographs) may be transformed into a different sequence or display. Transformation may also take the form of data consolidation, whereby data from different instruments, time periods, sites, cases, and so forth are merged into one overall data set. The development of indices representing multiple variables or constructs is one popular form of data consolidation. *It is also possible to transform one form of data into another—notably quantitative to qualitative and vice versa—and to consolidate different forms of data into one merged data set.* The primary purposes of transformation, including consolidation, are to enable further higher-order analyses.

4. Data correlation and comparison—This phase investigates patterns of relationship in the data set, marking clusters of variables, themes, or stories that appear to go together, as well as what importantly differentiates one data cluster from the others. Quantitative analyses in this phase can include correlations, cluster analyses, and various analyses of variation. Qualitative analyses can include matrix cross-tabulations of themes, contexts, critical incidents, and stories, as well as comparative analyses across cases or contexts or stories. *It is also possible to assess patterns of relationship across different forms of data (qualitative and quantitative) and to compare relational findings from one form of data to relational findings from a different form of data.*

5. Analyses for inquiry conclusions and inferences—In this final phase of analysis, higher-order analyses are conducted in support of study conclusions or inferences. For quantitative data, these characteristically include multivariate analyses, such as multiple regression and multivariate analyses of variance, as well as modeling techniques such as structural equation modeling, path analysis, and hierarchical linear modeling. For qualitative data, these analyses may include the inductive development of warranted assertions from the data, the creation of composite stories, the reordering and recoding of the data into a final set of coherent and cohesive themes, or sophisticated cross-node analyses with NVivo or another software system. *Once again, it is possible to conduct these higher-order analyses across data sets of different forms.*

The italicized entries in this list signal critical points for analyses across data sets of different forms; in other words, interactive mixed methods data analysis in an integrated mixed methods design. These critical points include the analytic phases of data transformation, data correlation and comparison, and analyses for inquiry conclusions and inferences. The discussion now turns to extant ideas and strategies for such interactive analyses for each of these critical points in the analytic process. It should be noted that the interactive strategies are not necessarily exclusive to the phase of the analysis in which they are discussed. In the adventurous spirit of interactive mixed methods data analysis, social inquirers are encouraged to imagine different enactments of at least some of these strategies for other junctures in their mixed methods analysis.

Data Transformation and Consolidation

In our empirical review of empirical mixed methods evaluation studies (Greene et al., 1989), we observed only a handful (five of fifty-seven studies) in which different forms of data were integrated during the analysis process. A closer look at these five studies yielded several initial ideas regarding interactive mixed methods data analysis (Caracelli & Greene, 1993).

One of these ideas was "data transformation—the conversion of one data type into the other so that both can be analyzed together. [Specifically], qualitative data are numerically coded and included with quantitative data in statistical analyses, [and] quantitative data are transformed into narrative and included with qualitative data in thematic or pattern analysis" (Caracelli & Greene, 1993, p. 197). Teddlie and Tashakkori (2003) also underscore the value of data transformation in mixed methods data analysis, using the concepts of *quantitized* and *qualitized* data to refer to this analytic strategy. And in their latest thinking, Teddlie and Tashakkori (2006) elevate this analytic approach to a mixed methods design feature, which they label *conversion*. In addition to sequential and concurrent options for the ordering and implementation of different methods in a mixed methods study, these authors suggest that conversion or transformation is a third option within this design dimension.

A second interactive mixed methods data analysis strategy that was yielded by our close examination of the five evaluation studies that had some kind of interactive analysis we labeled "data consolidation/merging—the joint review of both data types to create new or consolidated variables or data sets, which can be expressed in either quantitative or qualitative form. These consolidated variables or data sets are then typically used in further analyses" (Caracelli & Greene, 1993, p. 197). Consolidation is thus a particular form of transformation. To illustrate the potential power and reach of this analytic approach, I will quote at length from our earlier description of one of the evaluation studies that used this approach.

> Louis (1981, 1982) describes an interactive analytic model . . . [that] is explicitly focused on integrating the data obtained from different instruments, respondents, and observers. The model evolved during a multisite longitudinal evaluation of the Research and Development Utilization Program (RDU). This $8 million demonstration project was funded by the National Institute of Education between 1976 and 1979 to

promote the adoption and implementation of new curriculum and staff development materials in 300 local schools.

A variety of data collection methods were used throughout the project, including mini-ethnographies based on interviews, observations, and document analysis; . . . standardized site-visit field reports; "event-triggered" reports monitoring a school's progress through the project; and formal principal and teacher surveys. Site-level data were thus rich and diverse; however, no more than 20% of the sites had a complete data set, which seriously constrained cross-site analysis possibilities. To overcome this constraint, these evaluators created a transformed and consolidated site-level data set via the development and application of a "consolidated coding form" (CCF). The form constituted 240 dichotomous or Likert scale items, which were scored by senior staff members who had visited at least four of the sites and were involved in an intensive 2-day session in which common interpretations for consolidated coding were reached. Included on the CCF were variables that could not be readily obtained through traditional survey methods, for example, quality of the decision-making process and pattern of influence of different actors over decisions at various stages in the change process. Moreover, the consolidated data base reflected the holistic knowledge the site-visit team brought to the cases, as well as the reliability of standardized data, integrated both within and across sites.

The level of integration of qualitative and quantitative data achieved in the RDU evaluation is captured in the following summary statement: "Can a database composed of numbers that is entirely dependent on the iterative, holistic judgments of experienced site field teams be described as only quantitative? While the analysis procedures used to manipulate the data are statistical, the data itself [sic], and any interpretation of results is totally conditioned by its origins. On the other hand, as we approach any given analysis using case materials rather than quantified data, it has become genuinely impossible not to embed that activity in our knowledge of the descriptive statistics and correlational relationships that were available to us well before data collection had ended" (Louis, 1981, p. 21).

Louis cautions that this comprehensive, interactive approach requires constant attention by staff members who are skilled in both quantitative and qualitative data analysis techniques. Low rates of turnover among project staff, who are relatively free of paradigmatic preferences, would also be essential to achieving a high level of integration that was obtained in this evaluation. (Caracelli & Greene, 1993, pp. 201–202)

Data Correlation and Comparison

A third strategy that was yielded when we more carefully scrutinized the five evaluation studies that had some kind of interactive analysis we labeled "typology development—the analysis of one data type yields a typology (or set of substantive categories) that is then used as a framework applied in analyzing the contrasting data type" (Caracelli & Greene, 1993, p. 197). At this time, I would relabel this approach *data importation*, referring to the importation of midstream results from the analysis of one data type into the analysis of a different data type. This broader label is not restricted to the development of typologies but rather encompasses multiple and diverse ways that results of midstream analyses of diverse data sets might inform each other. This form of interactive mixed methods data analysis often also includes the analytic strategy of comparison. The key idea here is one of assessing the relational patterns in a data set and identifying what chiefly distinguishes one relational cluster from another, often through some kind of comparative analysis.

One natural example of this interactive mixed methods analytic strategy is to use the factors yielded from a factor analysis of data from a quantitative instrument to sort qualitative interview or observation data and then investigate patterns of commonality and difference among the different factor-groups of qualitative data. Conversely, another example is to use the descriptive themes from an analysis of qualitative interview data to group cases in a quantitative data set and then, again, investigate patterns of commonality and difference among the different theme-groups of quantitative cases. More generally, classificatory results of varying types from an analysis of one type of data could be imported into an analysis of a different type of data and used to group the data and then assess patterns of commonality and differences among the various groups.

The work of Australian Pat Bazeley (2003, 2006) catalogues computerized procedures—involving quantitative and qualitative software packages—for data importation of numerical and textual data into analyses of the other data type. Specifically, Bazeley concentrates on "the use of computers in combining qualitative and quantitative data and in integrating textual analyses (taken here to include analyses of pictorial, audio, and video material) and statistical analyses within the same project" (2003, p. 388). In doing so, Bazeley illustrates various interactive possibilities that engage data correlation and comparison. Some of these procedures involve data transformation as well, and Bazeley's discussion includes features of computer programs that facilitate transformation or conversion. A sampling of the interactive strategies Bazeley (2003) describes is offered next. (The reader is also encouraged to read Bazeley's writing in the original for details of which computer software enable these analyses and how, and also because her approach to analysis and especially her examples well illustrate a "mixed methods way of thinking.")

■ *Transferring quantitative data to a qualitative program.* This strategy is commonly used to include demographic data, or less commonly other scaled quantitative data, in an analysis of qualitative data. "The primary purpose of importing demographic and other categorical information into a qualitative database is to allow for comparative analysis of the responses of subgroups [formed by the quantitative responses] . . . with respect to themes, concepts, or issues raised in the qualitative material. It becomes possible to ask how those, say, in their 30s report an experience and then to determine whether this differs from the experience of those who are older and younger" (Bazeley, 2003, p. 396).

- *Transferring qualitative data to a quantitative program.* This strategy requires a transformation or coding of qualitative data into quantitative form, so that they can be analyzed along with the quantitative data, characteristically using nonparametric techniques. Codes can represent the presence or absence or the frequency of themes or categories, or ratings based on an interpretation of text. The inclusion of these indicators of qualitative information can substantially enrich an analysis and resulting conclusions. In an elaboration of this strategy, qualitative data can be arrayed in matrix form (following guidelines of Miles & Huberman, 1994) and then coded in this matrix form for exportation "to a statistical or mathematical database for further analysis using techniques such as cluster and correspondence analysis" (Bazeley, 2003, p. 400).

- *Other forms of data transfer and manipulation.* Bazeley notes that software other than statistical or textual analysis programs permit transfer across programs. In this discussion, she highlights the valuable contributions of mapping techniques to mixed methods analysis. "Programs that create a visual representation of links in data through network or concept maps provide a powerful extension to text or numerical descriptions of those data" (2003, p. 410). Examples provided include the graphical output of social network analysis and the relational maps generated by semantic network analysis and various forms of concept mapping.

Bazeley (2003) further offers some thoughtful and instructive reflections on the computer-related issues that can arise in conducting these kinds of interactive analyses. First are issues related to the fundamentally different meanings of codes in quantitative and qualitative data analysis tools.

> *Because codes are the only medium for communicating information in a quantitative data set, they are necessarily precise in what they are conveying. . . . Qualitative coding, by contrast, is often conceptually based and multidirectional in that all text about a particular issue, idea, or experience will be assigned the same code, regardless of the way in which it is expressed. . . . Given these differences in the way in which codes and coding are managed, the critical issue from the point of view of mixed methods computing becomes the meaning of the code that is exported from one type of analysis program to another. (Bazeley, 2003, pp. 414–415)*

Second are issues related to sampling and the goal of the analysis. Qualitative studies characteristically use small, purposefully selected samples aiming for in-depth understanding, whereas quantitative studies characteristically use large, representative samples that aim for generalizability. Applying statistical analyses to coded data from a small sample can be problematic, and applying qualitative inductive analyses to large data sets can be overwhelmingly daunting. Other issues include problems with segmentation of texts and exported coding and additional issues for statistical analysis of coded qualitative data. Bazeley concludes this *Handbook* chapter by reminding readers that all data analysis, including computer-assisted interactive mixed methods analyses, is not simply a technical activity but rather involves significant craftsmanship and must also be chosen and implemented in service to the overall inquiry questions.

Finally, the Amazon land use study by John Sydenstricker-Neto that was reported in Interlude One also illustrates a particular kind of data correlation and comparison analysis well suited to mixed methods inquiry: the use of fuzzy set analysis. Fuzzy set analysis is a clustering type of analysis that particularly useful for analyzing data representing complex constructs with multiple dimensions, data representing transitions or continua rather than discrete categories, or data that are heterogeneous.

Analyses for Inquiry Conclusions and Inferences

The final cluster of interactive analysis strategies involves joint analyses of datasets of different types that directly support inquiry inferences. This cluster refers not to analyses that follow data transformation or correlation and comparison (because those are implied in the preceding discussion), but rather to analysis strategies that are intended to directly generate study inferences or conclusions. Two promising strategies have appeared in the mixed methods literature and a third elsewhere, each of which relies quite extensively on inquirer judgment and interpretation.

The first is an adaptation by Mary Lee Smith (1997) of a qualitative data analysis technique originally developed by Fred Erickson (1986). Smith's study involved a large-scale, longitudinal policy study of the Arizona Student Assessment Program (ASAP) (1990–1995), which represented an early incarnation of now-widespread standards-based accountability measures in U.S. public education. The study's aim was "to understand educators' responses to this sweeping mandate, in particular how the introduction of the ASAP might have influenced curriculum, pedagogy, school organization, and teachers' meanings and actions" (Smith, 1997, p. 78). The first stage of the study was undertaken with an interpretivist mental model and involved case studies in four ASAP schools. The results revealed particular contextual conditions that influenced how educators in each context responded to the ASAP, including financial resources, the availability of a local reform expert, and the district's valuing of accountability and authority.

> Although our mental model predisposed us toward qualitative approaches, we believed that survey techniques could provide another angle on the program and could possibly allow us to generalize the working hypotheses and patterns that we developed in the case studies to broad and representative sample. We also recognized that some audiences attach greater credence to quantitative data. (p. 79)

So in a classic development design, the second stage of the research involved the use of the case study qualitative data to construct a survey assessing ASAP principles, test characteristics (validity and fairness), and testing program effects related to teaching and learning. The survey was administered to teachers and principals using survey-appropriate procedures for sample selection and data analysis. For the mixed methods purpose of complementarity, the survey was accompanied by teacher focus groups in four selected schools. Additional, nonrepresentative but rich qualitative data were available from the open-ended responses to the survey.

> *Taken together, the components of the study left us with a massive amount of data of such unevenness and apparent dissimilarity that they nearly defied synthesis. Although each component had been analyzed by appropriate methods and reported separately, we felt that the power of the study must lie in the integration of data. We decided to apply Erickson's modified method (1986) of analytic induction as a way to integrate these data.*

> *Erickson's method is based on the researcher's repeated reading of the data as a whole and then arriving inductively and intuitively at a set of credible [textual or qualitative] assertions. Assertions are statements that the researcher believes to be true based on an understanding of all the data. Next, the researcher goes through a process of establishing the warrant for each assertion, assembling the confirming evidence from the record of data, searching vigorously for disconfirming evidence, weighing the evidence one way or another, and then casting out unwarranted assertions or substantially altering them so they fit with the data. . . . [The assertions are presented, along with their supportive evidence,] striving for a credible, coherent report based on evidence adequate in amount and varied in kind. (pp. 80–81)*

Smith conducted Erickson's warranted assertion method with the whole ASAP data set, over 2,500 pages. She used data in their rawest form and, despite her own mental model, treated both quantitative and qualitative data as equivalent in "potential to inform" (p. 81). She also engaged the analysis as an exercise in disciplined skepticism. The result was eight warranted assertions (for example, "State inattention to the technical and administrative adequacy of the assessment and accountability system impeded coherent responses to ASAP intentions") and the evidence that supported them. The details of Smith's analytic process are commended to the reader.

The second mixed methods analysis strategy in direct support of inquiry inferences is a quantitative "results synthesis" procedure developed by McConney, Rudd, and Ayres (2002), specifically although perhaps not exclusively for evaluators. In this procedure, "quality of evidence assessments, in combination with judgment-based estimates of what each line of evidence says about program effect, can then be aggregated across diverse data-gathering methods to arrive at reasoned estimates of program effectiveness" (p. 124). The procedure consists of four steps, conducted separately for each program outcome:

1. Rate the program's effect according to each evidence set . . . positive effect, no effect, or negative effect [on a 5-point scale of −2 to +2].

2. Rate each evidence set's worth . . . according to a "CoW" [coefficient of worth] [using criteria] aligned with the particular program [and developed collaboratively with program stakeholders].

3. Combine [by multiplying] program effect ratings with "CoW" ratings, according to the program goal or outcome being examined.

4. Aggregate [by summing] combined ratings [for each outcome] to arrive at a summary program "effectiveness estimate." (p. 124)

These authors present this approach as especially relevant to contexts in need of summative evaluation conclusions "where data divergence is evident and not likely to be resolved (e.g., some lines of evidence suggest that the evaluand is effective, while others suggest that it is not)" (p. 124). As suggested throughout this book, it is also important to acknowledge and respect the value of divergence and dissonance as generative of unanticipated insights and understandings.

Finally, a pattern matching approach (originating with Donald Campbell, 1966) offers a characteristically graphical representational mode for analyzing mixed data sets for purposes of drawing inquiry conclusions and inferences. The essence of pattern matching is the comparison of empirically observed data with conceptually expected patterns of data. Expected patterns are commonly generated from a social science theory of intended effects or, in evaluation, a statement of the theory of the program being evaluated. Observed effects are derived from the data collected. Although not explicitly discussed as an analysis option in the mixed methods literature, pattern matching offers untapped potential for mixed methods analyses supporting inquiry conclusions and inferences. This is, in part, because patterns can be represented numerically, textually, or perhaps more usefully, in graphical and other pictorial form.

Jules Marquart (1990) made creative use of pattern matching ideas in an evaluation of an employer-sponsored child care program provided by a large medical complex in the Midwest. The evaluation focused on the connections between the child care program and employees' performance-related attitudes and behaviors, not on the program's effects on children. Marquart initiated the evaluation by generating a conceptual representation of the child care program based on the understandings of administrators in hospitals that offered the child care program. The representation focused on key employee attitudes and behaviors identified in the relevant literature (for example, recruitment, organizational commitment, stress in balancing work and family, absenteeism). The administrators were also asked to rate the expected causal effect of employer-sponsored child care programs on each of the attitudes and behaviors in the study. A questionnaire assessing these same concepts was also administered to samples of employees who used the child care program and employees who did not.

Marquart conducted two pattern matches comparing expected and observed patterns. The first, a "measurement pattern match," compared a concept map of the administrators' perceptions of the relationships among the key attitudes and behaviors being studied with a concept map representing the observed correlations among these attitudes and behaviors from the employee questionnaire. Comparisons were made with a "coefficient of configurational similarity," which is a Pearson correlation of the distances between the concepts on the two maps. This spatial correspondence coefficient was 0.76, thus supporting the construct validity of the evaluation questionnaire.

The second, an "outcomes pattern match," compared the administrators' ratings of expected causal effects with actual effects observed. This compared the order and magnitude of the effects. "A graphic representation of the two patterns was constructed by lining up the predicted and observed order of effects in columns, side by side, and drawing lines between the two. A Spearman correlation coefficient was calculated between the predicted means and the observed t-values," comparing program users and nonusers (Marquart, 1990, p. 103). The lines drawn evidenced many crisscrosses and the Spearman coefficient was but 0.23, suggesting only limited support for the correspondence between administrators' conceptualizations of significant program effects and those observed. "The implied theory of the causal effects of the program was not supported by the empirical data" (p. 104). (Marquart also used several other creative techniques for assessing pattern matches. The reader is encouraged to read the full article for these details.)

In this example, Marquart was creatively comparing expected and observed patterns of data. The logic and graphical power of pattern matching might also lend itself well to comparisons among different forms and types of data. The evaluation study of technology use in several middle schools (by Cooksy, Gill, and Kelly, 2001) that was presented in Chapter Five takes an initial step in using the logic of pattern matching for a mixed methods analysis. In this study, a program theory was developed to frame the overall evaluation, including data collection and analysis. During the analysis, all data relevant to *implementation* and use of the technology were reviewed and expectations were generated for program *outcomes*. The program theory thus provided both a substantive framework in which multiple data sets could be analyzed, as well as a chronological sequence of program components from which expectations about subsequent components could be generated.

Using Aspects of the Analytic Framework of One Methodological Tradition in the Analysis of Data from Another Tradition

There is one more set of analytic ideas in the mixed methods literature that is connected not to a particular analytic phase, but rather to a broad analytic concept. That is the idea of taking aspects of the analytic framework of one methodological tradition and using them in the analysis of data from another tradition. The idea of conducting ethnographic work—not with *purposeful* samples of people, places, and events, but rather with *random* samples of cases from both an experimental group and a comparison group (as discussed in Chapter Seven)—illustrates this concept in the domain of mixed methods design. Three incarnations of this concept in the domain of analysis follow.

First, more than a decade ago, Matthew Miles and Michael Huberman (1994) proposed the use of *matrices* and *displays* as integral parts of the analysis of qualitative data. A matrix represents an ordered cross-tabulation of data, and a display a characteristically spatial representation of relationships in a data set. Thus the idea of a matrix—specifically the notions of ordered dimensions and cross-tabulation—is rooted in more quantitative traditions. Yet this idea can be productively and generatively applied to qualitative data to assess possible relationships not otherwise pursued. (See also Lee, 2005, which will be referenced in Interlude Three, for a highly instructive example of a matrix display that combined multiple sets of qualitative and quantitative data.)

Second, the groundbreaking mixed methods work of comparative social scientist Charles Ragin (1987, 2000), briefly cited in Chapter Three, is organized around the contrasting conceptualizations of variable-oriented and case-oriented research. Variable-oriented research seeks explanations of human phenomena in the isolation of influential variables. Case-oriented research seeks to understand human phenomena in all of their historical and contextual complexity. Ragin has developed an application of Boolean algebra that permits joint analysis of variables and cases, especially useful with small samples. Briefly, in this analysis, the qualitative data for each case are coded 0 or 1 (that is, they are transformed) to indicate the absence or presence of selected descriptors, conditions, events, or outcomes. The selection of these descriptors, conditions, and so forth may well be based on a separate analysis of quantitative data. Boolean algebra is then applied to the coded data set to identify the critical configurations of codes that are needed to adequately describe each of the cases in the sample. A "truth table" is constructed that lists the configurations, the number of cases identified by each configuration, and relevant outcome values, leading to the construction of logical equations that summarize the revealed relationships. Boolean algebra enables the analyst to focus on patterns of covariation across cases and to see causal factors as conjunctural rather than additive: "that is, as working together to create an outcome rather than being potentially masked by an associated variable in a multivariate model. The ultimate goal of such analysis is the construction of typologies to describe the cases studied" (Bazeley, 2003, p. 412). Thus, again, an analytic procedure—algebraic processing of numbers—usually associated with quantitative data is used to assess conjunctural relationships among recoded descriptors, conditions, and themes in a case-oriented qualitative data set.

The third instance of mixed methods analysis in which aspects of one methodological tradition are brought over into the analysis of data from another methodological tradition is the work of Onwuegbuzie and Teddlie (2003). This handbook chapter presents a "framework for analyzing data in mixed methods research." This framework rests on two major rationales for mixed methods data analysis: (1) representation or the "ability to extract adequate information from the underlying data" and (2) legitimation or "the validity of data interpretations" (Onwuegbuzie & Teddlie, 2003, p. 353). These concepts of representation and legitimation are themselves taken from continuing conversations primarily in interpretivist and postmodern methodological circles, framed therein as *crises* of representation and legitimation (Schwandt, 2001). Thus, at the outset, these authors are constructing their analytic framework by using concepts that are of currency primarily in one methodological tradition. The authors also include in their framework a generative conceptualization of various kinds of effect sizes for qualitative data (from Onwuegbuzie, 2001), clearly borrowing an aspect of quantitative analysis and using it for legitimation purposes in qualitative data analysis. Finally, the authors propose a

TABLE 8.1.   **Summary of Mixed Methods Data Analysis Strategies.**

Phase of Analysis	Analysis Strategy
Data transformation	Data transformation, conversion Data consolidation, merging
Data correlation and comparison	Data importation
Analysis for inquiry conclusions and inferences	Qualitative warranted assertion analysis Quantitative results synthesis analysis Pattern matching
Broad idea: Using aspects of the analytic framework of one methodological tradition in the analysis of data from another tradition	Developing matrices and displays in qualitative data analysis Using Boolean algebra to generate a typology of cases from coded qualitative data Grounding a mixed methods analysis in rationales of representation and legitimation; generating effect sizes for qualitative data

seven-step process for mixed methods data analysis—data reduction, display, transformation, correlation, consolidation, comparison, and integration—that is quite similar to that offered in this chapter and that features iterative cycles of interaction among data from different sources and of different types.

Table 8.1 summarizes the mixed methods data analysis strategies discussed in this chapter.

MIXED METHODS DATA ANALYSIS EXEMPLARS

In this final section of this chapter, three highly instructive examples of mixed methods data analysis are presented. All come from large-scale educational inquiries, two representing research and one, evaluation. The description of the first one draws considerably from a previous description of this same study in a mixed methods journal article (Greene, Benjamin, & Goodyear, 2001).

Adopting a "Mixed Methods Way of Thinking" for Analyzing Data from a Study of Preschool Inclusion

In an oft-cited educational research study of the meanings and correlates of including children with developmental disabilities alongside their typically developing peers in preschool and child care contexts, Shouming Li, Jules Marquart, and Craig Zercher (2000) engaged in multiple, highly creative interactive analyses that epitomize the generative potential of a "mixed methods way of thinking." This study was conducted by the Early Childhood Research Institute on Inclusion, a consortium of five universities across the United States, as part of five-year program of research on preschool inclusion in the 1990s. The overall goal of this program of research was to identify promising strategies for inclusion.

> The foundational . . . study was an in-depth analysis of the ecological systems of inclusion . . . designed to answer questions about the goals that families, teachers, program administrators, and policy makers have for inclusion; multiple definitions and ways of implementing inclusion; and barriers to and facilitators of inclusion in various settings. (Li et al., 2000, p. 117)

The study was conducted on a sample of sixteen inclusive preschool programs, four each in four different sites around the country. The programs were identified as inclusive by key informants in each site. They were also purposively selected to demonstrate diversity on program model for inclusion and child and family demographics. In each program, seven children were purposively selected for study—five children were disabled and had an Individualized Educational Plan and two were typically developing peers in the same classroom—for a total of 112 children. In addition, these children's families and teachers and the administrators and policy makers for each program were studied.

The mixed methods design was broadly intended to "provide a broader perspective and deeper understanding of different levels of the ecological systems and the interactions among different levels than could be achieved by a single-method design" (p. 117). More specifically, the mix of methods was selected intentionally to gather both emic, contextualized meanings of key study constructs, and data representing etic, standardized definitions of these same and other constructs. This design thus well illustrates a dialectic paradigm stance (Chapter Five), engaged for mixed methods purposes of complementarity and initiation, among others. A summary of the classroom and family instruments and methods used in this study is presented in Table 8.2.

The analyses from this study were intentionally interactive (befitting the mixed methods paradigm stance and purposes) and included, for example, planned iterations of "qualitative—then quantitative—then qualitative" data analysis; inventive transformations of data from one type to the other; and planned stages of data reduction, transformation, comparison, and integration. During their work, the authors generated three distinct approaches to mixed methods data analysis: (1) a parallel tracks analysis, in which analysis of the different data sets "proceeds separately through the steps of data reduction and transformation until the point of data comparison and integration"

TABLE 8.2.   **Classroom and Family Measures in the Ecological Systems Study.**

Domain	Quantitative Measures	Qualitative Measures
Classroom	CASPERII (Code for Active Student Participation and Engagement, Revised), a direct observational measure of preschool environment and child and adult behavior Peer rating sociometric assessment Battelle Developmental Inventory, a standardized test of development	Participant observation Post-CASPER notes Teacher survey about children's friendships Teacher, service provider, and administrator interviews
Family	Telephone survey	Family interviews Family survey about children's friendships

Source: Li et al., 2000, p. 118.

(Li et al, 2000, p. 120); (2) a crossover tracks analysis, involving the ongoing concurrent analysis of both qualitative and quantitative data, with a focus on facilitating "data comparison, the central stage of mixed-method analysis, by transforming the formats of quantitative and qualitative data to make them more comparable" (p. 126); and (3) a single-track analysis formed by merging or consolidating the data sets early on (Marquart, 1997). The crossover tracks analysis recounted in Li et al. (2000) will be shared next.

This analysis involved the development of case summaries for each of the sixteen programs, which were intended "to provide an in-depth analysis of [the meanings of] inclusion in the programs, to determine barriers to and facilitators of inclusion, and to describe idiosyncratic issues" (p. 125). First, relevant data of both types were analyzed descriptively and reduced in standard ways—quantitative data to graphs and tables, and qualitative data to descriptive themes, narrative sums, and vignettes. Second, selected sets of these reduced data were transformed—the most salient points in quantitative tables and graphs were summed in narrative form, and ordered matrices were developed to capture the main points in the narrative sums. Third—and this is the heart of this analytic approach—the two sets of tables-graphs-matrices (the original quantitative set and the transformed qualitative set) were carefully *compared* for instances of convergence, complementarity, and discordance. Parallel comparisons were conducted on the two sets of narrative sums (the original qualitative set and the transformed quantitative set). Congruence in these comparisons led to stronger, more valid inferences, and incongruence to further probing and generative insights.

One example of one generative insight for one case summary follows.

▪ The *descriptive quantitative graphs* of observation data in this site revealed that one child with disabilities "spent more time than her peers staying by herself outside a group setting . . . [and] the least time in circle time, which was the main instructional time each day" (p. 128).

▪ A *comparison* of these graphs with the (transformed and ordered) matrices of qualitative observation notes pointed to some possible reasons for the initial observation. This comparison indicated that all of this child's "negative behaviors had something to do with her difficulty in staying with a group . . . [suggesting] that her problem was not confined to circle time alone, but might occur in any of the teacher-directed group activities such as work group, story time, and gym class" (pp. 128–129).

▪ *Further probing* of field notes and teacher interview data revealed a discrepancy in inclusion philosophy and child expectations between the regular teacher and the special education teacher, a discrepancy that was complex, nuanced, and multifaceted. Notably, the special education teacher gave this child tacit permission to leave the group whenever she felt like it, believing that "all children should try their best, but if they still could not follow the rules [for example, sitting still in group time], they should be given time to learn" (p. 129). The general education teacher, in contrast, said that high and consistent expectations are needed for all children so that they can get what they need from the educational program. When a child is exempted from the rules, like participating in group time, "'she is not getting what she should get because she is not staying with the group. She doesn't sit down long enough to pick up what we are doing . . . I feel she is not getting what she really needs as far as an education is concerned'" (p. 129).

This discrepancy in teacher philosophies was viewed as a major barrier to inclusion in this particular program.

Creativity in Analyzing Implementation Data from an Evaluation of the Reading Excellence Act in Illinois

The Reading Excellence Act (REA) was a precursor to Reading First, a federal educational program developed around research-based principles of learning to read. These principles included phonemic awareness (K–1 only), decoding, fluency, background knowledge and vocabulary, comprehension, and motivation. Both initiatives were designed to improve the reading skills of K–3 children in "low performing" schools. In 2001–2003, forty-eight schools in twelve Illinois districts received REA grants (of $100,000 to $200,000) to support the implementation of the REA model, including acquisition of new reading materials, teacher professional development, and extra staffing in the form of local reading coaches.

The two-year evaluation of REA was designed as a mixed methods study, emphasizing multiple data sources for primary purposes of triangulation and enhanced validity of inferences (DeStefano, Hammer, & Ryan, 2003; Ryan, DeStefano, & Greene, 2001). In particular, the evaluation used multiple methods in assessing implementation of the REA model. "Classroom instructional practices will be represented by local teachers' perceptions . . . data from independent observations of instruction . . . and ratings of student work assembled in school portfolios" (Ryan et al., 2001, pp. 19–20). Consistent with a triangulation intent, all of these measures were organized around the six principles of early reading that formed the substantive basis for the REA program.

In an enhancement of this original purpose, a subgroup of the evaluation team undertook a mixed methods analysis of the program implementation data, focusing on the classroom observation and teacher survey data (as the portfolio data collection was still in process at that time). The primary analytic question was an open one—what can be learned about the extent and quality of REA implementation from a joint analysis of the various data sources? This analysis well illustrates the iterative nature of interactive mixed methods data analysis, the considerable value of working with a team on this kind of analysis, and the spirit of adventure that can substantially enhance the results. In fact, in a conference presentation of the analytic process and findings, the team called their experience "our mixed methods journey" (Kallemeyn, Hammer, Zhu, DeStefano, & Greene, 2003). Using this metaphor, highlights from this analysis are presented next.

First, each member of the team selected one implementation data set to work with—Rongchun Zhu worked with the teacher survey data, Leanne Kallemeyn with the quantitative classroom observation data, and Victoria Hammer with the qualitative classroom observer notes. Second, the team decided to use the classification of sites (districts) into categories of high, medium, and low implementation as a *vehicle to initiate and facilitate the analysis,* not because this classification was of inherent interest and value. The interesting questions here were these: What basis was used for classifying sites into high, medium, and low implementation for each data set? Did the classificatory schemes yield similar or different results? And what sense could be made of patterns of both congruence and dissonance? Third, each team member began the journey by "traveling alone" and conducted the classificatory analysis on his or her own data set, striving to honor the rules of rigor and evidence in that methodological tradition while simultaneously anticipating the need to converse with the other data sets. These solo journeys featured the following highly creative and adventuresome analytic work:

- In working with the teacher survey data, Zhu created a set of rules, rooted in the logic of confidence intervals, for classifying each site as high, medium, or low implementation (for each early reading principle) based on its distance from the overall mean. Then, Zhu used the pattern of these deviations across the six reading principles to classify each site.

■ In analyzing the quantitative classroom observation data, Kallemeyn used a rule-guided visual analysis of bar graphs representing the extent of implementation of each reading principle in each site to sort the sites into the categories of high, medium, and low implementation.

■ In analyzing the qualitative classroom observer notes, Hammer sought to honor the contextual and holistic nature of observer perceptions and thus focused on the observers' accounts of classroom activities, teacher pedagogical strategies, salient contextual features, and unique characteristics of each observed site. Her classification system incorporated all of these strands of the data.

Fourth, the team "crossed paths" to share and compare the results of their site classifications. (This was actually an iterative process, involving several returns to the separate analyses and then back to the conversation, and back and forth several times.) Finally, a chart that identified the classifications of each site by each analyst was prepared (see Table 8.3). Extensive discussion of this chart—not to resolve the discrepancies but to learn from them—yielded a set of site and implementation characteristics believed to be importantly influential in the REA program. These included, for example, the centralized or decentralized nature of the program implementation leadership, the degree to which extant programs in each site align with the REA principles of early reading, and the degree of administrative knowledge of and support for the REA program. Without this mixed methods analysis, these insights would not have been generated.

Flexibility and Practical Judgment in Analyzing Data on Family Involvement in the School Transition Study

The final example of an instructive mixed methods data analysis illustrates the limitations of mixed methods theory in the midst of an adventuresome exploration about a complex issue in a complicated data set. The researchers in this case developed a thoughtful plan for their analysis, based on many of the ideas shared in this chapter. Yet they reflectively observed that

> studying different analytic models in advance and setting up collaborative team processes did not prepare us for the messiness and pragmatically driven nature of our analysis. . . . Our analytic tracks [those of the various team members] crossed over frequently as expected but not when we thought they would nor how we thought they would nor for the same reasons as anticipated. (Weiss, Kreider, Mayer, Hencke, & Vaughan, 2005, p. 55)

Excerpts from this analytic adventure follow. (See also Weiss, Mayer, Kreider, Vaughan, Dearing, Hencke, & Pinto, 2003, for additional discussion of the substantive findings of this analysis, and Greene, Kreider, & Mayer, 2005, for additional discussion of the mixed methods framework for the overall study.)

TABLE 8.3. **Site-level Implementation of the REA Reading Principles, by Data Set.**

Clusters	Class Observation Quantitative	Class Observation Qualitative	Teacher Survey	Overall
High	Site B	Site B		Site B
		Site E		
	Site F	Site F	Site F	Site F
		Site J	Site J	Site J
		Site G		
High/Medium			Site H	Site E
Medium	Site A			
			Site B	
			Site D	
	Site G		Site G	Site G?
	Site H			Site H?
	Site I		Site I	
Medium/Low	Site D			Site D
				Site I
Low	Site C	Site C	Site C	Site C
		Site A	Site A	Site A
		Site D		
		Site H		
		Site I		
Unidentified	Site E		Site E	
	Site J			

Source: Kallemeyn et al., 2003, reprinted with permission.

The data for this analysis came from the School Transition Study (STS), a large, mixed methods longitudinal study that followed approximately four hundred ethnically diverse children in low-income families from kindergarten through fifth grade (in the late 1990s). The study aimed ambitiously to "understand low-income children's successful pathways through middle childhood and through the school, family, and community contexts in which they live and learn" (Weiss et al., 2005, p. 47). The mixed methods design of the study included annual structured interviews with children's caregivers and teachers and the collection of academic and social indicators of achievement from the children's schools. A two-year ethnographic component studied in more depth a sample of twenty-three children when they were in first and second grade. These data included caregiver, teacher, and child interviews; community studies; and participant observation.

The researchers' prior interest in the meanings and influence of family involvement in children's developmental pathways, in particular their educational pathways, was piqued by repeated references in the STS interview data to the importance of parents' work. These interview references suggested positive connections between parent work and involvement, contrary to available evidence. So the researchers embarked on a mixed methods analysis of the nature and role of parental employment in the larger framework of family involvement. Their analytic plan was guided by the Li et al. (2000) model of crossover tracks analysis and also included planned and structured team meetings and reflections, as well as a strong mixed methods way of thinking. "A stance of openness and discovery is inherent in mixed-methods work . . . openness to other views and perspectives [including] not just rival explanatory hypotheses but more profoundly rival ways of thinking and valuing" (Weiss et al., 2005, p. 52).

At the outset, descriptive analyses of the quantitative data set (which focused on school-centric indicators of family involvement, such as attending parent-teacher conferences), yielded "varied and high levels of involvement to further explore" (p. 53). These analyses also "showed parental work as a perceived barrier to family involvement, especially through the time demands it imposed" (p. 53). Yet the initial qualitative analyses, which generated portraits of the work life of case study mothers, revealed a different picture. "Several working mothers described work as a resource for parenting, child learning, and family involvement. . . . Some mothers even took their children to work on a regular basis" (p. 54).

Back to the quantitative data: these qualitative findings generated the construction of several composite variables, from survey scales and factor analyses, to represent the combined time demands of mothers' employment and mothers' educational training (maternal work and education), as well as two family involvement variables—involvement in school and home teaching, or the ways in which mothers supported their child's education at home. Univariate and multivariate analyses with these composite variables indicated that maternal work and education (time demands) "was significantly associated not only with school involvement but also with broadly defined family involvement, which included both school and home activities" (p. 55). To make sense of and interpret these and other quantitative results, the case study members of the team relied increasingly on "their stores of internalized qualitative case study knowledge" (p. 56).

Building on this quantitative analysis, the qualitative data were further analyzed across cases to generate better understanding of the meanings and character of school and family involvement, and especially the role of work therein. The result was a typology of maternal strategies for being involved in their child's education. The categories included developing a complex "kith and kin network" that helped mothers support their child's learning and use their workplace as a home base for a variety of involvement activities usually performed in other settings, such as telephone conferences with their child's teacher.

Among the reflections offered by this team of analysts are the following:

Our contrasting findings about maternal work as a barrier and an opportunity for family involvement underscored the value of mixing methods. . . . This contrast led to new learning beyond what "everyone knows"—that work poses obstacles to involvement—to an understanding that work can also . . . support involvement at school, open up new avenues for family involvement, and contribute to children's learning beyond school walls. (p. 61)

Through this [mixed methods analysis] process we learned to be open to discovery . . . but also to be pragmatic and tolerate complexities. . . . [We learned] that mixed-methods approaches could only be rough guides and that intentional [analytic] designs might have to give way to real-world problems of data availability and deadlines. Accordingly, we developed a sense of our mixed-methods work as a dynamic, hands-on process, guided only very generally by mixed-methods analytic models. (p. 61)

These reflections underscore the craftspersonship required in mixed methods data analysis. As emphasized in Chapter Seven on mixed methods design, decisions about mixed methods practice involve thoughtful use of theoretical ideas, wise practical judgment, and considerable artistry.

REPRISE

This chapter has presented a portrait of interactive mixed methods data analysis as an adventurous journey. One can plan for this journey by mapping possible routes, scheduling rest stops for checking on progress and well-being, and traveling collaboratively and respectfully with others, even as parts of the journey may also be traversed solo. Yet the plans can only be rough guides, as the data landscapes being explored may present unanticipated challenges—as in missing data or a looming report deadline—*as well as* unanticipated opportunities—as in an empirical puzzle that needs further pursuit or a strand of especially enlightening evidence.

On the one hand, this portrait of mixed methods analysis is not all that different from analyses in other methodological traditions. All analyses are in part detective work and insight. On the other, the unique potential of mixed methods social inquiry is its promise of better understanding. So the mixed methods analysis team should embark on their analytic journey in ways perhaps a bit more open, flexible, creative, and adventuresome than those of other inquirers—with routes more imagined than fixed, with guideposts drawn from the travels of others (many recounted in this chapter), and with a commitment, if not fully to a mixed methods way of thinking, then more modestly to the importance of diverse ways of knowing and valuing.

CHAPTER

JUDGING THE QUALITY OF MIXED METHODS SOCIAL INQUIRY

PRACTICAL ISSUES of quality are the focus of this part of the mixed methods journey. The traveler will engage with the challenges of warranting inquiry claims from studies that include a mix of methods representing different inquiry traditions—and thus different ideas about what constitutes a valid or credible inquiry finding. Ideas related to inference quality and to legitimation are showcased in this chapter, along with additional ideas for practices that mixed methods inquirers can use to assess the quality and defensibility of their own inquiry findings. The traveler will be encouraged to add all of these ideas to his or her toolkit, along with a commitment to trying them out in practice, critically and reflectively.

■ ■ ■

When different forms of data, different kinds of methods, and, particularly, different mental models, or assumptive stances about the social world and social knowledge, are mixed in social inquiry, then how is the quality of that inquiry assessed and judged? What criteria or standards are employed to gauge the level and nature of confidence one can have in the data? What arguments are mounted to persuade readers of the warrants and justifications for the inquiry results?

In particular, if readers of this volume are engaged by a mixed methods way of thinking, which inherently values difference of multiple kinds, how are such differences respected when making judgments of inquiry quality? For example, some traditions of inquiry are judged by the representativeness of the samples and the generality of the inferences. Others are judged by the richness of the samples and the contextual meaningfulness of the inferences. And still others are judged by the actionability of the inquiry process and especially the knowledge generated. In mixed methods inquiry, are these different criteria and judgments also mixed, and if so, how? Or are there alternative ways of approaching the challenges of judging quality in mixed methods social inquiry?

There are few significant responses to these challenges of judging inquiry quality in the mixed methods literature. So, once again, adventuresome readers are encouraged to put their creativity and ingenuity to this task. Meanwhile, this chapter offers a way of thinking about inquiry quality in mixed methods inquiry, reviews extant work in this domain, and includes selected examples.

THINKING ABOUT INQUIRY CRITERIA IN MIXED METHODS SOCIAL INQUIRY

Mixed methods social inquiry that is conducted from *within* a given paradigm, mental model, or methodological tradition does not present serious challenges of validation, justification, or warrant, because conceptualizations of quality are rooted in philosophical frameworks and their assumptions. What constitutes defensible methods and warranted knowledge are fundamentally philosophical matters. From such philosophical assumptions come the methodological criteria, processes, and arguments about the quality of the methods used and the warrants or justification for the inferences reached. That is, "methodologies are discourses comprised of epistemological assumptions, principles, and procedures through which social scientists construct the aim of understanding" (Schwandt, 2004, p. 34). So in a study with only one paradigm or mental model, there is only one set of guidelines, criteria, and processes for warranting method and knowledge claim. Different understandings of inquiry quality are not being mixed in such a study.

To use some familiar examples, in a classic post-positivist world view or paradigm, objectivity—defined as the minimization of inquirer and methodological bias in the quest for truth—is considered a major criterion for inquiry quality. And methodological traditions that use a post-positivist framework have numerous procedures and techniques both for minimizing bias and error and for assessing how free the data actually are from such bias. These include standardization of measures and their administration, estimates of reliability and validity coefficients, as well as statistical adjustments for unwanted variation. In contrast, objectivity in some feminist traditions means the challenging of prevailing but false assumptions (such as the biological inferiority of women) through an intentional stance of political nonneutrality (Harding, 1993). In ideologically oriented inquiry frameworks—such as participatory action research (Kemmis & McTaggart, 2000) and democratic evaluation (House & Howe, 1999)—objectivity is supplanted by political ideals of fairness and equity, such that a good study is one that advances the interests and well-being of the most underserved. Some even argue that such inquiry is, in fact, more objective in the sense of being more impartial and fair, because it includes and gives voice to all legitimate perspectives and interests, rather than just the privileged few (House & Howe, 1999).

And, of course, there are philosophical frameworks and mental models in which objectivity is viewed as unattainable, given the intertwined relationship of the knower and the known. In these frameworks, including interpretivism and constructivism, warranted knowledge is attained not by distance or the protective shields of sophisticated methods, but rather by closeness, engagement, and sufficient time on site to understand the inside or emic perspective. In these frameworks, subjectivity is accepted as an inevitable strand of meaningful contextual understanding. And in hermeneutic traditions, inquiry is less a matter of producing scientific knowledge (distant or near) and more a dialogic process of understanding self and other, invoking aesthetics, imagination, and craftspersonship (Schwandt, 2004).

So in what kinds of mixed methods studies are paradigms, mental models, and methodological traditions mixed? This answer to this question depends, of course, on the individual study and individual inquirer—as I have said before, mixed methods practice is so much more complicated than mixed methods theory. Mixing at the level of paradigm or mental model is an inquirer decision, rather than a prescription of a particular mixed methods design or mix of methods. In general, however, the mixed methods paradigm stances presented in Chapter Five offer some rough guidance on this issue. Mixing at the paradigm or mental model level is precluded by definition for the *purist stance*, and required by definition for the *dialectic stance*. Mixing paradigms or mental models is less likely for the *a-paradigmatic stance*—as it is context, not philosophy, that drives methodological decisions in this stance—and for the *alternative paradigm stance*, as this stance intentionally adopts a single paradigm in which mixing at multiple levels is welcomed and not intrinsically problematic. Although the *complementary strengths stance* includes multiple paradigms, there is little mixing of them in order to maintain the integrity of each. Finally, the *substantive theory stance* could likely benefit from a mix of paradigms and mental models, but such mixing is a matter of inquirer discretion and choice.

For those mixed methods studies in which paradigms, mental models, and methodological traditions are being mixed, how then should we think about the challenges of inquiry quality? Here are two ideas.

1. For warranting the *quality of method* and the data obtained, adhere to the quality criteria and procedures of the tradition in which the method is being implemented. In survey methodology, for example, such quality criteria include minimization of response bias, maximization of the number of respondents, and measurement

considerations of reliability and validity. In participant observation, such criteria include appropriate balance of participant and observer roles, lengthy time on site, keen perceptive acuity, and reporting of observations in rich, descriptive contextualized detail.

2. For warranting the *quality of the inferences*, conclusions, and interpretations made, adopt a multiplistic stance that (a) focuses on the available data support for the inferences, using data of multiple and diverse kinds; (b) could include criteria or stances from different methodological traditions; (c) considers warrants for inquiry inferences a matter of persuasive argument, in addition to a matter of fulfilling established criteria; and (d) attends to the nature and extent of the better understanding that is reached with this mixed methods design, as that is the overall aim of mixed methods inquiry.

The idea of focusing on inference quality in judging the quality of mixed methods work is attributable to Teddlie and Tashakkori (2003). Their ideas about inference quality are presented in the next section. These ideas offer thoughtful starting points, in the form of various kinds or dimensions of inference quality, for engaging the challenges of warrant in mixed methods social inquiry. The multiplistic stance about inference quality that I just outlined incorporates Teddlie and Tashakkori's good thinking and also extends this thinking beyond a criterial approach to warranting inferences to include deliberative practices as well. This multiplistic stance further includes warrants anchored in the fundamental aim of mixed methods inquiry, and that is the better understanding of social and human phenomena.

INFERENCE QUALITY IN MIXED METHODS SOCIAL INQUIRY

Teddlie and Tashakkori (2003) consider an inference to be the investigator's interpretations of the study results. Inferences are study outcomes or conclusions; they can take the form of explanations, understandings, or other accounts of what was learned from the study. The term is attractive in a mixed methods context because it is generically applicable to multiple inquiry traditions.

Inference quality, then, is "the mixed methods term for the accuracy with which we have drawn both our inductively and deductively derived conclusions from a study" (Teddlie & Tashakkori, 2003, p. 36). (I must observe that the term *accuracy* in this definition suggests a realist ontology and a relatively conventional idea about the purpose of social inquiry. Likely omitted from this conceptualization are ideological, action-oriented, and postmodern social inquiry traditions. This fits with Teddlie and Tashakkori's concentration in their mixed methods work on customary understandings of basic qualitative and quantitative methodological frameworks, signaled in the foregoing definition by the use of both inductive and deductive reasoning, respectively. I would like to also note that throughout this discussion of inference quality these authors rely heavily on conventional criteria for quantitative inquiry, as presented in

Cook and Campbell, 1979, and on the trustworthiness criteria for qualitative inquiry articulated by Lincoln and Guba, 1985.)

Teddlie and Tashakkori further distinguish between "two important aspects of inference quality. The first we call *design quality*, which comprises the standards for the evaluation of the methodological rigor of the mixed methods research, and the second we call *interpretive rigor*, which comprises the standards for the evaluation of the accuracy or authenticity of the conclusions" (p. 37, emphasis in original). These two aspects parallel the distinction I made earlier between warranting the quality of method and warranting the quality of inference or interpretation. I also agree with these authors that extant criteria and standards from existing traditions can be used to assess design quality or the quality of method. Warranting study inferences, or interpretive rigor, however, is another matter altogether.

In this regard, Teddlie and Tashakkori offer ideas for more specific criteria related to mixed methods inference quality (see also Tashakkori & Teddlie, 2006). These include the following:

■ *Conceptual consistency* refers to the "degree to which the inferences are consistent with each other and with the known state of knowledge and theory" (p. 40).

■ *Interpretive agreement* refers to the consistency of interpretations across people, including scholars as well as the members of the setting being studied.

■ *Interpretive distinctiveness* refers to "the degree to which the inferences are distinctively different from other possible interpretations of the results and the rival explanations are ruled out" (p. 41). (Ruling out rival explanations is a time-honored practice in experimental inquiry but is less customary in many qualitative traditions, which often seek understanding rather than explanation.)

LEGITIMATION AS QUALITY IN MIXED METHODS SOCIAL INQUIRY

Onwuegbuzie and Johnson (2006) offer a variation of Teddlie and Tashakkori's conceptualization of mixed methods inference quality. Their argument is rooted in their own particular conceptualization of mixed methods inquiry as inquiry that combines complementary strengths and nonoverlapping weaknesses of quantitative and qualitative research. Their work concentrates on the concept of *legitimation* as a conceptual framework for mixed methods validity. Legitimation encompasses warrants for the quality of both method and inference and is construed as both an outcome of and a continuous process in mixed methods inquiry. This legitimation framework builds on the prior development of legitimation models for both quantitative and qualitative inquiry by Onwuegbuzie (2003) and Onwuegbuzie and Leech (in press), respectively. Onwuegbuzie and Johnson position their legitimation framework as directly engaging the mixed methods challenges of integrating data and interpretations from very different stances, methods, samples, and analyses.

Onwuegbuzie and Johnson offer nine different types of legitimation:

1. Samples for purposes of making statistical generalizations from research samples (qualitative and quantitative) to larger populations

2. The inclusion of both inside and outside perspectives

3. The degree to which one method well compensates for weaknesses in another

4. Inferences in a sequential design, specifically that the inferences do not arise singularly from the sequence used

5. Conversions or transformations of data from one type to another

6. The (single or multiple) paradigm assumptions being included in the study

7. The cognitive commensurability of different worldviews

8. The methodological soundness of each method used

9. The appropriate engagement with the politics of mixing methods in the context at hand

Each of these legitimation types is presented as a discussion of its distinctive complexities in mixed methods inquiry. For example, the sampling issues include the challenges of generalization when the inference is based on the integration of data from a large representative sample and a nonoverlapping small purposive sample. These legitimation ideas are richly complex and offer considerable potential to meaningfully inform the continued development of responses to the challenges of warrant in mixed methods social inquiry.

WARRANTING THE QUALITY OF INFERENCES IN MIXED METHODS INQUIRY

The discussion now turns to my own thinking about the criteria and processes for warranting the quality of inferences from mixed methods social inquiry. Like Teddlie and Tashakkori, I construe an inference as the overall conclusion, interpretation, or learning achieved in a study. As presented previously, my ideas about warranting the quality of the inferences in mixed methods inquiry feature the adoption of a multiplistic stance that (1) focuses on the available data support for the inferences, using data of multiple and diverse kinds; (2) could include criteria or stances from different methodological traditions; (3) considers warrants for inquiry inferences a matter of persuasive argument, in addition to a matter of fulfilling established criteria; and (4) attends to the nature and extent of the better understanding that is reached with this mixed methods design, as that is the overall aim of mixed methods inquiry. I will attend to each of these considerations in the discussion that follows.

Providing Data Support for Inferences

In Chapter Eight on data analysis, Mary Lee Smith's (1997) adaptation of Fred Erickson's (1986) "warranted assertion" approach to analyzing qualitative data was presented as a strong candidate for mixed methods analyses for purposes of directly generating inquiry conclusions. In this approach, an iterative and critical review of all of the data available in a study—*without prejudice to data type or source*—is used to establish study assertions or conclusions. *Data of all types* are then assembled and displayed in support of each assertion.

I believe that this idea of presenting the data that support a given mixed methods inference is of generally valuable use, in contexts beyond those in which this particular mixed methods analysis approach is used. In particular, depending on the inquirer's mixed methods stance, purpose, and design, data of different types could be presented without prejudice as to source and only on their merits to inform and substantiate the inference. Such a presentation could itself support particular mixed methods stances and purposes, notably those with dialectic, interactive, and integrative intent.

Including Criteria or Stances from Different Methodological Traditions

When warranting the inferences attained from a mixed methods data analysis involving data gathered in multiple methodological traditions, it is also possible to use criteria that are resident in one tradition or another. Yet this would not be an automatic or conventional application of inquiry criteria, but rather a more nuanced way of judging the quality of an integrated set of inquiry findings from multiple perspectives. That is, it would not likely make sense to judge the quality of an integrated set of inferences by applying within-paradigm criteria as they are usually applied, because neither the form of the analysis nor the form of the inferences would conform to usual standards. But it still may be relevant and useful to use the concepts represented in criteria from various inquiry traditions, again in a more nuanced way, for judging inference quality. Here are two different arguments for doing this.

First, also discussed in Chapter Eight was the idea of using aspects of the analytic framework of one methodological tradition in the analysis of data from another tradition. The examples of this analytic idea provided included the use of traditionally quantitative matrices and displays for qualitative data (Miles & Huberman, 1994); the use of Boolean algebra to jointly analyze data from cases and from variables (Ragin, 1987); and the use of the concepts of legitimation and representation—substantially from interpretive traditions—as anchoring rationales for a mixed methods data analysis framework (Onwuegbuzie & Teddlie, 2003). This same idea could be applied to judging the quality of inferences from mixed data analyses. Aspects of the *criterial frameworks of multiple inquiry traditions* could be applied to help judge inference quality. These would need to be aspects of importance to the respective inquiry traditions, but probably not aspects that represent one pole of long-standing dualisms in philosophical thought. For how can an inference be simultaneously objective—free from inquirer bias and predispositions—and subjective—representing an engaged and contextually embedded inquirer stance?

Valerie Caracelli and I identified several characteristics of traditional interpretivist and post-positivist inquiry traditions

> that constitute important facets of [these] inquiry traditions and therefore war-rant our attention and respect but that are also not logically irreconcilable when juxtaposed with contrasting characteristics. Contrasts, conflicts, and tensions between different . . . findings are an expected, even welcome dimension of mixed-method inquiry, for it is in the tension that the boundaries of what is known are most generatively challenged and stretched. The analytic space created by the tension, however, must offer the possibility of coordination, integration, and synthesis. [Thus] the constitutive characteristics must be other than irrecon-cilable philosophical assumptions. (Greene & Caracelli, 1997a)

Some of the characteristics we identified pertain to the criteria for judging the quality and soundness of inquiry inferences. For the interpretivist and post-positivist traditions, these include the following:

- Particularity and generality

- Closeness and distance

- Meaning and causality

- The unusual and the representative

- The diversity within the range and the central tendency of the average

- Micro- and macro-lenses, or setting and structural perspectives

- Insider and outsider viewpoints

- The contextualized understanding of local meanings and the general identification of recurring regularities

Our argument at that time for this idea fits the current argument very well.

> A mixed method[s] study that combines these two traditions would strive for knowl-edge claims that are grounded in the lives of the participants studied and that also have some generality to other participants and other contexts, that enhance under-standing of both the unusual and the typical case, that isolate factors of particular significance while also integrating the whole, that are full of emic meaning at the same time as they offer causal connections of broad significance. (Greene & Caracelli, 1997a, p. 13)

A second idea for using inquiry criteria from different traditions for warranting inferences from mixed methods studies involves logical and philosophical challenges to historic dualisms themselves. Clearly, those advancing an alternative paradigm for mixed methods inquiry, or social inquiry more broadly, do just this, as illustrated in chapters Four and Five when discussing American pragmatism and a transformative, emancipatory framework for social inquiry. Another form of challenge to dualistic thinking is to argue for a reconceptualization of traditionally opposed inquiry characteristics and warrants more as continua than as either/or competitors. Evaluation theorist Michael Patton has done this as part of his argument for a "paradigm of choices" in evaluation practice (1980). He argues, for example, that program evaluators do not have choose whether to have standardized, quantitative measures of constructs or contextualized, emergent conversations with inquiry participants. Rather, both standardization and contextualization can be conceptualized as continua, so that a given study can partake of both kinds of measurement and data collection.

A recent and more elaborated argument in this genre was offered by Ercikan & Roth (2006). These educational researchers argue first that quantity and quality are inherent characteristics of phenomena in diverse natural and social fields, and then that objectivity and subjectivity are inevitable strands of both qualitative and quantitative social inquiry traditions. In a move "beyond dichotomies," Ercikan and Roth then reframe eight core "knowledge characteristics" of educational inquiry as continua along a dimension of low-level to high-level inference. These eight characteristics are standardization, contingency, universality, particularity, distance, being affected, abstraction, and concretization. With this framework, "the aim of education research should be to produce research results that are characterized simultaneously by high and low inference levels, with results that include the standardizing, universalizing, distancing, and abstracting aspects of knowledge, as well as the contingent, particular, and concrete aspects" (p. 22). These authors conclude their argument by restating the priority of the research question over method and by encouraging researchers from diverse traditions to work together.

Considering Warrants for Inquiry Inferences a Matter of Persuasive Argument as Well as Fulfilling Criteria

This multiplistic approach to warranting the inferences from mixed methods social inquiry further advances the importance of warrants that are a matter of deliberation, in addition to warrants that are a matter of the procedural application of criteria. The rationale for this stance is rooted in Thomas Schwandt's eloquent appeal for a social science (particularly evaluation) framed by the tenets of "practical philosophy," as the nonfoundational heir to outdated and, for the most part, discarded foundational philosophies (notably logical positivism) (Schwandt, 2002). Social inquirers guided by practical philosophy (1) seek not explanatory knowledge but better understanding of *praxis* (or the human actions and practices of everyday life); (2) must attend to the moral, ethical, and political dimensions of human endeavor, because these are central to praxis; and (3) envision the "rationality of everyday life . . . *as intrinsically dialogical and communicative*" (Schwandt, 1996, p. 62, emphasis added). Social inquiry guided by practical philosophy is descriptive and normative, seeking to enable practitioners to refine the rationality of their own practices through data-informed critical reflection and dialogue. This form of social inquiry is thus collaborative and cogenerative, inquiry *with* rather than *on* participants, deliberations *with* participants rather than *about* them.

With a turn toward social inquiry as practical philosophy, argued Schwandt (1996), judgments about the goodness of the practice and its inferences must seek an alternative to the criterial approach to judging quality and warranting inferences. This is because the criterial approach is historically rooted in foundationalist epistemologies, which used criteria to establish a firm foundation for scientific knowledge and to distinguish true scientific knowledge from biased knowledge and mere belief. As an alternative to criteria, Schwandt proposed a "guiding ideal" of democracy and several enabling conditions that emphasize deliberation and dialogue because, again, social inquiry as practical philosophy is intrinsically dialogic and communicative. Among these conditions is this view:

> The activity of deliberation is inescapably rhetorical in character. We aim to persuade other interpreters of a particular interpretation through a discourse that is characterized by qualities such as coherence, expansiveness, interpretive insight, relevance, rhetorical force, beauty and texture of argument, and so forth. The conversation among interpreters is an act of persuasion and involves using language infected by partisan agendas and interests. . . .

> [However] parties to the encounter are not viewed as opponents who seek to expose the weaknesses in each other's arguments. Rather, the conversation begins with the assumption that "the other has something to say to us and to contribute to our understanding. . . . The other is not an adversary or opponent, but a conversational partner" (Bernstein, 1991, p. 337). (Schwandt, 1996, pp. 66–67)

It is indeed consistent with a mixed methods way of thinking to envision dialogues and other conversations held among interested parties regarding the quality of and warrant for particular study inferences. Such dialogues would complement, not replace, the use of multiple forms of inquiry criteria themselves. Such dialogues could engage possible dissonance in judgments yielded by multiple criteria, could assess the consequential or "so what?" character of inquiry conclusions, or could involve a range and variety of people with a vested interest in the matter at hand—conversing with "coherence, expansiveness, interpretive insight, relevance . . . [and] beauty" (Schwandt, 1996, p. 66) and with respect and acceptance, one of the other. The broader literature on dialogue in social inquiry is highly relevant to this set of ideas (for example, Abma, 1998, 2001; Schwandt, 2002).

Attending to the Nature and Extent of the Better Understanding That Is Reached with This Mixed Methods Design

Finally, I propose that the quality of inferences in mixed methods social inquiry be judged by the ways in which and the extent to which the study contributed to better understanding. This is primarily a conceptual challenge but also one of resources.

The conceptual challenge is one of demonstrating that the understandings and insights generated in the mixed methods study would not have been attained with a single methodology. The book edited by Tom Weisner (2005) presents mixed methods studies in the domain of child development. The papers in the book were originally offered at a working conference, orchestrated specifically to showcase empirical examples of mixed methods inquiry that led to conclusions not attainable with a single methodology. This volume thus offers excellent examples of this kind of demonstration. For the most part, the contributors to this volume were able to single out insights and understandings achieved through their mix of methods and to demonstrate just how they were attained. The resource question is also important. With fixed resources, the decision to use more than one kind of method may risk the quality of implementation of each method; for example, in smaller than desired sample sizes (Chen, 1997). Moreover, there is always the important question of when a mixed methods study is not a justifiable choice (Datta, 1997b).

Reprise

The knotty issue of judging the quality of inferences yielded by a study with multiple and interactive assumptions and stances remains a conceptual and procedural challenge. In this chapter, I have offered several different ways of thinking about and engaging with this challenge, not all of which would be expected to be used in a single study. Yet collectively they offer a multiplicity of perspectives on just what constitutes a defensible and warranted inference in social inquiry. They also ideally offer an invitation to invoke imagination and creativity as part of rationality. In these ways they well illustrate a mixed methods way of thinking.

AN ILLUSTRATION

Examples of these various ways of warranting inference quality in mixed methods social inquiry are now offered in a hypothetical adaptation and elaboration of a mixed methods dissertation study. (The illustration is invented because actual examples of these ideas for warranting inference quality remain for future encounters, if then.) Yang Yang (2005) studied the effects of a traditional Tai Chi movement program for seniors using standardized physiological measures, as well as personalized interviews with a purposeful sample of participants who were observed to have especially intense engagement during the six-month program. This example is anchored in Yang's exceptionally thoughtful work, but no parts of the example should be attributed to Yang or interpreted as other than inventive elaborations of his work.

> *Many seniors who are otherwise in fine health are at major risk for falling and breaking a bone (often a hip), or otherwise damaging muscles and tissues, such that their mobility is permanently restricted. This study investigated the beneficial effects of Tai Chi on seniors' balance, stride, and strength. In addition, given the emphasis in traditional Tai Chi on the*

*movement and channeling of qigong (which includes mental and spiritual dimensions
like confidence, connectedness, and tranquility), the researcher was also interested in
participants' experiences of these broader and potentially deeper benefits. The study used
a wait-list comparison group. Seniors who agreed to participate in the study were randomly assigned to the main intervention or to the same Tai Chi program that started six
months later (n = 50 in each at the start, though attrition from the comparison group was
greater than attrition from the treatment group). All participants in both groups were
administered a battery of physiological measures and a short survey at pretest, at midpoint of the intervention, and again at posttest. The physiological measures focused on
balance, stride, agility, flexibility, and strength. The short survey gathered seniors' self-
reports of the kind and extent of both social and cognitive activities in which they had
participated during the previous week. At the end of the six months of intervention, a
small sample of five Tai Chi participants who were observed to have especially intense
engagement in the program were also personally interviewed, with a narrative approach
that asked, "Tell me the story of your participation in the Tai Chi program."*

Primary inferences from the study included the following two:

1. Participation in Tai Chi afforded seniors sustainable improvements in balance,
    stride, and strength, as well as modest to marked changes in their social and
    cognitive activity patterns, compared with a similar group who did not participate
    in the Tai Chi intervention.

2. For a small group of seniors, participation in Tai Chi can be a life-transforming
    experience, marked most significantly by an integrated and profound sense of
    well-being, permeating all aspects of life, including physical balance and strength,
    social and cognitive engagement, and deep spiritual renewal.

Illustrations of the ideas just presented for warranting inferences in mixed methods studies will be provided for these two hypothetical inferences.

Inference: Participation in Tai Chi afforded seniors sustainable improvements in balance,
stride, and strength, as well as modest to marked changes in their social and cognitive
activity patterns, compared with a similar group who did not participate in the Tai Chi
intervention.

Warranting this inference by providing available data support could include the
following:

-   Controlling for the small demographic differences in the two groups, the aver-
    age scores of seniors who participated in Tai Chi were significantly higher on the
    balance, stride, and strength measures than were the average scores of seniors in

the comparison group. This difference was noticeable at the program midpoint and sustained through the end of the program. And there were no average differences at pretest.

▪ Seniors who participated in Tai Chi reported a modest to significant increase in the frequency and variety of their social and cognitive activities while in the program, whereas comparison group seniors reported maintaining a similar level and variety of social and cognitive activities. These differences were again noticeable at midpoint and sustained through the end of the program.

▪ Senior interviewees were enthusiastic about what one called "major changes in my daily quality of life," attributed to their Tai Chi participation. These changes included a dramatic increase in physical activity—for example, walking daily around an exercise track—as well as significantly more active engagement in family and community activities; for example, caring for grandchildren once a week and volunteering at a local library.

Inference: For a small group of seniors, participation in Tai Chi can be a life-transforming experience, marked most significantly by an integrated and profound sense of well-being, permeating all aspects of life, including physical balance and strength, social and cognitive engagement, and deep spiritual renewal.

Warranting this inference by providing available data support could include the following:

▪ A highly distinguishing feature of the Tai Chi stories told by the interviewees (who were all intensely engaged in the program) was their integrated and holistic character. When recounting the profound differences Tai Chi has made in their lives, these participants blended and interwove in ways not separable the various physical, socioemotional, intellectual, and spiritual ("life affirming") dimensions and activities of their daily life.

▪ Scores on the balance, stride, and strength measures for the five interviewees were, without exception, the highest in the treatment group at midpoint and posttest, whereas they were near the average of the treatment group at pretest.

Warranting this inference by including criteria or stances from different methodological traditions might take the following form:

Although not distinguishable from others in the treatment group at the outset of the intervention, the five interviewees reported a remarkable life-transforming experience during their Tai Chi participation. Their own narratives are linguistically and rhetorically compelling and again marked by the integrative and holistic character of their experience. Moreover, the pattern of their scores on all other measures in the study exhibits similar interconnections. Nonparametric indicators of relationship among all scores are consistently strong for this subgroup of participants and consistently stronger than these relational indicators for all others in the treatment group.

Warranting both inferences through deliberation, in addition to fulfilling criteria might include the following excerpt from a follow-up discussion among a handful of seniors who participated in the Tai Chi program and the medical staff at the nursing home where they reside:

> *Mr. A: You know, I haven't felt this good in about ten years! I used to walk every day, but I stopped walking . . . hmm, I don't remember when. But now, I can't tell you how enjoyable it is to get out there again in the sunshine and warm breeze and feel so nourished by mother nature.*

> *Mrs. B: And I started doing those Sudoku puzzles, you know, the ones with the numbers. I used to love to do puzzles, but couldn't really muster the energy to do them after a while. Now, I join the lunchtime Sudoku competition, which is more of a collaboration than a competition. But I still love it when I get one all on my own!*

> *Nurse C: What do you think accounts for this increase in energy? You know, both of you have stopped taking your energy medication, yet I can just look at you and see that you have more energy than before and that you are doing things you haven't done in a long time.*

> *Dr. D: I wonder if maybe it has something to do with blood flow and better circulation. I was reading some recent research out of China that suggested this was one medical explanation for the benefits of Tai Chi.*

> *Mr. A: Well, now that you mention that, I haven't experienced the numbness or cramping in my legs that I had earlier in the year. But I think it also has to do with mental energy and acuity. I seem to simply be able to notice and pay attention to things more and better than I did before Tai Chi. And lots of these things that I notice catch my attention, and I get engaged. I think that is one reason I enjoy my walks so much. I really attend to what is around me when I am walking.*

> *Nurse C: Maybe it is like being more present in the world, more connected to people and actions around you?*

> *Mrs. B: Yes, exactly! It's like feeling part of a global web of interconnections, with strands in all directions full of possibility and even mystery.*

> *Dr. D: Can we bottle it and share it with others?*

Warranting both inferences by attending to the nature and extent of the better understanding that is reached with this mixed methods design could include the following argument:

> This study's main inferences—that Tai Chi can significantly and sustainably enhance life quality for some seniors, in a moderate to transformative way—were attained primarily because of the combination of methods used. Absent one method or another, the study could have identified the comparative physiological benefits of Tai Chi on the average or the contextualized transformative potential of Tai Chi for selected seniors. In combination, these methods enabled assessments of both the magnitude of measured and experienced differences as well as their contextual meaningfulness for the seniors involved. In particular, the mix of methods helped to identify and substantiate the integrated and holistic nature of these life changes and their enhancing or transforming import for some seniors' daily lives.

In the next and final chapter on mixed methods practice, issues of writing and reporting the work of mixed methods inquirers are taken up and discussed. A brief concluding chapter brings this journey to a close.

CHAPTER

WRITING UP AND REPORTING MIXED METHODS SOCIAL INQUIRY

THE JOURNEY nears its end in this chapter on writing up mixed methods studies. Like other territories of mixed methods practice, this one engages the challenges of respecting multiple traditions of social inquiry while simultaneously endeavoring to integrate them in the process of writing up and reporting inquiry results. These multiple inquiry traditions have their own modes of persuasive writing and voice, not all of which are congruent one with the other. Ideas of multiple representational forms are offered in this chapter as one valuable strategy to both respect and integrate different writing traditions.

▪ ▪ ▪

It was 9:00 AM on Wednesday. The HIV/AIDS work group of the Foundation was meeting in the seventh floor conference room to discuss the annual evaluation reports on the Foundation's extensive work in HIV/AIDS education, prevention, and treatment around the globe, with a major concentration of resources in Africa. Over the past two years, the Foundation had funded several new and exciting initiatives, many of them developed for Africa by African nongovernmental organizations (NGOs), and the HIV/AIDS group was especially eager to learn about the progress of these initiatives this past year and if indeed they were demonstrating their promise for meaningful and sustainable success.

The meeting began as usual with brief summary comments about the evaluation reports from each regional leader. Also as usual, these reports concentrated on the Foundation's own set of approved indicators of program quality. Sojung, the leader of the Foundation's far east Asia region, observed that the village health organizations in the rural areas of southeastern Asia had become considerably more active in AIDS education and treatment over the past year, and this was at least in part attributable to the Foundation's concerted outreach to rural areas over the past few years. Henrik, the leader for the western Europe region, commented that the new multimedia programs for youth funded by the Foundation were showing early success in knowledge gains and in self-reported decreases in risky behaviors among the program participants. Rose, a coleader for the African region, cited several population health indicators monitored by Foundation evaluations. The rate of the spread of HIV in western Africa remained steady, which was very good news compared to many years of increase. Yet the number of AIDS orphans in southern Africa continues to grow with each assessment, a report greeted with genuine sadness around the table.

Then Robert, the other coleader of the African region, said, "Even in the face of this continuing tragedy of so many, many children orphaned by this scourge on the earth, there are some stories of hope in some of these evaluation reports. These are the reports from some of the new programs we just recently funded. As you recall, a number of them ambitiously endeavor to 'do something' meaningful about the AIDS orphan crisis. Here I have copied a couple of excerpts from these reports to share with you. The first is a photo-essay of three orphaned siblings being welcomed into their new family, and the second is a set of collages of artwork and stories by children in an AIDS orphanage. I realize that these portrayals don't directly capture our quality indicators, but look what powerful information they do convey! The faces of these children in the photos are so poignant—suggesting a profound confusion of rescue and despair. The children's own work, in contrast, is full of bright colors and stories about happy times—they make you smile all over, and they also make you want to know so much more about this orphanage. What are they doing there to engender this kind of optimism in these children? There is something very special about these ways of sharing what is happening on the ground in these projects and about what these experiences mean to some of those involved, even when, or perhaps especially when, these images and stories present a different portrait from the indicator data!"

WRITING UP MIXED METHODS SOCIAL INQUIRY

Mixed methods studies engender a "crisis of representation" . . . all their own as they mandate that researchers/writers communicate across entrenched divides often separating writers from readers, in general, and qualitative from quantitative writers and readers, in particular. (Sandelowski, 2003, p. 321)

In her chapter in the *Handbook of Mixed Methods*, Margarete Sandelowski (2003) offers a very thoughtful and helpful discussion of the challenges of writing up mixed methods social inquiry. Of particular value is her presentation of these challenges as involving quite different communication traditions that incorporate different technical criteria and norms, *as well as* different rhetorical and aesthetic criteria and norms. Sandelowski argues that qualitative and quantitative inquirers, specifically, belong to different "interpretive communities," with different understandings and expectations of a research text or an evaluation report—in particular, what makes such a text or report appealing and persuasive. Mixed methods studies thus "call into question which appeals will produce the most convincing texts" (p. 322), especially when the anticipated readership of such texts itself comprises members from diverse communities.

Sandelowski further observes that the process of writing in traditional quantitative inquiry is "the end product of a clearly defined and sequentially arranged process of inquiry" (p. 329), whereas "in qualitative research, the write-up is conceived less as an end product of inquiry than inquiry in the making . . . to analyze and interpret is to write" (p. 330). In parallel, there is a well-accepted genre—the scientific report—for writing up quantitative studies that includes the use of third-person passive voice and neutral language, the separation of method from findings and findings from interpretation, and a linear model for research inference (p. 329). Yet qualitative inquiry traditions have no such standardized format, even as they commonly embrace a clear statement of inquirer authorship and thus the use of first person, expressive language, and in-depth contextual description. As discussed in the next section, qualitative traditions, inquirers, and inquiry contexts all differ on the ways in which and the extent to which expressive forms drawn from the humanities—poetry, performance, narrative—are welcomed as part of the write-up.

In short, just as the analysis phase of mixed methods inquiry constitutes the heart of the investigative and interpretive process, the writing-up phase constitutes the heart of the communication and presentation process. As all social inquirers know, crafting a text that presents the story of your work that you wish to tell in clear and compelling language is a significant challenge. This challenge is compounded in mixed methods social inquiry by varied traditions of writing and varied norms for just what makes a text compelling.

These challenges are especially acute for mixed methods studies that mix different aspects of paradigmatic traditions or mental models with relative equity of voice and that integrate data during the process of analysis. It is quite important that the write-up from such inquiries be respectful of the different traditions that have contributed to the study, as this respect signals legitimation of multiple ways of knowing and acceptance of diverse experiences, perspectives, and understandings. This respect is fundamental to a mixed methods way of thinking. These writing challenges are less acute—though not absent—when writing up mixed methods studies conducted with a mix of paradigmatic characteristics within a component design, in which the different methods serve different roles or remain separate until the point of drawing conclusions. In some component studies, results may even be reported separately for the different methods. Yet each inquiry tradition still needs to be visibly present and respected in the written product. Finally, writing up mixed methods studies that are conducted *within* a single inquiry tradition, even though there is a mix of methods, is not problematic, as the norms and expectations of that single tradition can be sensibly and defensibly used for the mixed methods write-up.

Good persuasive writing is also a matter of attending to the anticipated information needs and rhetorical customs or familiarities of the audiences for the write-up. A mixed methods study may well have a more diverse set of audiences than a mono-method study, precisely because a mix of methods can speak effectively to the concerns and interests of more than one intended audience. Indeed, sometimes this ability to respond to diverse audiences' information needs is referred to as a political rationale for mixing methods, notably within the evaluation community. So in addition to demonstrating respect for multiple inquiry traditions and ways of knowing, a mixed methods write-up must also convey respect for the various communities that have participated in the inquiry or are intended audiences of the study. Such a text must be accessible, interpretable, and persuasive to these various and multiple communities. In short, writing up a mixed methods study entails both "craft and responsibility" (Sandelowski, 2003, p. 344), or careful attention to the technical and rhetorical norms of multiple traditions and equally careful respect for these multiple traditions and their diverse constituencies and audiences.

In the remainder of this brief chapter, the contemporary "crisis of representation" in applied social inquiry—referred to in the previous quote from Sandelowski—will be discussed and illustrated, with special emphasis on its implications and potential for writing up mixed methods inquiry. The chapter will conclude with two preliminary suggestions of principles for mixed methods writing and reporting. The brevity of the chapter signals the considerable work yet to be done in this domain of writing up and reporting mixed methods inquiry.

REPRESENTATION IN SOCIAL INQUIRY

Representation refers to the portrayal of the findings, conclusions, and interpretations resulting from all forms of social inquiry; that is, to the public presentation or write-up of the empirical work. And although in today's world few social inquirers naively believe that their representations are a faithful and accurate mirror of an external reality, there remain serious schisms in the social science community regarding the possibility and defensibility of any realist claim in representation. This is the "crisis of representation." Schwandt describes this crisis as rooted in the noncontroversial claim that "no interpretive account can ever directly or completely capture lived *experience*. [Moreover] the crisis [of representation] is part of a more general set of ideas across the human sciences that challenge long-standing beliefs about the role of encompassing, generalizable . . . frameworks that guide empirical research within a discipline" (Schwandt, 2001, p. 41, emphasis in original). These challenges constitute many of the critical epistemological, methodological, and political debates of this contemporary era.

Post-positivists aspire to representations of the human phenomena they study that are as accurate and "true" as possible, for that remains the central job of the social scientist in post-positivist thought—to be able to explain, and thus control and predict, the external social world. Many interpretivists and constructivists, in contrast, accept the inevitable interpreted and authored character of social science findings and conclusions. These inquirers aspire not so much to explain an external reality as to enhance our understanding of complex and dynamic human phenomena, through insightful and artful work. These inquirers also reject rigid disciplinary boundaries and traditions and have looked recently to the humanities for inspiration and guidance, especially in the writing up of their work. And "radically skeptical" postmodern scholars eschew all representations as arbitrary, misleading, even fraudulent. They "insist that what we are faced with are only texts—that is, particular inscriptions that create different accounts of lived experience. . . . The language of representation is only rhetoric" (Schwandt, 2001, pp. 41–42). These scholars thus aspire in their work not to represent human phenomena through realist or humanistic texts, but rather to create evocative texts that challenge, question, and critique even their own legitimacy.

From this crisis of representation has come considerable creative experimentation with alternative forms of representation in the writing up of social science research, especially within the broad and diverse community of qualitative inquirers, and also within the smaller circle of postmodern skeptics. In particular, qualitative inquirers have experimented with forms of representation drawn from the humanities— narratives, poems, and performances, as well as art, music, and dance. Some academic journals, including *Qualitative Inquiry*, have become actually enjoyable, even entertaining, to read in ways that engage emotions and personal commitments—well beyond the intellectual engagement of a good traditional write-up of an empirical study for a scholarly journal. And many of these same authors who experiment with alternative forms of representation, as well as critics who do not, continue to critically reflect on the defensibility of and warrants for a poem or a fictionalized story as a way to write up the results and conclusions from social scientific inquiry. The argument is lively within the academic and scholarly communities. Extending these alternative forms of representation to write-ups and reports of empirical work in the worlds of policy and practice remains quite a bit more tentative.

The vignette offered at the beginning of this chapter is intended to illustrate some of the continuing strands of controversy as manifested in the applied inquiry domain of program evaluation. In this vignette, members of the HIV/AIDS working group of the Foundation were sharing evaluation information from their respective regions, primarily in the form of indicator data—data on the performance indicators the Foundation itself had identified as gauges of program progress and quality. These indicators included the geographic reach of a program, the nature and extent of local organizational participation in or support for the program, specific short-term outcomes such as knowledge gain and attitude change, and population indices such as the rate and prevalence of HIV infection. This kind of information is clearly valuable, especially for those responsible for program funding, direction, and impact—like the Foundation's HIV/AIDS working group. Data on important indicators provide a record of the HIV/AIDS landscape at an aggregate level of program or country or region. Such data help decision makers, like the Foundation working group, monitor the reach and consequence of their investments, identify emerging problems or crises (such as the tragic increase in AIDS orphans in southern Africa), and, as appropriate, redirect resources or take other kinds of ameliorative action.

Yet, as Robert pointed out, many other facets and dimensions of the human experience are missed in the indicator data. Contextuality, emotion, pathos, expressiveness, and creativity—these can be better captured in particular pictures and stories. These can offer a glimpse of the daily lived experiences of people in these Foundation-funded programs. These can offer a window into the hope and despair of individual lives in particular places and times. These can well enrich an aggregate portrait comprising indicator data. These can thus contribute to a better understanding of the complex and multifaceted character of human experience.

An Illustration

Leslie Goodyear (2001) conducted a doctoral dissertation investigating various constituent views of both standard and alternative representations in reporting evaluation results from an HIV/AIDS education program. Goodyear identified three different types of evaluations conducted in this domain—a quasi-experiment, a survey study, and a case study. For each, she created a standard and an alternative representation of the results. She presented these representations to groups of state health decision makers, AIDS educators, AIDS advocates, and evaluators, then collected data on their reactions and responses.

Figures 10.1 and 10.2 present samples of the representations created for the evaluation conducted with a survey methodology. Figure 10.1 offers a histogram that represents responses to a question on the survey, disaggregated by race or ethnicity. Figure 10.2 offers a poem.

Goodyear's interesting results clearly indicated that most evaluation audiences appreciated the various kinds of representation and expressed a preference for evaluation reports that included multiple forms of representation. One could imagine an evaluation report of an HIV/AIDS education program presenting an array of charts and graphs that depict epidemiological trends as well as particular program outcomes for different groups of participants, alongside poems and stories that convey some of the lived experiences of people living with AIDS and of the street-level educators endeavoring to stem the tide of this dreadful epidemic, all interconnected with an artful and compelling narrative. Would not this be a more comprehensive portrayal of the

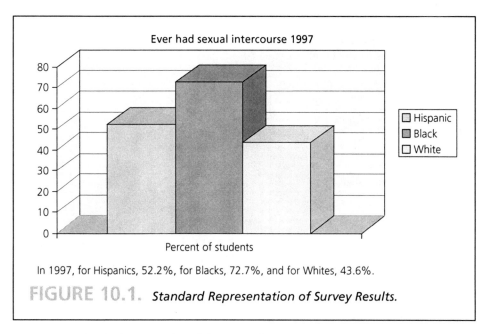

In 1997, for Hispanics, 52.2%, for Blacks, 72.7%, and for Whites, 43.6%.

FIGURE 10.1. *Standard Representation of Survey Results.*

Source: Reproduced with permission of the author (Goodyear, 2001, p. 43).

quality and effectiveness of this educational program? Would not this offer a better understanding of the promise and potential this program has to offer?

WRITING UP MIXED METHODS SOCIAL INQUIRY: TWO PRELIMINARY PRINCIPLES

Whether or not one is attracted to the possibilities of alternative representational forms, they offer an important message for writing up the findings and conclusions of mixed methods inquiry. Few would argue that images, narratives, and performances engage dimensions of human experience that are not very well represented in a standard scientific text. Few would argue that important human phenomena are simple and unidimensional or can be meaningfully captured in a few numbers or words. Indeed, the express purpose of a mixed methods approach to social inquiry is to develop a better understanding of the multiple dimensions, facets, and complexities of human experience.

Remembering also the responsibility of the mixed methods inquirer to write up his or her work in ways respectful of difference—differences in ways of knowing, differences in methodological and rhetorical traditions, differences in values and priorities, differences among our readers and listeners—the mixed methods inquirer is strongly encouraged to adopt a mixed approach to writing up the results and conclusions of his or her work. This is the first suggested principle for mixed methods writing. The mixing could be in voice, perspective, language, as well as in representational

Survey time, same questions every time.
Analyze, categorize, what's my prize?

Race?
Hispanic.
Minority.

Sex?
Yes. Ha, no really, female.
Majority.

Age?
17.
Majority.

Ever had sex?
Yes.
Majority and minority, depends.

Used a condom?
No.
Minority and majority, depends again.

Talked with parents?
Yes.
Majority.

So who am I?
I'm a **minority** who,
in the **majority** of cases
IS the **majority.**

Does that make me a standard deviation?

FIGURE 10.2. *Alternative Representation of Survey Results.*

Source: Reproduced with permission of the author (Goodyear, 2001, pp. 60–61).

form. That is, one could mix rhetorical forms, traditions of language, perspective of the speaker, and norms of persuasion and appeal, even if the construction of a story or poem or the inclusion of photos, artwork, or other images is judged out of bounds for a particular context. And the mixing should be responsibly and artfully crafted in ways that maximize the clarity and persuasiveness of the inquiry story being told.

I recognize that this principle constitutes a significant challenge, even to the best writers among us. Let me share a story that underscores the importance of endeavoring to rise to this challenge. Some years ago, I was coediting a *New Directions for Evaluation* volume with Tineke Abma that captured new developments in the tradition of responsive evaluation (Greene & Abma, 2001). One of the authors contributing to the volume, Stafford Hood—who is a good colleague and friend of mine—was not responding to my repeated editorial suggestions to trim and streamline a particular section of his chapter. Stafford had responded to other suggestions but had left this one section pretty much as he had originally written it. After several electronic exchanges, we finally spoke on the phone. Following updates on families and work, I turned to that one section and again recommended some streamlining. I said I found it somewhat repetitive and thought it could be productively edited. Stafford responded by explaining that in this section, he was endeavoring to model the "call and response" tradition of the African American language, especially the African American spiritual language. And he was doing so because his chapter was about reclaiming some of the history of African American thought in the field of evaluation. He believed that using the "call and response" rhetorical form of expression both reinforced the content of his chapter and signaled his profound respect for those who had gone before. I was deeply impressed and learned a lot that day. This lesson in voice constitutes an exemplary inspiration for my own call herein for a mixed methods way of writing.

The second suggested principle for writing up the results of mixed methods inquiry is particularly germane to integrated studies, but may also have relevance for some component studies. It is very well captured metaphorically in a story on National Public Radio's "This I Believe" series by renowned and esteemed educator Lee Shulman. Shulman wrote,

I believe in pastrami—well-marbled pastrami. Hot, thinly sliced, piled on fresh rye bread with dark mustard and a crisp dill pickle.

I believe that pastrami is a metaphor for a well-lived life, for a well-designed institution and even for healthy relationships. Pastrami is marbled rather than layered. Its parts, the lean and the fat, are mixed together rather than neatly separated. Too much of life is lived by adding layers that don't really connect with one another. . . .

Separate layers [make it] much easier to trim [the fat] from the brisket. Separate layers are much easier to build, to schedule and to design. But I believe that marbling demands that we work with the messy world of people, relationships and obligations in their full, rich complexity. The diet mavens inform us that marbling can be dangerous for our health, but as an educator I'm willing—even obligated—to take the risk. I want to

marble habits of mind, habits of practice and habits of the heart with my students—
just like pastrami. (http://www.npr.org/templates/story/story.php?storyId=6696794)

And I believe that effective mixed methods writing is also marbled, like good pastrami. The different perspectives, voices, understandings, representational forms that are mixed in the writing are not layered or offered separately or sequentially; rather, they are mixed together, interwoven, interconnected. They collectively tell the story to be told from a given mixed methods study, not so much taking turns as joining in one chorus, likely both harmonious and discordant. The challenges of this preliminary principle for mixed methods writing are also considerable. The rewards, once again, are to realize the mixed methods promise of better understanding of vital and valuable "habits of mind, habits of practice, and habits of the heart."

INTERLUDE

MORE CREATIVITY IN MIXED METHODS DATA ANALYSIS AND DISPLAY

In 2002, science education evaluation specialists Frances Lawrenz and Douglas Huffman presented an "archipelago" framework for mixed methods evaluation. Their work uses the spatial, geological, and ecological characteristics of an archipelago as a creative metaphor for mixed methods inquiry, in particular for data analysis and display. In this final interlude, I share their ideas and their example, as well as a second application of them in an educational measurement dissertation by Young-ju Lee (2005).

THE METAPHOR

Lawrenz and Huffman first remind us that an archipelago is a group of islands connected by a large underwater peninsula. In their metaphor, this underlying peninsula is viewed as the foundational "truth" of the program being evaluated, a truth that is mostly hidden from view. The islands, representing evaluative data, are then visible ways of probing the truth, but what is visible is much smaller than what is hidden. The islands can also be characterized in multiple ways—in terms of their topography, geology, ecology, and climate, among other attributes. As evaluators, we use various islands of data to try to understand the experiences and outcomes of a program. We endeavor to ascertain the interrelationships among the islands, sometimes finding that one is an outlier, not really connected to the others underwater. Other times we find connections between some aspects of an island, as in geological history and climate conditions, but not others, perhaps the current ecology of species living on the island. It is through examination of the individual islands, within the context of the overall archipelago, that a comprehensive understanding of the underlying foundation is developed (p. 332).

THE EXAMPLE

The example provided by Lawrenz and Huffman concerns an evaluation of a science teacher professional development program sponsored by the U.S. National Science Teachers Association (NTSA). This program involved science teachers in thirteen high schools across the country and included two summer workshops followed by implementation of curriculum materials developed by the NTSA. The program aspired to encourage all high school students to study science every year "in a rigorous, inquiry oriented, hands-on, connected, and spiraling matter" (p. 333). In what was a politically charged context, the evaluators needed to provide information that was credible and persuasive to multiple stakeholders in the science education domain, including national standards-setters, science education researchers, and science teachers themselves. A mixed methods design was an "obvious choice" (p. 333).

The evaluators present their three-part evaluation design using the archipelago metaphor. The first part involved a quasi-experimental design that used both quantitative and qualitative assessments of student learning and that contributed about half of the data islands in the archipelago (because it consumed about half of the evaluation resources and was considered most important by the evaluators). The student achievement data islands all had some "descriptive similarity" because they all assessed student learning. Metaphorically, the different levels of achievement indicated on these various achievement data islands could be viewed as varying levels of rock strata on each island. These achievement islands also had their own distinctive details, corresponding to the different assessments used—metaphorically, varying island shorelines and other waterways.

The second part of the evaluation, which contributed about one-third of the data islands, used a "social interactionist" approach to gather data on the nature and quality of teachers' application of the program in their own classrooms. The methods used included on-site observations; interviews with teachers, principals, and students; and student and teacher surveys. "The archipelago metaphor allows us to consider these social interactionist data in a much more interactive and integrative manner. [Like the student achievement islands] we considered each of the data sources as different islands with its own unique characteristics, but also with some characteristics in common" (pp. 335–336). For example, all of these islands could provide information on climate, but the measures of climate might differ from island to island, based on different perspectives of the meanings of climate. The archipelago metaphor enabled an in-depth and interactive consideration of these different perspectives and thus the interrelationships among the linked but still distinct social interactionist islands.

Finally, the third part of this evaluation consisted of a phenomenological mini-case study of six teachers as they implemented the curriculum. This part of the evaluation concentrated on teachers' experiences. This part of the evaluation—the remaining one-sixth of the overall effort—produced a third set of islands, one for each teacher—again with some common features, such as flora, but also some distinctive fauna on each island.

The usefulness of the archipelago metaphor continued through the data interpretation and display and the inference phases of this evaluation. In particular, the metaphor enabled the evaluators to visually arrange the various data islands in terms of their relationships to other islands within their cluster *and* in terms of their relationships to other islands in other clusters. For example, from within the social interactionist cluster of islands, the comments of the classroom observers demonstrated a stronger relationship with student performance on the multiple-choice test than did teacher comments. Thus the observer island could be visualized as closer to the multiple-choice student achievement island than the teacher comments island. In addition, the archipelago metaphor helped the evaluators respect and preserve individual school differences (recall that there were thirteen schools in this study), while also analyzing and presenting cross-school trends and patterns in the results. In sum, the archipelago metaphor "allowed us to link the different methods in a way that respected the uniqueness of different data and analysis methods while at the same time helping to form inferences about the 'truth' of the program we were evaluating" (p. 337).

AN APPLICATION OF THE ARCHIPELAGO METAPHOR

Young-ju Lee (2005) applied this archipelago metaphor for mixed methods display and interpretation in her dissertation study of the predictive validity of an English proficiency placement test. This study investigated the relationships between scores on an English as a Second Language (ESL) placement test and three measures of academic performance in a graduate education context. The three measures of academic performance were grade point average (GPA), faculty evaluations, and student self-assessments. The faculty and student assessments were each gathered with both interviews and questionnaires. The study was premised on the idea that academic performance is a complex, multifaceted phenomenon that is not readily captured in just one assessment, especially at the graduate level. Rather, in a complementary mixed methods design, Lee investigated the possible differential predictive validity of the ESL test for varying assessments of international graduate students' first-semester academic performance.

Following statistical and interpretive analyses of the individual relationships between the ESL test scores and the various indicators of academic performance, Lee endeavored to portray the overall pattern of interconnections and relationships by using the archipelago metaphor. She envisioned five islands, each representing the *relationship* between the predictor and one of the five sources used in assessing academic performance: GPA, faculty evaluations via a questionnaire, faculty evaluations via an interview, student self-evaluations via a questionnaire, and student self-evaluations via an interview. She developed an expected spatial pattern of arrangement for these five islands and then used pattern matching logic to assess the extent to which and ways in which the observed data fit the expected pattern. (See the Chapter Eight discussion of this pattern matching approach to mixed methods analysis and interpretation.) Lee found it challenging to visually array these five islands to represent their interconnections, as each one already represented a relationship. A more straightforward use of the archipelago metaphor may have been to envision six islands—scores on the ESL placement test and assessments of academic performance from each of the five distinct sources—and then spatially arrange these six islands to convey the overall holistic portrait of their interconnections, or the underlying truth of the relationship between English language proficiency and academic performance for international graduate students in their first semester of graduate study.

3

VALUING MIXED METHODS SOCIAL INQUIRY

In Part Three, one final chapter positions mixed methods social inquiry as crucial to the contributions of social scientists to better understanding of today's urgent social problems and to envisioning possible resolutions of these problems.

CHAPTER

11

THE POTENTIAL AND PROMISE OF MIXED METHODS SOCIAL INQUIRY

AND SO our shared mixed methods journey ends, even as each traveler's journey continues on, revisiting the various territories and domains and thereby reshaping the potential and promise of mixed methods social inquiry.

The contemporary university, both in the United States and around the globe, is a wondrous place. Universities in the United States, even with their bumbling bureaucracies and notoriously cantankerous characters, are filled with many interesting people doing many interesting things. One scholar is developing new techniques to conserve the colors and original patterns of tile mosaics set in the floors and walls of thousand-year-old buildings in Africa and Asia. Another is using the powers of a supercomputer to develop new econometric models that include estimates of the influence of global markets and cultural exchanges on family income and well-being. A professor on the quad is studying the reproductive cycle of the mosquito, so that perhaps it can be disrupted and diseases like malaria wiped out. And in the studios a young artist has just completed a haunting holographic image she calls "the petrified soldier."

As a long-term resident of the American university, I have on occasion bumped into some of these interesting people doing interesting things, including some from the natural science sectors of the university's scientific community. Most recently, I bumped into nanotechnologists, a varied group of scientists—including physicists, chemists, biologists, and engineers—who are studying applications of new developments in nano science. Did you know that a nanometer is so small that the diameter of a human hair is about eighty thousand nanometers across? And did you know that nano particles of gold are not gold in color, but red? Did you also know that scientists have developed filters that can trap particles that are only twenty nanometers wide? These kinds of scientific developments in nanotechnology hold exciting promise for both material goods and inventions—for example, tiny nano-robots that could enter the bloodstream of a person with cancer, travel to the cancer cells site, and destroy only them without destroying healthy cells. Wow! Quite amazing, I must say.

Yet, however mind-boggling the nano world may be, the worlds entered by my social science colleagues are that much more complicated, that much more daunting, that much more humbling (Berliner, 2002). Here are some examples of these worlds currently being studied by social scientists.

- Latina women in the United States, compared with Caucasian women, participate less often in breast and cervical cancer screening procedures—specifically, mammograms and Pap smears. Latina women have a higher incidence of breast and cervical cancer and lower survivorship rates, again compared with Caucasian women in the United States This observed difference is likely attributable to a complex entanglement of culture and class with the ways in which the U.S. health system is structured. These differences, that is, are attributable to cultural differences in health beliefs, socialization practices, understandings of the role of women, as well as differential access to health care information and to actual health care. Moreover, there are also intragroup differences in these health dynamics for Latina women from different Spanish-speaking countries and with different immigration statuses and different experiences with acculturation. (See Buki, 1999.)

- Methamphetamine production and use among adults living in rural areas of the United States continues to increase. Among the tragedies of this heartbreaking addiction are the children in methamphetamine-using families. These children are characteristically neglected, even left to fend for themselves when their parents are high on meth. Many of these children do not attend school, do not eat a balanced diet or sleep in an actual bed, never see a doctor or a dentist, and may not even be immunized. Understandably, the physical and mental health of these children is severely challenged, often severely damaged. Then, when their meth-using parents are arrested, these children go into foster care, where many struggle mightily to find a sense of safety and to claim a sense of healthy identity, all without betraying their birth parents. (See Haight, Jacobsen, Black, Kingery, Sheridan, & Mulder, 2005.)

- Some African American children and youth, especially boys, intentionally choose not to engage with school, do their homework, or try to learn what is being offered, because they believe that to do well in school is to "act white." They believe they are protecting and preserving their own cultural identity by failing in school. In addition, when African Americans (and other racial and ethnic minorities in the United States) take achievement tests, their performance is sometimes interrupted by a phenomenon called "stereotype threat." This refers to the test taker's fear that he or she will in fact confirm negative stereotypes of his or her people by doing poorly on the test. The fear itself can contribute significantly to poor test performance. Given these psychological complexities, alongside generational legacies of discrimination, what really importantly accounts for the persistent achievement gap in the United States between majority and minority children, and how can educators best redress persistent inequities? (See Ryan & Ryan, 2005; Steele, Perry, & Hilliard III, 2004.)

- Early in the twenty-first century, South Africa continues on its path of restoring the life worlds and life opportunities of its majority black population, after so many devastating decades of apartheid. Programs for youth are a top national priority, as this generation of young people has already been denied opportunities for a meaningful education, for adequate food and shelter, and for sustaining employment. It is very telling that youth in South Africa are defined as young people ages fifteen to thirty-five. The older ones in this age span never had a real childhood. Yet the ruinous legacies of apartheid remain, even within the black and colored populations, but in complex ways sometimes turned against outsiders. One such outsider is the evaluator of a youth development program in Capetown designed to provide training in generic work skills (such as responsibility and teamwork) and also to help the youth participants secure sustainable employment. The evaluator is white and American. She has been living and working in South Africa for more than ten years and is acutely sensitive to her status as an outsider, especially to the privileges her heritage has randomly granted to her and not to the youth she is working with. She has extensive experience working with youth and is usually able to build trust and reciprocity in the relationships she establishes with youth. Yet in the relational spaces defined by the employment training program, this evaluator finds herself frequently discounted, ignored, and the target of barbed and cutting racial slurs. What complex constellation of sociopolitical factors can explain the misdirected anger of these young South Africans? And in the face of such emotionality, is the employment training program completely missing the mark? (See Podems, 2004.)

- The world of early childhood in the United States, and in most other places around the globe, is a world of women and children. Over recent generations, this world has been transformed and decentralized from the individual home, wherein the mother of the family stayed home and took care of her young children, to a diverse array of child care locations, programs, and providers. The majority of mothers of young children now work outside the home, and the care of young children is now a business as well as a profession for early childhood caretakers. But the economics of this business and this profession remain seriously depressed, largely because it is a place traditionally, and still today, inhabited and managed by women, and our society remains economically sexist. It is in no small degree highly ironic that we collectively devalue one of life's most precious and vital responsibilities—that of nurturing the health and well-being of our children. Beyond this and other ironies, however, some planners and community development specialists see enormous economic potential in the early child care industry and are working to reposition early child care as a strategy for economic development. These planners are seeking to forge collaborations between the world of early childhood care and the domain of economic development. Such collaborations would be of social and economic benefit to all partners. Yet among the considerable challenges facing this important endeavor are different gender histories and norms of interaction, different perspectives and standards for what constitutes good social research and trustworthy evidence, and policy inertia in all sectors of government. (See Warner, 2006; Warner & Liu, 2006; and for further work, Warner's website http://government. cce.cornell.edu/warner/.)

- The Kyoto Protocol to the United Nations Framework Convention on Climate Change is an amendment to the international treaty on climate change, assigning mandatory targets for the reduction of greenhouse gas emissions to signatory nations and financial penalties if targets are not reached. As of August 2006, a total of 165 countries and other governmental entities had ratified the agreement (representing over 61 percent of emissions from developed countries). Advocates of the Kyoto Protocol claim that reducing these emissions is crucially important; carbon dioxide, they believe, is causing the earth's atmosphere to heat up. This is strongly supported by recent reports from the Intergovernmental Panel on Climate Change (2007a, 2007b, 2007c). Most prominent among advocates of Kyoto have been the European Union and many environmentalist organizations. The United Nations and some individual nations' scientific advisory bodies (including the G8 national science academies) have also issued reports favoring the Kyoto Protocol. The two major countries currently opposed to the treaty are the United States and Australia. Some environmental economists in these countries see the costs of the Kyoto Protocol as outweighing the benefits; some believe the standards that Kyoto sets to be too optimistic, others see a highly inequitable and inefficient agreement that would do little to curb greenhouse gas emissions. This complex scenario involves multiple disciplines—from climatology to chemistry and engineering (needed to reduce toxic emissions), as well as multiple traditions of science and evidence related to both the natural and the social worlds, and clearly, above all, the political delicacy of international relationships and negotiations. Although it is a complex mix of both natural and social science, the resolution of this continuing dispute rests not on environmental evidence but on political theories and practices involving international relationships, balances of power, and commitments to good will—all so very challenging in today's global and political economy. (Adapted from http://en.wikipedia.org/wiki/Kyoto_Protocol.)

So the challenges engaged by applied social scientists in the early part of the twenty-first century are considerable. They involve tangled webs of factors, influences, and experiences that cross the neat disciplinary lines of the academy; the contested boundaries of competing theories; and the ways of thinking of scientists, citizens, politicians, advocates, and artists. The work of applied social inquirers alone will not solve these challenges, as such solutions will require science to work in concert with politics, ethics, spirituality, and vision. But the work of applied social inquirers can and will contribute in important ways to our understandings of persistent and emerging challenges in our global society, to the way we think about these challenges, to which strands of their tangled webs we see and which ones remain obscured from view, and to what solutions appear as possible and what possibilities are not even envisioned.

In service of this work of applied social scientists, a mixed methods way of thinking as enacted in a mixed methods approach to social inquiry offers many multiplisms. A mixed methods social science crosses borders and boundaries once fenced and defended, invites diverse ways of thinking to dialogue one with the other, and models the acceptance of difference indispensable to the sustainability of our crowded little planet.

REFERENCES

Abma, T. A. (1998). Writing for dialogue, text in an evaluative context. *Evaluation, 4*(4), 434–454.

Abma, T. A. (Ed.). (2001). Dialogue in evaluation [Special issue]. *Evaluation, 7*(2).

Bazeley, P. (2003). Computerized data analysis for mixed methods research. In A. Tashakkori and C. Teddlie (Eds.), *Handbook of mixed methods in social and behavioral research* (pp. 385–422). Thousand Oaks, CA: Sage.

Bazeley, P. (2006). The contribution of computer software to integrating qualitative and quantitative data analyses. *Research in the Schools, 13*(1), 64–74.

Berliner, D. C. (2002). Educational research: The hardest science of all. *Educational Researcher, 31*(8), 18–20.

Bernstein, R. J. (1983). *Beyond objectivism and relativism: Science, hermeneutics, and praxis.* Philadelphia: University of Pennsylvania Press.

Bickman, L. (Ed.). (1987). *Using program theory in evaluation. New Directions for Evaluation, 33.* San Francisco: Jossey-Bass.

Bickman, L. (Ed.). (1990). *Advances in program theory. New Directions for Evaluation, 47.* San Francisco: Jossey-Bass.

Biesta, G. J. J., & Burbules, N. C. (2003). *Pragmatism and educational research.* Lanham, MD: Rowman & Littlefield.

Brewer, J. D., & Hunter, A. (1989). *Multimethod research: A synthesis of styles.* Thousand Oaks, CA: Sage.

Brewer, J. D., & Hunter, A. (2005). *Foundations of multimethod research: Synthesizing styles.* Thousand Oaks, CA: Sage.

Bryman, A. (1988). *Quantity and quality in social research.* London: Unwin Hyman.

Buki, L. P. (1999). Early detection of breast and cervical cancer among medically underserved Latinas. In M. Sotomayor and A. Garcia (Eds.), *La familia: traditions and realities* (pp. 67–85). Washington, DC: National Hispanic Council on Aging.

Burbules, N. C., & Rice, S. (1991). Dialogue across differences: Continuing the conversation. *Harvard Educational Review, 61,* 393–416.

Campbell, D. T. (1966). Pattern matching as an essential in distal knowing. In K. R. Hammond (Ed.), *The psychology of Egon Brunswick* (pp. 81–106). New York: Holt, Rinehart, & Winston.

Campbell, D. T. (1978). Qualitative knowing in action research. In M. Brenner, P. Marsh, & M. Brenner (Eds.), *The social context of methods* (pp. 184–209). London: Croom Helm.

Campbell, D. T. (1979). "Degrees of freedom" and the case study. In T. D. Cook and C. S. Reichardt (Eds.), *Qualitative and quantitative methods in evaluation research* (pp. 49–67). Thousand Oaks, CA: Sage.

Campbell, D. T. (1984). Can we be scientific in applied social science? In R. F. Connor, D. G. Altman, & C. Jackson (Eds.), *Evaluation studies review annual* (Vol. 9) (pp. 26–48). Thousand Oaks, CA: Sage.

Campbell, D. T., & Fiske, D. W. (1959). Convergent and discriminant validation by the multitrait-multimethod matrix. *Psychological Bulletin, 56*(2), 81–105.

Caracelli, V. J., & Greene, J. C. (1993). Data analysis strategies for mixed-method evaluation designs. *Educational Evaluation and Policy Analysis, 15*(2), 195–207.

Caracelli, V. J., & Greene, J. C. (1997). Crafting mixed-method evaluation designs. In J. C. Greene and V. J. Caracelli (Eds.), *Advances in mixed-method evaluation: The challenges and benefits of integrating diverse paradigms. New Directions for Evaluation, 74.* San Francisco: Jossey-Bass.

Chatterji, M. (2005). Evidence on "what works": An argument for extended-term mixed-method (ETMM) evaluation designs. *Educational Researcher, 34*(5), 14–24.

Chelimsky, E. (2007). Factors influencing the choice of methods in federal evaluation practice. In G. Julnes and D. J. Rog (Eds.), *Informing federal policies on evaluation methodology: Building the evidence base for method choice in government sponsored evaluation. New Directions for Evaluation, 113.* San Francisco: Jossey-Bass.

Chen, H.-T. (1990). *Theory-driven evaluation.* Thousand Oaks, CA: Sage.

Chen, H.-T. (1997). Applying mixed methods under the framework of theory-driven evaluations. In J. C. Greene and V. J. Caracelli (Eds.), *Advances in mixed-method evaluation: The challenges and benefits of integrating diverse paradigms. New Directions for Evaluation, 74.* San Francisco: Jossey-Bass.

Chen, H.-T., & Rossi, P. H. (1983). Evaluating with sense: The theory-driven approach. *Evaluation Review, 7,* 283–302.

Cook, T. D. (1985). Postpositivist critical multiplism. In R. L. Shotland and M. M. Mark (Eds.), *Social science and social policy* (pp. 21–62). Thousand Oaks, CA: Sage.

Cook, T. D. (2002). Randomized experiments in educational policy research: A critical examination of the reasons the educational evaluation community has offered for not doing them. *Educational Evaluation and Policy Analysis, 24*(3), 175–199.

Cook, T. D. (2004). Causal generalization: How Campbell and Cronbach influenced my theoretical thinking on this topic, including in Shadish, Cook, & Campbell. In M. C. Alkin (Ed.), *Evaluation roots: Tracing theorists' views and influences* (pp. 88–113). Thousand Oaks, CA: Sage.

Cook, T. D., & Campbell, D. T. (1979). *Quasi-experimentation: Design and analysis issues for social research in field settings.* Boston: Houghton Mifflin.

Cook, T. D., & Reichardt, C. S. (Eds.). (1979). *Qualitative and quantitative methods in evaluation research.* Thousand Oaks, CA: Sage.

Cooksy, L. J., Gill, P., & Kelly, P. A. (2001). The program logic model as an integrative framework for a multimethod evaluation. *Evaluation and Program Planning, 24*(1), 119–128.

Creswell, J. W. (2002). *Research design: Qualitative, quantitative and mixed methods approaches* (2nd ed.). Thousand Oaks, CA: Sage.

Creswell, J. W., Plano Clark, V. L., Gutmann, M. L., & Hanson, W. E. (2003). Advanced mixed methods research designs. In A. Tashakkori and C. Teddlie (Eds.), *Handbook of mixed methods in social and behavioral research* (pp. 209–240). Thousand Oaks, CA: Sage.

Cronbach, L. J. (1975). Beyond the two disciplines of scientific psychology. *American Psychologist, 30*(1), 116–127.

Cronbach, L. J., & Associates (1980). *Toward reform of program evaluation.* San Francisco: Jossey-Bass.

Datta, L.-E. (1994). Paradigm wars: A basis for peaceful coexistence and beyond. In C. S. Reichardt and S. F. Rallis (Eds.), *The qualitative-quantitative debate: New perspectives. New Directions for Program Evaluation, 61.* San Francisco: Jossey-Bass.

Datta, L.-E. (1997a). Multimethod evaluations: Using case studies together with other methods. In E. Chelimsky and W. R. Shadish (Eds.), *Evaluation for the 21st century* (pp. 344–359). Thousand Oaks, CA: Sage.

Datta, L.-E. (1997b). A pragmatic basis for mixed-method designs. In J. C. Greene and V. J. Caracelli (Eds.), *Advances in mixed-method evaluation: The challenges and benefits of integrating diverse paradigms. New Directions for Evaluation, 74.* San Francisco: Jossey-Bass.

Datta, L.-E. (2005). Mixed methods, more justified conclusions: The case of the Abt evaluation of the Comer program in Detroit. In T. S. Weisner (Ed.), *Discovering successful pathways in children's development: Mixed methods in the study of childhood and family life* (pp. 65–83). Chicago: University of Chicago Press.

Denzin, N. K. (1978). *The research act: A theoretical introduction to sociological methods.* New York: McGraw-Hill.

Denzin, N. K., & Lincoln, Y. S. (2000). Introduction: The discipline and practice of qualitative research. In N. K. Denzin and Y. S. Lincoln (Eds.), *Handbook of qualitative research* (2nd ed.) (pp. 1–29). Thousand Oaks, CA: Sage.

Denzin, N. K., Van Maanen, J., & Manning, P. K. (1989). *Interpretive biography.* Thousand Oaks, CA: Sage.

DeStefano, L., Hammer, V. L., & Ryan, K. (2003). *Final report of the external evaluation of the Illinois Reading Excellence Act Program*. Springfield, IL: Illinois State Board of Education.

Eckert, J. K. (1987). Ethnographic research on aging. In S. Reinharz and G. D. Rowles (Eds.), *Qualitative gerontology* (pp. 241–255). New York: Spring.

Eisner, E. W., & Peshkin, A. (1990). *Qualitative inquiry in education: The continuing debate*. New York: Teachers College Press.

Ercikan, K., & Roth, W.-M. (2006). What good is polarizing research into qualitative and quantitative? *Educational Researcher, 35*(5), 14–23.

Erickson, F. E. (1986). Qualitative methods in research on teaching. In M. Wittrock (Ed.), *Handbook of research on teaching* (3rd ed.) (pp. 119–161). Old Tappan, NJ: Macmillan.

Erzberger, C., & Kelle, U. (2003). Making inferences in mixed methods: The rules of integration. In A. Tashakkori and C. Teddlie (Eds.), *Handbook of mixed methods in social and behavioral research* (pp. 457–488). Thousand Oaks, CA: Sage.

Fielding, N. G., & Fielding, J. L. (1986). *Linking data*. Thousand Oaks, CA: Sage.

Filstead, W. J. (Ed.). (1970). *Qualitative methodology: Firsthand involvement with the social world*. Chicago: Markham.

Filstead, W. J. (1979). Qualitative methods: A needed perspective in evaluation research. In T. D. Cook and C. S. Reichardt (Eds.), *Qualitative and quantitative methods in evaluation research* (pp. 33–48). Thousand Oaks, CA: Sage.

Gage, N. L. (1989). The paradigm wars and their aftermath: A "historical" sketch of research on teaching since 1989. *Educational Researcher, 18*(7), 4–10.

Geertz, C. (1983). "From the native's point of view": On the nature of anthropological understanding. *Local knowledge: Further essays in interpretive anthropology*. New York: Basic Books.

Gibson-Davis, C. M., & Duncan, G. J. (2005). Qualitative/quantitative synergies in a random-assignment program evaluation. In T. S. Weisner (Ed.), *Discovering successful pathways in children's development: Mixed methods in the study of childhood and family life* (pp. 283–303). Chicago: University of Chicago Press.

Goodyear, L. K. (2001). *Representational form and audience understanding in evaluation: Advancing use and engaging postmodern pluralism*. Unpublished doctoral dissertation, Department of Human Service Studies, Cornell University, Ithaca, NY.

Greene, J. C. (1996). Qualitative evaluation and scientific citizenship: Reflections and refractions. *Evaluation, 2*(3), 277–289.

Greene, J. C. (2000). Understanding social programs through evaluation. In N. K. Denzin and Y. S. Lincoln (Eds.), *Handbook of qualitative research* (2nd ed.) (pp. 981–999). Thousand Oaks, CA: Sage.

Greene, J. C. (2001). Mixing social inquiry methodologies. In V. Richardson (Ed.), *Handbook of research on teaching, fourth edition* (pp. 251–258). Washington, DC: American Educational Research Association.

Greene, J. C. (2002). With a splash of soda, please: Towards active engagement with difference. *Evaluation, 8*(2), 259–266.

Greene, J. C. (2005a). Synthesis: A reprise on mixing methods. In T. S. Weisner (Ed.), *Discovering successful pathways in children's development: Mixed methods in the study of childhood and family life* (pp. 405–419). Chicago: University of Chicago Press.

Greene, J. C. (2005b). Evaluators as stewards of the public good. In S. Hood, R. K. Hopson, & H. T. Frierson (Eds.), *The role of culture and cultural context: A mandate for inclusion, truth, and understanding in evaluation theory and practice, Evaluation and Society Series* (pp. 7–20). Greenwich, CT: Information Age Publishing.

Greene, J. C. (2005c). The generative potential of mixed methods inquiry. *International Journal of Research & Method in Education, 28*(2), 207–211.

Greene, J. C. (2006). Toward a methodology of mixed methods social inquiry. *Research in the Schools, 13*(1), 93–99.

Greene, J. C., & Abma, T. A. (Eds.). (2001). *Responsive evaluation. New Directions for Evaluation, 92*. San Francisco: Jossey-Bass.

Greene, J. C., Benjamin, L., & Goodyear, L. K. (2001). The merits of mixing methods in evaluation. *Evaluation*, *7*(1), 25–44.

Greene, J. C., & Caracelli, V. J. (1997a). Defining and describing the paradigm issue in mixed-method evaluation. In J. C. Greene and V. J. Caracelli (Eds.), *Advances in mixed-method evaluation: The challenges and benefits of integrating diverse paradigms. New Directions for Evaluation, 74.* San Francisco: Jossey-Bass.

Greene, J. C., & Caracelli, V. J. (Eds.). (1997b). *Advances in mixed-method evaluation: The challenges and benefits of integrating diverse paradigms. New Directions for Evaluation, 74.* San Francisco: Jossey-Bass.

Greene, J. C., & Caracelli, V. J. (2003). Making paradigmatic sense of mixed methods practice. In A. Tashakkori and C. Teddlie (Eds.), *Handbook of mixed methods in social and behavioral research* (pp. 91–110). Thousand Oaks, CA: Sage.

Greene, J. C., Caracelli, V. J., & Graham, W. F. (1989). Toward a conceptual framework for mixed-method evaluation designs. *Educational Evaluation and Policy Analysis*, *11*(3), 255–274.

Greene, J. C., & Henry, G. T. (2005). The qualitative-quantitative debate in evaluation. In S. Mathison (Ed.), *The encyclopedia of evaluation* (pp. 345–350). Thousand Oaks, CA: Sage.

Greene, J. C., Kreider, H., & Mayer, E. (2005). Combining qualitative and quantitative methods in social inquiry. In B. Somekh and C. Lewin (Eds.), *Research methods in the social sciences* (pp. 274–281). London: Sage.

Greene, J. C., & McClintock, C. (1985). Triangulation in action: Design and analysis issues. *Evaluation Review*, *9*(5), 523–545.

Guba, E. G. (1985). The context of emergent paradigm research. In Y. S. Lincoln (Ed.), *Organizational theory and inquiry: The paradigm revolution* (pp. 79–104). Thousand Oaks, CA: Sage.

Guba, E. G. (Ed.). (1990). *The paradigm dialog.* Thousand Oaks, CA: Sage.

Haight, W., Jacobsen, T., Black, J., Kingery, L., Sheridan, K., & Mulder, C. (2005). "In these bleak days": Parent methamphetamine abuse and child welfare in the rural Midwest. *Child Youth Services Review*, *27*, 949–971.

Hammersley, M. (1992). The paradigm wars: Reports from the front. *British Journal of Sociology of Education*, *13*(1), 131–143.

Harding, S. (1993). Rethinking standpoint epistemology: What is "strong objectivity"? In L. Alcoff and E. Potter (Eds.), *Feminist epistemologies* (pp. 49–82). New York: Routledge.

Harding, S., & Hintikka, M. B. (Eds.). (1983). *Discovering reality: Feminist perspectives on epistemology, metaphysics, methodology, and philosophy of science.* Dordrecht, The Netherlands: D. Reidel.

Hargreaves, D. H. (1985). The micro-macro problem in the sociology of education. In R. G. Burgess (Ed.), *Issues in educational research: Qualitative methods* (pp. 21–47). London: Falmer Press.

House, E. R. (1993). *Professional evaluation: Social impact and political consequences.* Thousand Oaks, CA: Sage.

House, E. R. (1994). Integrating the quantitative and qualitative. In C. S. Reichardt and S. F. Rallis (Eds.), *The qualitative-quantitative debate: New perspectives. New Directions for Evaluation, 61.* San Francisco: Jossey-Bass.

House, E. R., & Howe, K. R. (1999). *Values in evaluation and social research.* Thousand Oaks, CA: Sage.

Howe, K. R. (1985). Two dogmas of educational research. *Educational Researcher*, *14*(8), 10–18.

Howe, K. R. (1988). Against the quantitative-qualitative incompatibility thesis (or dogmas die hard). *Educational Researcher*, *17*(8), 10–16.

Howe, K. R. (2003). *Closing methodological divides.* Boston: Kluwer Academic Publishing.

Institute of Medicine. (2004). *Preventing childhood obesity: Health in the balance.* Washington, DC: National Academies of Science.

Institute of Medicine. (2006). *Progress in preventing childhood obesity: How do we measure up?* Washington, DC: National Academies of Science.

Intergovernmental Panel on Climate Change (2007a). *Climate change 2007: The physical basis.* Contribution of Working Group I to the Fourth Assessment Report of the Intergovernmental Panel on Climate Change.

Intergovernmental Panel on Climate Change (2007b). *Climate change 2007: Impacts, adaptation, and vulnerability.* Contribution of Working Group II to the Fourth Assessment Report of the Intergovernmental Panel on Climate Change.

Intergovernmental Panel on Climate Change (2007c). *Climate change 2007: Mitigation of climate change*. Contribution of Working Group III to the Fourth Assessment Report of the Intergovernmental Panel on Climate Change.

Jick, T. D. (1983). Mixing qualitative and quantitative methods: Triangulation in action. In J. Van Maanen (Ed.), *Qualitative methodology* (pp. 135–148). Thousand Oaks, CA: Sage.

Johnson, R. B., & Onwuegbuzie, A. J. (2004). Mixed methods research: A research paradigm whose time has come. *Educational Researcher, 33*(7), 14–26.

Kallemeyn, L., Hammer, V., Zhu, R., DeStefano, L., & Greene, J. C. (2003, November). A purposeful mixed-method journey in the Illinois Reading Excellence Act (REA) Evaluation. Paper presented at the annual meeting of the American Evaluation Association, Reno, NV.

Kemmis, S., & McTaggart, R. (2000). Participatory action research. In N. K. Denzin and Y. S. Lincoln (Eds.), *Handbook of qualitative research* (2nd ed.) (pp. 567–605). Thousand Oaks, CA: Sage.

Kennedy, M. M. (1979). Generalizing from single case studies. *Evaluation Quarterly, 3*(4), 661–678.

Kidder, L. H., & Fine, M. (1987). Qualitative and quantitative methods: When stories converge. In M. M. Mark and R. L. Shotland (Eds.), *Multiple methods in program evaluation. New Directions for Evaluation, 35*. San Francisco: Jossey-Bass.

Kincheloe, J. L. (2001). Describing the Bricolage: Conceptualizing a new rigor in qualitative research. *Qualitative Inquiry, 7*(6), 679–692.

Kling, J. R., Liebman, J. B., & Katz, L. F. (2005). Bullets don't got no name: Consequences of fear in the ghetto. In T. S. Weisner (Ed.), *Discovering successful pathways in children's development: Mixed methods in the study of childhood and family life* (pp. 243–281). Chicago: University of Chicago Press.

Kuhn, T. S. (1970). *The structure of scientific revolutions*. Chicago: University of Chicago Press.

Kushner, S. (2002). I'll take mine neat: Multiple methods but a single methodology. *Evaluation, 8*(2), 249–258.

Lawrenz, F., & Huffman, D. (2002). The archipelago approach to mixed method evaluation. *American Journal of Evaluation, 23*(3), 331–338.

LeCroy, C. W., & Whitaker, K. (2005). Improving the quality of home visitation: An exploratory study of difficult situations. *Child Abuse & Neglect, 29*, 1003–1012.

Lee, C. D. (2003). Why we need to re-think race and ethnicity in educational research. *Educational Researcher, 32*(5), 3–5.

Lee, Y. (2005). *Construct validation of an integrated, process-oriented, and computerized English for academic purposes (EAP) placement test: A mixed method approach*. Unpublished doctoral dissertation, Department of Educational Psychology, University of Illinois, Urbana-Champaign.

Li, S., Marquart, J. M., & Zercher, C. (2000). Conceptual issues and analytic strategies in mixed-method studies of preschool inclusion. *Journal of Early Intervention, 23*(1), 116–132.

Lincoln, Y. S. (1991). The arts and sciences of program evaluation. *Evaluation Practice, 12*(1), 1–7.

Lincoln, Y. S., & Guba, E. G. (1985). *Naturalistic inquiry*. Thousand Oaks, CA: Sage.

Lincoln, Y. S., & Guba, E. G. (2000). Paradigmatic controversies, contradictions, and emerging confluences. In N. K. Denzin and Y. S. Lincoln (Eds.), *Handbook of qualitative research* (2nd ed.) (pp. 163–188). Thousand Oaks, CA: Sage.

Louis, K. S. (1981, April). Policy researcher as sleuth: New approaches to integrating qualitative and quantitative methods. Paper presented at the annual meeting of the American Educational Research Association, Los Angeles. (ED 207 256).

Louis, K. S. (1982). Sociologist as sleuth: Integrating methods in the RDU study. *American Behavioral Scientist, 26*(1), 101–120.

Lyotard, J.-F. (1984). *The postmodern condition: A report on knowledge*. Minneapolis: University of Minnesota Press.

Madey, D. L. (1982). Some benefits of integrating qualitative and quantitative methods in program evaluation, with illustrations. *Educational Evaluation and Policy Analysis, 4*, 223–236.

Mark, M. M., & Shotland, R. L. (Eds.). (1987a). *Multiple methods in program evaluation. New Directions for Evaluation, 35.* San Francisco: Jossey-Bass.

Mark, M. M., & Shotland, R. L. (1987b). Alternative models for the use of multiple methods. In M. M. Mark and R. L. Shotland (Eds.), *Multiple methods in program evaluation. New Directions for Evaluation, 35.* San Francisco: Jossey-Bass.

Marquart, J. M. (1990). A pattern-matching approach to link program theory and evaluation data. In L. Bickman (Ed.), *Advances in program theory. New Directions for Evaluation, 47.* San Francisco: Jossey-Bass.

Marquart, J. M. (1997, November). Mixed-method studies: Design and analysis dilemmas and solutions. Paper presented at the annual meeting of the American Evaluation Association, San Diego, CA.

Marris, P., & Rein, M. (1982). *Dilemmas of social reform: Poverty and community action in the United States* (2nd ed.). Chicago: University of Chicago Press.

Mason, J., Cheung, I., & Walker, L. (2004). Substance use, social networks, and the geography of urban adolescents. *Substance Use & Abuse, 39,* 1751–1777.

Mathison, S. (1988). Why triangulate? *Educational Researcher, 17*(2), 13–17.

Maxwell, J. A. (1996). *Qualitative research design: An interactive approach.* Thousand Oaks, CA: Sage.

Maxwell, J. A. (2004a). Realism as a stance for mixed methods research. Paper presented at the annual meeting of the American Educational Research Association, Chicago.

Maxwell, J. A. (2004b). Causal explanation, qualitative research, and scientific inquiry in education. *Educational Researcher, 33*(2), 3–11.

Maxwell, J. A., Bashook, P. G., & Sandlow, C. J. (1986). Combining ethnographic and experimental methods in educational evaluation. In D. M. Fetterman and M. A. Pittman (Eds.), *Educational evaluation: Ethnography in theory, practice, and politics* (pp. 121–143). Thousand Oaks, CA: Sage.

Maxwell, J. A., & Loomis, D. M. (2003). Mixed methods design: An alternative approach. In A. Tashakkori and C. Teddlie (Eds.), *Handbook of mixed methods in social and behavioral research* (pp. 241–271). Thousand Oaks, CA: Sage.

McCarthy, T. (1981). *The critical theory of Jurgen Habermas.* Cambridge, MA: MIT Press.

McConney, A., Rudd, A., & Ayres, R. (2002). Getting to the bottom line: A method for synthesizing findings within mixed-method program evaluations. *American Journal of Evaluation, 23*(2), 121–140.

Mertens, D. M. (1999). Inclusive evaluation: Implications of a transformative theory for evaluation. *American Journal of Evaluation, 20*(1), 1–14.

Mertens, D. M. (2003). Mixed methods and the politics of human research: The transformative-emancipatory perspective. In A. Tashakkori and C. Teddlie (Eds.), *Handbook of mixed methods in social and behavioral research* (pp. 135–164). Thousand Oaks, CA: Sage.

Miles, M. B., & Huberman, A. M. (1984). Drawing valid meaning from qualitative data: Toward a shared craft. *Educational Researcher, 13*(5), 20–30.

Miles, M. B., & Huberman, A. M. (1994). *Qualitative data analysis: An expanded sourcebook* (2nd ed.). Thousand Oaks, CA: Sage.

Morse, J. M. (2003). Principles in mixed methods and multimethod research design. In A. Tashakkori and C. Teddlie (Eds.), *Handbook of mixed methods in social and behavioral research* (pp. 189–208). Thousand Oaks, CA: Sage.

Newman, I., Ridenour, C. S., Newman, C., & DeMarco, G. M. P., Jr. (2003). A typology of research purposes and its relationship to mixed methods. In A. Tashakkori and C. Teddlie (Eds.), *Handbook of mixed methods in social and behavioral research* (pp. 167–188). Thousand Oaks, CA: Sage.

Niglas, K. (1999, September). Quantitative and qualitative inquiry in educational research: Is there a paradigmatic difference between them? Paper presented at the European Conference on Educational Research, Lahti, Finland.

Niglas, K. (2004). *The combined use of qualitative and quantitative methods in educational research.* Dissertation, Faculty of Educational Sciences, Tallinn Pedagogical University, Tallinn, Estonia.

Onwuegbuzie, A. J. (2001, April). Effects sizes in qualitative research: A prolegomenon. Paper presented at the annual meeting of the American Educational Research Association, Seattle, WA.

Onwuegbuzie, A. J. (2003). Expanding the framework of internal and external validity in quantitative research. *Research in the Schools, 10*(1), 71–90.

Onwuegbuzie, A. J., & Johnson, R. B. (2006). The validity issue in mixed research. *Research in the Schools, 13*(1), 48–63.

Onwuegbuzie, A. J., & Leech, N. L. (in press). Validity and qualitative research: An oxymoron? *Quality & Quantity: An International Journal of Methodology.*

Onwuegbuzie, A. J., & Teddlie, C. (2003). A framework for analyzing data in mixed methods research. In A. Tashakkori and C. Teddlie (Eds.), *Handbook of mixed methods in social and behavioral research* (pp. 351–383). Thousand Oaks, CA: Sage.

Orellena, M. F., & Bowman, P. (2003). Cultural diversity research on learning and development: Conceptual, methodological, and strategic considerations. *Educational Researcher, 32*(5), 26–32.

Patton, M. Q. (1980). *Qualitative evaluation methods.* Thousand Oaks, CA: Sage.

Patton, M. Q. (2000). *Utilization-focused evaluation* (New century ed.). Thousand Oaks, CA: Sage.

Patton, M. Q. (2002). *Qualitative research and evaluation methods* (3rd ed.). Thousand Oaks, CA: Sage.

Pawson, R., & Tilly, N. (1997). *Realistic evaluation.* London: Sage.

Phelan, P. (1987). Compatibility of qualitative and quantitative methods: Studying child sexual abuse in America. *Education and Urban Society, 20*(1), 35–41.

Phillips, D. C. (1990). Postpositivistic science: Myths and realities. In E. G. Guba (Ed.), *The paradigm dialog* (pp. 31–45). Thousand Oaks, CA: Sage.

Phillips, D. C. (1996). Philosophical perspectives. In D. C. Berliner and R. C. Calfee (Eds.), *Handbook of educational psychology* (pp. 1005–1019). Old Tappan, NJ: Macmillan.

Phillips, D. C. (2000). *The expanded social scientist's bestiary.* Lanham, MD: Rowman and Littlefield. (Original edition Oxford: Pergamon, 1992)

Phillips, D. C. (2005). *A guide for the perplexed: Scientific educational research, methodolatry, and the gold versus platinum standards.* Invited lecture, University of Illinois, Urbana Champaign, IL.

Phillips, D. C., & Burbules, N. C. (2000). *Postpositivism and educational research.* Lanham, MD: Rowman & Littlefield.

Podems, D. R. (2004). *A monitoring and evaluation intervention for donor-funded NPOs in the developing world: A case study.* Unpublished doctoral dissertation, The Union Institute and University, Cincinnati, OH.

Power, M. (1999). *The audit society: Rituals of verification.* Oxford: Oxford University Press.

Pressman, J., & Wildavsky, A. (1979). *Implementation: How great expectations in Washington are dashed in Oakland* (2nd ed.). Berkeley: University of California Press.

Radimer, K. L. (1990). *Understanding hunger and developing indicators to assess it.* Unpublished doctoral dissertation, Division of International Nutrition, Cornell University, Ithaca, NY.

Ragin, C. C. (1987). *The comparative method: Moving beyond qualitative and quantitative strategies.* Berkeley: The University of California Press.

Ragin, C. C. (2000). *Fuzzy-set social science.* Chicago: University of Chicago Press.

Raudenbush, S. W. (2005). Learning from attempts to improve schooling: The contribution of methodological diversity. *Educational Researcher, 34*(5), 25–31.

Reichardt, C. S., & Cook, T. D. (1979). Beyond qualitative versus quantitative methods. In T. D. Cook and C. S. Reichardt (Eds.), *Qualitative and quantitative methods in evaluation research* (pp. 7–32). Thousand Oaks, CA: Sage.

Reichardt, C. S., & Rallis, S. F. (1994). Qualitative and quantitative inquiries are not incompatible: A call for a new partnership. In C. S. Reichardt and S. F. Rallis (Eds.), *The qualitative-quantitative debate: New perspectives. New Directions for Evaluation, 61.* San Francisco: Jossey-Bass.

Rist, R. C. (1980). Blitzkreig ethnography: On the transformation of a method into a movement. *Educational Researcher, 8*(2), 8–10.

Rogers, P. J., Hacsi, T. A., Petrosino, A., & Huebner, T. A. (Eds.). (2000). *Program theory in evaluation: Challenges and opportunities. New Directions for Evaluation, 87.* San Francisco: Jossey-Bass.

Rossman, G. B., & Wilson, B. L. (1985). Numbers and words: Combining quantitative and qualitative methods in a single large-scale evaluation study. *Evaluation Review, 9*(5), 627–643.

Ryan, K. R., DeStefano, L., and Greene, J. C. (2001). *External evaluation of the Reading Excellence Act Implementation in Illinois.* Proposal submitted to the Illinois State Board of Education by the University of Illinois, Urbana-Champaign.

Ryan, K. R., & Ryan, A. M. (2005). The psychological processes underlying stereotype threat and standardized math test performance. *Educational Psychologist, 40*(1), 53–63.

Salmon, W. C. (1998). *Causality and explanation.* New York: Oxford University Press.

Salomon, G. (1991). Transcending the qualitative-quantitative debate: The analytic and systemic approaches to educational research. *Educational Researcher, 20*(6), 10–18.

Sanchez-Ayendez, M. (1998). Middle-aged Puerto Rican women as primary caregivers to the elderly: A qualitative analysis of everyday dynamics. In M. Delgado (Ed.), *Latino elders and the twenty-first century: Issues and challenges* (pp. 75–97). Binghamton, NY: The Haworth Press.

Sandelowski, M. (2003). Tables or tableaux? The challenges of writing and reading mixed methods studies. In A. Tashakkori and C. Teddlie (Eds.), *Handbook of mixed methods in social and behavioral research* (pp. 321–350). Thousand Oaks, CA: Sage.

Schwandt, T. A. (1996). Farewell to criteriology. *Qualitative Inquiry, 2*(1), 58–72.

Schwandt, T. A. (2000). Three epistemological stances for qualitative inquiry: Interpretivism, hermeneutics, and social constructionism. In N. L. Denzin and Y. S. Lincoln (Eds.), *Handbook of qualitative research* (2nd ed.) (pp. 189–214). Thousand Oaks, CA: Sage.

Schwandt, T. A. (2001). *Dictionary of qualitative inquiry* (2nd ed.). Thousand Oaks, CA: Sage.

Schwandt, T. A. (2002). *Evaluation practice reconsidered.* New York: Peter Lang.

Schwandt, T. A. (2003). "Back to the rough ground!" Beyond theory to practice in evaluation. *Evaluation, 9*(3), 353–364.

Schwandt, T. A. (2004). Hermeneutics: A poetics of inquiry versus a methodology for research. In H. Piper and I. Stronach (Eds.), *Educational research: Difference and diversity* (pp. 31–44). Aldershot, UK: Ashgate Publishing.

Scriven, M. (1999). The nature of evaluation part I: Relation to psychology. *Practical Assessment, Research & Evaluation, 6*(11). Retrieved February 2, 2007, from http://PAREonline.net/getvn.asp?v=6&n=11.

Sechrest, L. (1992). Roots: Back to our first generations. *Evaluation Practice, 13*(1), 1–7.

Sieber, S. (1973). The integration of field work and survey methods. *American Journal of Sociology, 78,* 1335–1359.

Smith, A. G., & Louis, K. S. (Eds.). (1982). Multi-method policy research: Issues and applications [Special issue]. *American Behavioral Scientist, 26.*

Smith, J. K. (1983). Quantitative versus qualitative research: An attempt to clarify the issue. *Educational Researcher, 12*(3), 6–13.

Smith, J. K., (1985). The problem of criteria for judging interpretive inquiry. *Educational Evaluation and Policy Analysis, 6*(4), 379–391.

Smith, J. K. (1989). *The nature of social and educational inquiry: Empiricism versus interpretivism.* Norwood, NJ: Ablex Publishing.

Smith, J. K., & Heshusius, L. (1986). Closing down the conversation: The end of the qualitative-quantitative debate among educational inquirers. *Educational Researcher, 15*(1), 4–12.

Smith, M. L. (1986). The whole is greater: Combining qualitative and quantitative approaches in evaluation studies. In D. D. Williams (Ed.), *Naturalistic evaluation. New Directions for Program Evaluation, 30.* San Francisco: Jossey-Bass.

Smith, M. L. (1997). Mixing and matching: Methods and models. In J. C. Greene and V. J. Caracelli (Eds.), *Advances in mixed-method evaluation: The challenges and benefits of integrating diverse paradigms. New Directions for Evaluation, 74*. San Francisco: Jossey-Bass.

Steele, C., Perry, T., & Hilliard, A., III. (2004). *Young, gifted, and black: Promoting high achievement among African American students*. Boston: Beacon Press.

Sydenstricker-Neto, J. M. (2004). *Land-cover change and social organization in Brazilian Amazonia*. Unpublished doctoral dissertation, Department of Rural Sociology, Cornell University, Ithaca, NY.

Sydenstricker-Neto, J. M. (2006). Population and deforestation in Brazilian Amazonia: A mediating perspective and a mixed-method analysis. Paper submitted for publication.

Tashakkori, A., & Teddlie, C. (1998). *Mixed methodology: Combining qualitative and quantitative approaches*. Thousand Oaks, CA: Sage.

Tashakkori, A., & Teddlie, C. (2003a). *Handbook of mixed methods in social and behavioral research*. Thousand Oaks, CA: Sage.

Tashakkori, A., & Teddlie, C. (2003b). The past and future of mixed methods research: From data triangulation to mixed model designs. In A. Tashakkori and C. Teddlie (Eds.), *Handbook of mixed methods in social and behavioral research* (pp. 671–701). Thousand Oaks, CA: Sage.

Tashakkori, A., & Teddlie, C. (2006, April). Validity issues in mixed methods research: Calling for an integrative framework. Paper presented at the annual meeting of the American Educational Research Association, San Francisco.

Teddlie, C., & Tashakkori, A. (2003). Major issues and controversies in the use of mixed methods in the social and behavioral sciences. In A. Tashakkori and C. Teddlie (Eds.), *Handbook of mixed methods in social and behavioral research* (pp. 3–50). Thousand Oaks, CA: Sage.

Teddlie, C., & Tashakkori, A. (2006). A general typology of research designs featuring mixed methods. *Research in the Schools, 13*(1), 12–28.

Trend, M. G. (1979). On the reconciliation of qualitative and quantitative analyses: A case study. In T. D. Cook and C. S. Reichardt (Eds.), *Qualitative and quantitative methods in evaluation research* (pp. 68–86). Thousand Oaks, CA: Sage.

Van der Knaap, P. (2004). Theory-based evaluation and learning: Possibilities and challenges. *Evaluation, 10*(1), 16–34.

Van Maanen, J. (1995). Editor's introduction. In J. Van Maanen (Ed.), *Representation in ethnography*. Thousand Oaks, CA: Sage.

Warner, M. E. (2006). Putting child care in the regional economy: Empirical and conceptual challenges and economic development prospects. *Community Development: Journal of the Community Development Society, 37*(2), 7–22.

Warner, M. E., & Liu, Z. (2006). The importance of child care in economic development: A comparative analysis of regional economic linkage. *Economic Development Quarterly, 20*(1), 97–103.

Waysman, M., & Savaya, R. (1997). Mixed method evaluation: A case study. *Evaluation Practice, 18*(1), 227–237.

Webb, E. J., Campbell, D. T., Schwartz, R. D., & Sechrest, L. (1966). *Unobtrusive measures: Nonreactive research in the social sciences*. New York: Rand McNally.

Weisner, T. S. (Ed.). (2005). *Discovering successful pathways in children's development: Mixed methods in the study of childhood and family life*. Chicago: University of Chicago Press.

Weiss, C. H. (Ed.). (1972). *Evaluating action programs: Readings in social action and education*. Boston: Allyn & Bacon.

Weiss, C. H. (1998). *Evaluation* (2nd ed.). Upper Saddle River, NJ: Prentice-Hall.

Weiss, H. B., Kreider, H., Mayer, E., Hencke, R., & Vaughan, M. A. (2005). Working it out: The chronicle of a mixed-methods analysis. In T. S. Weisner (Ed.), *Discovering successful pathways in children's development: Mixed methods in the study of childhood and family life* (pp. 47–64). Chicago: University of Chicago Press.

Weiss, H. B., Mayer, E., Kreider, H., Vaughan, M., Dearing, E., Hencke, R., & Pinto, K. (2003). Making it work: Low-income working mothers' involvement in their children's education. *American Educational Research Journal, 40*(4), 879–901.

Yang, Y. (2005). Yin and Yang: *Quantitative and qualitative research investigating physical and psychological effects following a 6-month Taiji (T'ai Chi) and Qigong (Ch'i Kung) intervention with older adults.* Unpublished doctoral dissertation, Department of Kinesiology, University of Illinois, Urbana, IL.

Yin, R. K. (2006). Mixed methods research: Are the methods genuinely integrated or merely parallel? *Research in the Schools, 13*(1), 41–47.

INDEX